# DOCTOR DOOM™
## THE CHAOS ENGINE
### BOOK 1

Author STEVEN A. ROMAN made his professional writing debut in 1993 with the publication of his comic book horror series *Lorelei*. Outside the comics industry, Roman was a contributor to the prose anthologies *Untold Tales of Spider-Man* and *The Ultimate Hulk*, and was the editor of the ibooks, inc. novels *Heavy Metal: F.A.K.K.²*, *Moebius' Arzach*, and, yes, even *Britney Spears is a Three-Headed Alien*. Currently, he's working on Book 2 of *The Chaos Engine*. Roman lives in Queens, New York.

Illustrator MARK BUCKINGHAM is presently the artist on Marvel's *Peter Parker: Spider-Man*. Before that, in the years since he became a comic book artist, he juggled his time among DC Comics' *Titans* and almost every book in the Vertigo line, and Marvel's *Dr. Strange*, *Amazing Spider-Man*, *Star Trek Unlimited*, and *Generation X*. He lives with his wife, Gail, and three cats in the Victorian seaside town of Clevedon, England.

# X-MEN®

# DOCTOR DOOM™

## THE CHAOS ENGINE

### BOOK 1

## STEVEN A. ROMAN

ILLUSTRATIONS BY MARK BUCKINGHAM

BP BOOKS, INC.

DISTRIBUTED BY SIMON & SCHUSTER, INC

BP Books, Inc.
24 West 25th Street
New York, NY 10010

The ibooks World Wide Web Site Address is:
http://www.ibooksinc.com

ISBN 0-7434-3483-8

PRINTING HISTORY
BP Books, Inc. trade paperback edition/ July 2000
BP Books, Inc. mass-market paperback edition/ September 2001
10 9 8 7 6 5 4 3 2 1

Edited by Dwight Jon Zimmerman
Cover art by Bob Larkin
Cover design by Mike Rivilis
Interior design by Michael Mendelsohn and MM Design 2000, Inc.

Printed in the U.S.A.

For
my brother Frank,
who understands my pursuit of "The Dream,"
and
Stan Lee and Jack Kirby,
without whose dreams *none* of this would have been possible.

# ACKNOWLEDGMENTS

While it's often been said that writers work in a vacuum, this project in particular wouldn't have gone anywhere without the hard work of people who shared my dedication to making this one of the more unusual X-Men prose adventures you're ever liable to come across. Thus, I'd like to thank the following folks—without their help in the creation of this series, I might've still been sitting around in a dark room, contemplating my navel:

Byron Preiss, for coming up with the initial concept, and then allowing a loose cannon to see how far he could run with it; Mike Thomas and Mike Stewart, who were willing to go with an edgier approach for this series, and who provided some much-appreciated input to help get it started; Dwight Jon Zimmerman, for his editorial guidance; Managing Editor Clarice Levin, for keeping everything on track; Bob Larkin, for providing such an incredible cover painting; Mark Buckingham, for once again proving why he's one of the most talented artists in the comics industry; Mike Rivilis, for his wonderful cover design; Alex Gadd and Frank Roman, for answering all X-questions put to them by a writer who hadn't read more than a handful of the bazillions of X-Men comics released in the past ten years; Howard Zimmerman, for kibitzing above and beyond the call of duty; the folks at X-Men.com, and webmasters Victor Moore (*Codename: Psylocke*), Christine Feliciano (*The Inner Psyche*), and J. Logan Meller (*Children of the Atom*), whose sites provided a lot of information on the X-Universe in general, and all things Psylocke in particular.

Take a bow, folks!

# X-MEN

# DOCTOR DOOM™

## THE CHAOS ENGINE

### BOOK 1

Deep into that darkness peering, long I stood
    there wondering, fearing,
Doubting, dreaming dreams no mortal ever dared
    to dream before.

Edgar Allan Poe
"The Raven"

T HE FORCE of the explosion roared outward from the lobby of the General Electric office tower, toppling the gigantic lighted tree that stood before the building's glass doors, then continuing across the expanse of Rockefeller Center and through the wide walkway that led to Fifth Avenue; on the opposite side of the street, the windows of Saks department store imploded, showering the colorful Christmas displays inside with shards of flying glass. Decapitated and amputated mannequins and dummies collapsed in plastic heaps among the bright ribbons and tangled blinking lights.

For a moment, a disturbing silence hung over the streets and sidewalks that, just moments before, had been congested with holiday shoppers and rubbernecking tourists—or was the quiet merely a result of the temporary loss of hearing caused by the blast? Whatever the reason, the icy December air was soon filled with a mind-numbing cacophony: the screams of the injured; the keening for the dead; the wail of sirens in the distance; the ear-piercing screech of car alarms.

And the peal of insane laughter.

For the few souls not suffering from shock or crippling injuries, the sight of the madman responsible for the debacle was more than enough to send their minds spiraling into a dark pit from which they might never recover.

Floating above the skating rink—which was now filled with the shattered remains of the mammoth Norway spruce tree that had, just moments before, towered above it—clad in garments of the bloodiest red, seemed to be none other than the devil himself, given human form. His yellow eyes fairly glowed with arcane energy from beneath the shadows of a gladiator-like helmet—shadows that did well to hide the features of this spawn of hell. Looking from one side of the plaza to the other, then out toward Fifth Avenue, he surveyed the damage wrought by his handiwork: the broken bodies; the blood that flowed like a river down to the skating rink, where it quickly congealed; the lopsided buildings and overturned vehicles.

And found it good.

Slowly, his lips split open to reveal yellowed, dagger-like teeth flecked with bits of blood . . . and flesh.

" 'And now was acknowledged the presence of the Red Death,' " he said, voice rumbling like storm clouds. " 'And one by one dropped the revelers in the blood-bedewed halls of their revel, and died each in the despairing posture of his fall. And the life of the ebony clock went out with that of the last of the gay. And the flames of the tripods expired. And Darkness and Decay and the Red Death held illimitable dominion over all.' "

"Not here they don't, Magneto!" shouted a male voice from behind the costumed terrorist. "Not now, not ever!"

A predatory smile chiseled onto his features, the self-proclaimed Master of Magnetism turned in midair and looked down at the group of colorfully-garbed men and women gathered at the spot where the one-hundred-foot Christmas tree had stood. Six in all, they comprised the membership of Earth's greatest team of super heroes: Storm—a tall, beautiful African woman, her flowing white hair in sharp contrast to the black leather outfit she wore, a billowing satin cape attached to her shoulders and slender wrists; Wonder Man—the world's greatest superpowered adventurer, garbed in a black-and-red bodysuit, a stylized "W" emblazoned across his chest; Spider-Woman—a mysterious heroine dressed in black and silver, scarlet hair streaming out like a fountain of blood through the open top of her mask; the incredible Hulk—the green-skinned, gamma-spawned monster whose short temper was as well known—and feared—as his tremendous strength; and Iron Man—the Armored Avenger, resplendent in his red-and-gold battlesuit. Standing in front of the group was their leader—a man unafraid to put his life at risk in order to attain his ultimate goal of creating a world in which all men and women might live in peace. Clad from head to toe in gleaming armor, wrapped in a cape of the darkest green velvet, he was the world's foremost scientific genius—and its all-powerful ruler.

"Doctor Doom," Magneto said, the words spilling like curdled milk from between his rotted teeth. "I was wondering when you and your little band of merrymakers would show up to spoil my fun."

Doom extended an arm and dramatically swept it across the plaza to indicate the chaos created by his enemy. *"Fun?"* he roared, the anger in his voice amplified by the speaker built into his helmet's faceplate. "You injure and kill hundreds of my subjects, cause hundreds of thousands of dollars in property damage, make a mockery of this festive season—all for your amusement?"

Magneto shrugged. "What can I say? I was bored."

Doom started, as though he had been slapped.

"Oh, come now, von Doom," Magneto replied. "You of all people should know how it is ruling over lesser beings—keeping the rabble in line, constantly guarding against possible invaders, oppressing personal freedoms. Sometimes a monarch needs to find a way to fight off the tedium." He nodded toward the injured and dying below him. "This is mine."

"Monster!" Spider-Woman cried, her cheeks almost as red as her mane of fiery tresses. "You'd destroy innocent lives *just to pass the time?"* Her hands clenched into fists, and she snarled. *"I'll give you something to fight off!"* She tensed, preparing to leap at the red-hued villain.

A gauntleted hand gently placed on her shoulder, though, halted her ill-considered attack.

"No, Spider-Woman," Doom said calmly. "We will not allow Magneto to force us into careless actions. Only a level head will prevail against such a madman."

Behind them, the Hulk grunted. "Yeah, but I'd *still* like to smash in that bedpan he's wearin' on his skull," he mumbled.

The black-and-silver-clad heroine glared at Magneto through polarized lenses, then turned to face Doom. Slowly, her muscles relaxed, fists unclenching. She exhaled sharply.

"All right, Doctor," she said, almost in a whisper. "Sorry."

Doom consolingly patted her on the shoulder, then looked toward his old enemy. "You're wrong, Magneto. Latveria under my rule, as the rest of the world is today, has ever been governed with a caring, yet firm, hand. My subjects are as dear to me as my own children—" he glanced toward Storm, who smiled beatifically "—or my loving wife. What I do for them is no more than any father would do for his family, or a true monarch for his people: providing for their comfort, ensuring their safety, guiding them towards a bright future. But then, I am not surprised by your attitude—I have *heard* of the atrocities you enacted on the fair people of Genosha . . ."

"Lies! All lies!" Magneto barked. "I, too, did what was necessary for my subjects. I, too, provided for them, gave them safety and a future—"

"You gave them *death!*" Wonder Man interjected. "You took away their hopes, their freedom, their very lives!"

"Hope. Freedom." Magneto sneered. "Mere *words*, you muscle-bound ape. What use has the typical man or woman for such concepts? Feed and clothe them, and they are happy. Protect their homes, and they are content. I did all that, and more, for my followers, yet still they turned against me. All I asked in return was—"

4

"Their children as fodder for your body banks?" Iron Man shouted. "Yeah, that sounds like a *real* fair deal to me." Even through the metal helmet encasing his head, the sarcasm in his voice was unmistakable.

"Armored fool!" Magneto spat. "With but a thought, I could crush that tin can in which you hide, until flesh and bone ooze out upon the ground like the juice of a freshly squeezed orange. And *then* where would your much-vaunted technological strength be?"

"Good God, who *writes* this crap?"

Sitting in the darkened movie theater, Elisabeth Braddock turned to face the commentator to her left—her boyfriend, millionaire Warren Worthington III.

"Warren, please!" she whispered.

"Oh, come on, Betsy," Warren muttered, leaning over to speak into her ear. Her skin tingled as his lips gently brushed the lobe. He pointed toward the movie screen, where Magneto continued to face off with Doom and his team. "*Nobody* talks like that! And besides, when's all the hitting gonna start? This is supposed to be a big action blockbuster. It isn't *Shakespeare*, for crying out—"

Betsy placed an index finger against his lips to quiet him. He smiled and kissed the tip of it, and she had to bite her bottom lip to keep from giggling; she settled for smiling back. Silently, she gazed at the man sitting beside her.

Silhouetted by the flickering images cast from the projector at the back of the theater, his handsome features and shoulder-length blonde hair made her think of all the times they had lain by the fireplace in his Battery Park City apartment, staring out at the starry sky that was draped across New York Harbor like a velvet curtain. They were times she always wished would never end, even as the rising sun washed away the indigo color of the night, replacing it with the rosy pink of dawn.

It was on one such night, as the fire crackled and the city slept around them, that she realized she was truly in love with this man.

A man who was always supportive, and understanding. Who let her live her own life, with no strings attached.

Who kissed her fingertips in dark movie theaters.

Apparently uncertain of what to make of her silence, Warren cocked his head to one side, a quizzical expression etched on his face.

"What is it?" he asked.

Her smile widened. "You're incorrigible," she said breathlessly.

"And *you're* a regular chatterbox," said the man to her right. With a start, Betsy turned to face him. She recognized him as J. Jonah Jameson, publisher of the New York *Daily Bugle*. Clad in an ill-fitting tuxedo, his stern features, salt-and-pepper crewcut, and Charlie Chaplinesque mustache contrasted sharply with the softer visage and stylish attire of his wife, Marla. "If you two love-birds are more interested in each other than the movie," Jameson continued, "get a room. Otherwise, let the rest of us watch this in peace." His beady eyes narrowed. "All right?"

"Sorry," Betsy mumbled. She turned back to Warren, who stuck out his upper teeth and crossed his eyes in a moronic expression. Betsy placed a hand over her mouth to suppress a laugh, then rested her head against his shoulder. He responded by placing his arm around her and drawing her even closer.

And there they remained until the end credits had rolled and the house lights had come on.


"I'm tellin' you, Betsy, *Doom's Patrol* is gonna be *the* movie event of the summer! I *guarantee* it's gonna blow *Titanic* outta the water . . . figuratively speaking, of course."

Smiling politely, Betsy gazed up at the chiseled features of Simon Williams, who, in both his personal and professional lives, was better known throughout the world as actor and box office darling Wonder Man. Standing well over six feet tall, dark hair dramatically swept back from his forehead, Williams was garbed in his traditional red leather safari jacket, with tight black slacks tucked into a pair of red boots; a pair of thick, red-lensed sun-glasses covered his eyes so completely that Betsy had trouble telling if he even *had* eyes. He certainly cut an impressive figure, she thought—a combination of Arnold Schwarzenegger's body, Kevin Sorbo's face, and Antonio Banderas's hair.

Not that she was anything to sneeze at, though. Waist-length, lavender-colored hair piled stylishly upon her head, Betsy was clad in a body-hugging black velvet cocktail dress that accentuated her curves to the point of distraction for every man in the room. Her Japanese features were just as striking: high cheekbones; button nose; full lips; jade-green eyes that shone with the fires of life.

And having shapely legs that seemed to go up to her neck didn't hurt, either.

But even in three-inch stiletto heels, the top of her head just even with Williams' powerful jaw, she looked like a child in comparison to his larger-than-life appearance.

"I'm glad the picture turned out so well for you, Mr. Williams," Betsy said. "Have there been any reports on what the Emperor thought of it?"

Williams grinned broadly, flashing an impressive set of capped teeth. "Not yet, but how could he *not* love it? Besides, von Doom had total script approval—even took the time to work with Val Kilmer on how to play him. He's *gotta* be happy with the finished product. I gotta tell you, though," he said in a conspiratorial murmur, "I thought Chris Walken spent a *little* too much time chewin' the scenery as Magneto." He shrugged. "But Naomi Campbell as Storm?" He exhaled sharply. "Talk about your major hotties! Man, I'd give my right arm for a chance to do a love scene with her!"

"Er . . . yes," Betsy said, continuing to smile as she nodded. "An inspired bit of casting, I thought—I'm certain the Empress is pleased. Not that you were so bad yourself."

"Thanks," Williams said. The grin widened further, until it practically threatened to split his head apart. The image suddenly made Betsy think of a child set loose in a toy store on Christmas day.

"I've got one question, though," Betsy said. "Don't you find the whole thing somewhat . . . propagandist?"

Williams's smile faded, and he tilted his head to one side. "What do you mean?"

"Well, I know Emperor von Doom's had his share of problems with Magneto over the years, but would he really act so incredibly infantile, blowing up Christmas trees in the middle of New York and spouting lines from Edgar Allan Poe? I'd say that's being more than a tad ridiculous with dramatic license—wouldn't you? And the Emperor preserving the spirit of the holidays for all the good little children of the world—a bit much, don't you think?" Before Williams could respond, Betsy continued. "And isn't Magneto supposed to be a survivor of the Holocaust? What could really make a man like that—who's already experienced, first-hand, the kind of horrors the human race can create—lower himself to the very depths of cruelty enacted by the Nazis, in order to terrorize the Empire? Now, *that's* the sort of story I would have liked to have seen, not some senseless knockabout with flashy effects."

Williams's head slowly swung from side to side. From similar conversations she'd had with other people over the years, Betsy knew he was looking for any sign of an armor-clad Guardsman—a number of them had been assigned as a security detail for the party—or a none-too-casual observer in the service of von Doom. Of course, Williams would be wasting his time if the stories Betsy had heard of the Emperor's psychic watchdogs were true—with their mental powers, the Psi Division could be miles away and still eavesdrop on their every word.

"I-I wouldn't know about any of that stuff, Betsy," Williams said, a slight hitch in his voice. "I'm just an actor."

A wicked smile played at Betsy's lips, but she fought back the urge to let it transform into a full-out Cheshire Cat-like grin. It was childish, really, but seeing the massive actor squirm a bit almost made up for having to tolerate his overbearing personality.

Any sense of victory quickly faded, however, with the next words to spill from his mouth as he quickly changed the subject: "So, where'd you two meet—Tokyo, right?"

"I beg your pardon?" Betsy asked, startled.

"You and Worthington," Williams said. An easy, knowing smile crept across his face. It was clear from his expression that he enjoyed catching Betsy off-guard—returning the favor for her Magneto comments, obviously. "Way I've heard it, you and Prince Charming met during one of his fact-finding tours of the Orient. You were working in some karaoke bar, cranking out 'I Will Survive' and 'Boogie Nights' for the locals, and he was meeting with some potential investors for his company. But he took one look at you, and it was love at first sight." He shook his head. "You must feel like the luckiest girl in the world, meeting a guy who sweeps you off your feet and brings you to America. Even sets you up as the A-Number One singer in his nightclub."

"B-but . . . I-I'm British . . ." Betsy said, voice trailing off. "A-and it never happened like that . . ." She felt her cheeks grow hot. How had this conversation taken such a bizarre turn? And, more importantly, when would this annoying man go away?

Williams shrugged. "Oh. Guess you can't believe everything you read in the *Enquirer*, right?"

"I-I should say not . . ." Betsy stammered.

Williams looked back over his shoulder, then turned to Betsy. He smiled his winnigest smile. "Hey, look—I've gotta go. My publicist hates it if I don't try to mingle with every person in the room. Gets the idea I'm not doing enough of her job for her." He grabbed Betsy's hand, shaking it so hard she half expected it to snap off at the wrist. "Nice talking to you."

Without waiting for a reply, he turned and walked off, the crowd parting around him like the Red Sea.

Betsy's eyes narrowed as she watched him stomp away. "Wish I could say the same . . . you *git,*" she growled softly.

Betsy closed her eyes and sighed. She'd forgotten all about those stories—the rumors of how she and Warren had met. Looking back, she had to admit that it *had* seemed the unlikeliest of pairings—the azure-skinned millionaire playboy, and the purple-tressed British chanteuse who had been struggling for years to move beyond the small West Village clubs and Alphabet City bars in which she had been performing. "Worlds apart" was a mild description for the situation.

But then, Warren had never been a typical millionaire—as comfortable with old college friends in a smoky bar as he was when in control of Worthington Enterprises' boardroom. And the fact that wings sprouted from between his shoulder blades, giving him the power of flight, also tended to make him stand out from the other CEOs listed in *Fortune* magazine. As for Betsy, she had never been a typical British singer—especially when one considered she was actually a member of the House of Braddock, one of Britain's most prestigious families ... though she tended to keep that information to herself. Only Warren and her brother, Brian, knew of her real origins.

Over the past three years, friends often said that she and Warren had been destined to meet from birth, even though they lived an ocean apart. And Destiny must certainly have been holding Warren by the hand, leading him on that night when he and two friends showed up at The Gilded Cage to hear a lavender-tressed nightingale sing.

And, she thought contentedly, her song had yet to end ...

With a smile, Betsy opened her eyes and made a slow pirouette, hoping to catch a glimpse of Warren, wherever he might have gotten to in the spacious room. After the world premier of *Doom's Patrol* at the cavernous Ziegfeld Theater in midtown Manhattan, the attendees had traveled uptown to a major celebration being held here at Tavern on the Green, a sumptuous restaurant on the western edge of Central Park. Despite her natural tendency to avoid large gatherings of people she didn't know—and, therefore, people with whom she'd be completely uncomfortable—Betsy had put on her most supportive face and accompanied her beau to the festivities. Unfortunately, being one of the world's foremost powerbrokers meant that anyone and everyone wanted to be Warren's friend, so it was only moments after they arrived that Betsy suddenly found herself alone ... and, thus, an easy target for Simon Williams and his inappropriate questions.

"Is he gone?" said a voice off to one side. Betsy looked out of the corner of one eye to find Warren standing a step behind her, tilting his head back just enough that his face was hidden from view by her skyscraping hairstyle.

"And who would that be?" Betsy asked without turning around.

"Man-Mountain Marko over there," Warren replied, pointing past her shoulder. She followed the direction of his index finger; it led straight to Williams, who was involved in another pointless conversation with some other poor soul unlucky enough to have lacked the speed to avoid him. With a bemused smirk, Betsy recognized the actor's new sounding board: Jean-Paul Beaubier, the famed Canadian skier. She'd noticed the lithe athlete casting furtive glances at Williams from across the room while she was trapped in her conversation with him.

*Poor dear,* she thought. *I'm sure "Wonder Man" doesn't seem half as attractive now as he did before he opened his mouth....*

"You're referring, of course, to the annoying Mr. Williams," Betsy remarked to Warren. With a start, she saw the actor glance in her direction, as though he had heard her from across the room. She waved to him and smiled, silently praying he didn't think it was an invitation to return to talk off her remaining ear. Thankfully, he only waved back and continued toying with his victim.

"Yeah," Warren said, his voice slightly muffled by her hair. "That's the guy."

Teeth still locked in a sardonic grin, Betsy turned to face her boyfriend. "Warren, *dear,* how long have you been standing there?"

"Well, I've only been *here* a few seconds." Warren gestured back over his shoulder, toward a gigantic ice sculpture of a swan, its long neck bent gracefully so that the bird's beak could touch the surface of the large punch bowl beneath it. "But I was standing behind that swan, talking to Mary Jane Watson-Parker—she's the actress who played Spider-Woman—and her husband for about five minutes. A really nice couple—no pretensions, unlike what you'd normally find in most Hollywood marriages."

"And were you aware of the *hell* you were putting me through while you gabbed the night away with your new friends?"

"Oh, it couldn't have been *that* bad, honey. Right?" Warren paused. "You know, you're starting to freak me out with that death's-head stare you've got going. Didn't your mother ever warn you your face could freeze like that?"

"That's not the *only* thing that's going to be cold tonight," Betsy said in a warning tone.

Warren cocked his head to one side. "Huh?" Then his eyes widened as the realization hit him. He winced. "Ouch. Am *I* in trouble." He flashed a warm smile, and lowered his head until his chin touched his chest. "What if I said I was sorry, and it'll never happen again?"

The muscles in Betsy's face slowly relaxed. "It's a start."

Warren beamed brightly, and raised his head. "That's what makes me such a great warrior in the arena we powerbrokers call 'global finances,' Betts." He leaned forward to kiss her lightly on the forehead. "Like any smart businessman, I know when to let the other party establish the ground rules for negotiations."

Betsy smiled, and wrapped her arms around his waist. "You mean you'll take what you can get."

Warren nodded. "Exactly."

"Glad to be out of there?"

Staring off into space, Betsy started, then glanced around. She and Warren were walking hand-in-hand along Central Park West, the tree-lined, four-lane avenue that extended from Columbus Circle in the south to 110th Street in the north. To their left, the park—with its architectural symbiosis of nature's rocks and trees combined with man's winding footpaths and brass-plated lampposts—stretched out into the darkness; to their right, on the other side of the street, elegant, cream-colored, Art Deco-designed apartment buildings pierced the night sky, reaching up toward the heavens. For a Saturday night in late June, traffic—both vehicular and pedestrian—was surprisingly light in this part of Manhattan; occasionally, Betsy and Warren were passed on the sidewalk by another couple or the odd bicyclist.

And echoing in the night, the sounds of merrymaking from the restaurant could still be heard, even though it was blocks behind them.

"I asked if you were glad to get away from the party," Warren said.

"Umm . . . yes, actually." Betsy bit her bottom lip. She hadn't meant to be that brutally honest, but there it was, out in the open with just two words. She gazed at her beau, then cast her eyes downward. "I'm sorry, Warren. I know how important it was for you to make an appearance tonight, what with the movie and all—"

"And I did," Warren commented. "I showed up, shook some hands, let some wannabe movers-and-shakers suck up to me, made it clear how much I *loved* the movie . . ." He rolled his eyes toward the night sky. "I've done my part for the Empire tonight." He gently took her chin between thumb and forefinger and lifted it so she could look directly into his cool, blue eyes. "And my reward for such dedication is to spend the rest of the evening with the most beautiful woman in this—or any other—world."

Betsy's lips parted, but she suddenly found herself at a loss for words. It was one of those moments when Warren was so completely serious—so confident in expressing his feelings for her—that she wasn't quite certain what to say in response.

*But really, though—there's only* one *thing that needs to be said, isn't there?* she thought, reaching up to stroke his cheek.

"I love you," she whispered, her eyes sparkling in the moonlight.

"And I, you, Betts." Warren smiled and shook his head. "You know, a few years ago, I would've been surprised to hear me say that. But when I first saw you, that night in the bar . . ."

The light in Betsy's eyes suddenly dimmed, her brow furrowing.

"What's wrong?" Warren asked.

Betsy looked away. "It's—"

*"Don't* say it's nothing," Warren said. "You *know* it makes me crazy when you try to avoid discussing something that's bothering you. So, out with it."

Betsy took a deep breath, held it for a moment, then slowly released it. There was no point in avoiding the issue, now that she'd allowed it to spring back into the front of her mind; Warren would just keep nagging her until she cracked. The best thing to do was to just say it, get it out of the way and move on.

"It was a comment someone made at the party," she said at last.

"Who?" Warren asked. "Was it Stark? He tried to come on to you, didn't he?" He paused, then snapped his fingers. "It was that Rasputin guy, right? Wanted to show you his 'etchings.' " He nodded, as though agreeing with himself. "Yeah, I've heard about *him.*"

"It doesn't *matter,*" Betsy said, a tad too brusquely. "Besides, it's the *comment* that bothered me, not the person who said it."

"And that comment would be . . . ?"

Betsy stopped walking; Warren immediately halted.

"About us," Betsy said. "About me. About my place in your life. In life in general."

Warren exhaled. "Sounds pretty intense. What exactly did this anonymous person say that got you thinking about all this?"

Betsy grimaced. "He mentioned the rumors . . ."

"Oh, for Pete's sake!" Warren exclaimed, throwing his hands in the air. "Betts, we've been through all of that before! It didn't bother me back then what people were thinking, and it sure as hell doesn't bother me now. Remember all the things I had to deal with even before I met you, just because I was, you know, *different* from all the other kids?" He shook his head in resignation. "They're *always* gonna talk about us, hon—it comes with the territory when you're a public figure." He placed his hands on her shoulders. "You've gotta put that kind of nonsense behind you, Betts," he said gently, "before it destroys you."

"I *have* put it behind me," Betsy countered. She paused. "At least, I *thought* I had." She gnawed on her bottom lip for a few moments; Warren patiently waited for her to continue. "It's just that . . . ever since we met, I stopped being Betsy Braddock; stopped being *me*. I had a career, a good bit of word of mouth going, a life that had its share of problems, but I was able to handle them." She frowned. "Now, I'm just 'Warren Worthington's gal pal,' jetting around the world, eating at the finest restaurants, doing five shows a week at the Starlight Room."

"And that's a *bad* thing?" Warren said sarcastically.

"You know what I mean," Betsy replied. "It's wonderful—I wouldn't trade the time we've spent together for anything in the world. But . . ." *Go ahead, get it all out.* "But the public doesn't take me seriously as an artist; the press, too. They treat me like I'm some bit of Page Three fluff you'd find posing for the tabloids back home—just a pretty face and a nice pair of . . . legs." She sneered. "As far as they're concerned, I'm nothing more than window dressing for your arm."

"That's not how *I* see you," Warren said.

"I know that, and I appreciate it. I really do. You've always been there for me, always been respectful of my wishes, never interfering with my decisions, never using your station to force other people to do things for me." Betsy looked up to meet Warren's warm gaze. "But it all comes down to perceptions—how the public sees you. You know how important that can be."

"True," Warren said.

"And what people think of when they see *you* is a man who overcame adversity and prejudice, who rose to become the head of an international corporation." Betsy's head slowly dipped, until she was staring at her clasped hands; the knuckles were white from the pressure. "But when they see *me* . . . when they see me, they think of a hanger-on. An oriental . . . 'golddigger,' I think is the term. Anything but a singer."

"Betsy . . ." Warren began.

She shook her head. "I've never made my mark, you see. My

place in history. Never made people stand up and pay attention to me. I've always been relegated to the background—first with my brother, Brian, and his athletic awards. . . . That's why I've never told too many people about my heritage—then I'd just be 'Brian Braddock's sister.' " She glanced at Warren. "And then it happened anyway . . . with you." Betsy laughed curtly, a small, trembling note, as tears formed in the corners of her eyes. "Pretty silly, wouldn't you say? The luckiest woman on two continents, with the most beautiful man in this—or any other—world, and she's worried about having future generations remember her." She sniffed loudly.

Warren reached out to brush away her tears. "I don't think it's silly at all," he said softly.

Betsy reached into her small leather purse and took out a pair of Kleenex from a small portable dispenser. Wiping her nose, then dabbing at her eyes, she managed a small smile. "Oh, you're just being kind," she said in a phlegmy half-whisper.

"No, I'm entirely serious," Warren said. "So, what do you want to do about it?"

"Do?"

"About making your mark in history."

Betsy was confused. "I really hadn't—" she began.

"What's the matter—you talk a good game, but you never took the time to figure out how to make it happen?" Warren playfully pressed the tip of her nose with his index finger. "Come on, Braddock—what's it gonna take for you to smack around all those half-wits to get their attention and then rub their faces in it?"

For the second time that evening, Betsy was at a loss for words.

"I . . . I don't know," she said softly.

Warren nodded. "Okay, okay . . . there must be *something* we can do about this . . ." He stared off into space, pinching his bottom lip between thumb and forefinger. Betsy silently watched as his face underwent a series of comical expressions, the smooth, blue-tinted skin contorting and stretching as he reviewed whatever options were running through his mind.

*"He puzzled and puzzled, until his puzzler was sore . . ."* she thought, remembering a line from Dr. Seuss's classic children's book, *How the Grinch Stole Christmas*. She bit her tongue to keep from laughing.

Warren's face suddenly brightened. "I've got it! How would you like an opportunity to perform for von Doom himself?"

"And how would I do that?"

"Well, next week is the tenth anniversary of his rise to power. And the celebration's going to be held in Washington, right?"

Betsy slowly nodded in agreement. She had a feeling she knew where this was going, but decided to say nothing for the moment.

"So, what if you were picked to be on the entertainment bill that night?" Warren continued. "The ceremony's going to be televised around the world—that's over three billion people watching. And with your talent, they'll have no choice but to see how wrong they've been about you. You'll *never* have a better showcase in your entire life. Would *that* qualify as making your mark?"

Betsy frowned, then pursed her lips.

"What?" Warren asked.

"It's a wonderful idea, Warren," Betsy said hesitantly, "and I appreciate the offer, but it's not the kind of thing that could happen to just any cabaret singer living in the West Village . . ."

Warren smiled. "Oh, I get it. Not without her well-respected boyfriend pulling some strings, is that it?" He drew an X across his chest with the point of an index finger. "I swear—" he glanced up at the night sky "—as God is my witness, I will in no way influence anyone's decision to give you a shot at the anniversary performance. The Minister of Entertainment is in town for a couple of days to check out potential acts for the gala. All I'll do is invite him to the Starlight Room; then we'll see what happens after he's heard you sing." His smile widened. "You know me, Betts—I only use these powers of mine for good, not evil."

Betsy raised a quizzical eyebrow. "Really?"

Warren patted the pockets of his tuxedo. "Well, I don't have my Bible with me," he mumbled, "but I *am* telling you the truth."

Betsy stared at him for a moment, then walked over to a nearby park bench and sat down; the wood felt wonderfully cool against her legs. Hunched forward, elbows placed on her knees, she rested her chin in the palms of her hands to think.

He was right—performing for the Emperor on a worldwide telecast *would* be a once-in-a-lifetime opportunity. She'd be an utter fool to pass it up, even if Warren went back on his promise . . . which she half expected him to do, anyway. It was just that, when one came right down to it, she had always been reluctant to accept help from anyone—family, friends, even lovers. It made her feel beholden to them, even if they expected nothing in return for their actions; made her feel as though she were incapable of achieving her goals on her own. And Warren was no exception.

Still and all, it *was* the Emperor. *And* three billion TV viewers . . .

"All right," she said at last. "I'll do it."

Warren clapped his hands. "Excellent!" He strode over and helped Betsy to her feet, then embraced her. "But it's all going to be up to *you*, hon. I'm just gonna take a seat in the back and watch."

Suuuure, *you will* . . . Betsy thought, her chin happily resting on his shoulder. But she didn't mind at all.

"Warren?" she said softly.

"Yes?" he asked.

"Do you *really* consider me the most beautiful woman in the world?"

Taking a step back, Betsy smiled wickedly as she stared at her lover. Her eyes narrowed, daring him to change his earlier comment.

"Well . . . sure," Warren slowly replied. "With the exception of Claudia Schiffer, of course." He started to look away, then paused. "And Cindy Crawford." A boyish grin slowly spread across his face. "And—" He tapped the side of his head with the knuckle of one finger, as though trying to shake loose a hidden memory.

"What *was* the name of that cute little red-headed waitress in Glasgow . . . ?"

The scarlet lips that playfully covered his mouth to silence him soon made him forget about any woman but the one in his arms.

# 2

**M**ORNING IN America—and another work day for the citizens of Washington, D.C.

At Union Station, the first trains were arriving, full of high school students—and their teachers—excited about leaving behind the familiar surroundings of their New York and Philadelphia and Boston neighborhoods for an opportunity to tour the district that had become home to the undisputed leader of the world. Government employees hurried to their jobs at L'Enfant Plaza and Federal Center and Judiciary Square, while tourists lined up to visit Ford's Theatre and the Smithsonian Institute and the Jefferson Memorial. On The Mall—the expansive parkscape that stretches from the Capitol building in the east to the Lincoln Memorial in the west—Parks Department workers moved across carefully-tended fields of green in small hover-vehicles; from the bottom of the craft, whirring blades dipped down to trim the grass to a uniform height, while water and nutrients were pumped directly into the soil from large drums built behind the drivers' seats.

At the Latverian Monument—once a monolithic structure named in honor of George Washington, and now referred to as "The Monument of Doom" only by those who ran the risk of punishment for their disrespect—armed guards dressed in deep-blue armor patrolled the grounds, occasionally stopping people—even small children—to run quick scans for weapons or explosives. Golden Age of Mankind though it might be, these were still times for caution—one never knew when one of Emperor von Doom's cowardly enemies—few though they were—might come out of hiding long enough to threaten the lives of the noble citizens who lived under his protection. And a child—even one possessing the sweetest of smiles and the face of an angel—was just as capable of carrying a bomb as any crazed adult bent on destruction.

Cautious times, indeed.

And at 1600 Pennsylvania Avenue, in the master bedroom of the White House, in private living quarters once occupied by forty presidents and their families over a 193-year span, the planet's Empress slowly awoke to face the new day.

As resting places go, the room was somewhat at odds with what one would normally expect to find in a mansion that, for nearly two centuries, had been a representation of the hopes and dreams of the country's population. Its walls a deep blue, its carpeting a lush red, the sanctum's furnishings were a strange mixture of antique fittings—French settee, Viennese crystal chandelier, Louis XVI-era chairs and sofa—and hi-tech gadgetry—viewing screen, holographic projector, a cell phone or three—though, oddly enough, the combination seemed to go well together. To the left of the Empress's oaken four-poster bed, on the western wall, hung an ornate tapestry of the coat-of-arms of Latveria—a golden eagle, wings spread wide, beak open as though it were shrieking a cry of victory over its fallen enemies; below it, an ornate "L." And all set against a blood-red background. On the eastern wall was a 4' × 6' oil painting of Victor von Doom, his strong, handsome features those of a stern, but loving, father—a likeness of the subject perfectly recreated by the artist who had been assigned the daunting task of capturing the power and majesty of the Lion of Latveria on canvas. Indeed, there was almost a lifelike quality to the hypnotic brown eyes that stared out at the room—watching, always watching.

Rubbing her own sleep-crusted eyes with the edges of her hands, Ororo I—the sovereign formerly known as Ororo Munroe—blinked three times to clear her blurry vision, then sat up in bed. But even before she could look up to face the northeastward window that stood across from her to greet the sun, she was plunged into darkness once more as a mountain of white hair cascaded down over her face.

*I really* should *start tying it back before I go to bed*... she thought with a chuckle. But then, Victor always preferred her hair loose.

Throwing back her head, Ororo kicked away the white satin sheets that covered her and sinuously stepped onto the lush carpeting; her feet sank deep into the pile. She crossed the room quickly, stepping into the light that poured through the window; the warmth of the rays made her skin tingle.

She smiled. Mild, bright mornings like this reminded her of her years as a "goddess" on the plains of Kenya, in East Africa—back when she really thought she might be some sort of Earth-bound deity, possessing an innate ability to control the weather; how this might be so, considering both her parents had been "mortals," had never troubled her. But whatever the source of her powers, if drought threatened the land, it only took a single thought to summon a modest-sized storm that prevented the crops—or her faithful worshippers—from dying; too much rainfall, and she could banish the clouds before the precious topsoil was washed away. It was a simple life, with simple responsibilities—one light years away from the days she had spent as a child on the streets of Cairo, Egypt, following her parents' deaths.

Ororo frowned, her thoughts turning dark from the unbidden memory. And above the streets of Washington, a thundercloud suddenly formed, its icy fingers reaching out to block off the sunlight; it was quickly joined by another. The sky filled with an ominous rumbling.

A knock at the bedroom door snapped Ororo out of her reverie. "W-who is it?" she asked.

"Paterson, Your Majesty," replied a deep, male voice. "Is everything all right?"

"Yes, Joseph," Ororo called back. "Why do you a—" Her attention was drawn to the dark clouds that continued to form in the skies directly above the historic mansion, threatening to wash out the streets of the world's capital in a deluge of biblical proportions. Wincing slightly, she realized that she'd allowed her wandering mind to affect the weather patterns in the area. "Oh. I see what you mean."

Closing her eyes, the dark-skinned maharani cleared her mind, letting her psionic powers reach out, beyond the mansion, to the farthest edges of the district, searching for—

There.

A jet stream of air coming down from Canada. She could practically feel the cool wind playing across her skin; goose flesh prickled its way along her arms and legs. It would miss Washington by a few miles . . . unless it had some help.

All it took was a thought.

Outside the White House, trash receptacles overturned, spilling their contents; papers and food containers fluttered down Pennsylvania Avenue, then leapt skyward like a murder of crows taken flight. Caught in the sudden gale, the storm clouds swiftly retreated from the capitol, bound for the Atlantic Ocean.

Eyes still closed, Ororo smiled as warm sunlight once more bathed her face.

"Ma'am?" Paterson asked.

"It is all right now, Joseph," Ororo replied, opening her eyes. "I have taken care of the situation. And please—stop talking to me through the door. You know how much I find it distasteful. Come in."

"Sorry, Ma'am," Paterson said. The door opened, and Ororo's personal bodyguard entered the room. At six feet, five inches, and 240 pounds, forty-year-old Joseph Paterson cut a dashing figure in his emerald Guardsman armor, which shone brightly in the restored sunlight. The protective helmet that normally covered his

head was tucked under his arm, allowing Ororo to see his rugged features: squarish jaw, piercing blue eyes, a slightly off-center nose that showed signs of having been broken a time or two, and closely-cropped dark hair. A former field operative of the international law enforcement organization called S.H.I.E.L.D.—an acronym for Strategic Hazard Intervention Espionage Logistic Directorate—he had been assigned to the Empress by Doctor Doom himself on the basis of Paterson's service record, having fought against such terrorist groups as Hydra and A.I.M.—Advanced Idea Mechanics—when they had attempted to overthrow the Emperor on more than one occasion. It also didn't hurt that Paterson had been recommended for the job by S.H.I.E.L.D.'s beautiful and oh-so-deadly director, Viper... though she had wisely neglected to mention to von Doom that she and the handsome agent were lovers.

Neither the Emperor, nor Joe's wife, Maria, would have understood that to refuse the director's bed was to invite an early retirement—at the wrong end of a gun.

But for all the dangerous situations in which he'd been involved, none had prepared Joe Paterson for the sight that greeted him when he walked into the master bedroom: his Empress *in puris naturalibus*. And facing him.

"Ah, jeez!" he cried, eyes wide and cheeks turning a bright red. He quickly averted his gaze, concentrating instead on the portrait of von Doom to his left.

Ororo raised a hand to suppress a laugh. No matter how long she lived in the United States, she would never become used to its conservative climate. Back in Kenya, no one worried about such inconsequentials as modesty, not when there were far more important concerns to address. Certainly, her people would never have asked their goddess to cover herself up with strips of cloth—it would have been an insult.

Of course, her attititude toward clothing had eventually changed, once she had met...

Had met...

26

Ororo frowned. How odd that she couldn't remember the name of the man who had come to visit her in Kenya four years ago; who had explained that she was no deity, but a mutant—a "child of the atom," as others of her kind were later referred to. A human being, not a goddess, gifted with wondrous powers that could help shape the future of the world. Her brow furrowed as she struggled to conjure up a mental picture of the strange man who had changed her life. But none came.

"Umm...bad dreams again, Ma'am?" Paterson kept his eyes fixed on the painting...and the stern face that seemed to glare down at him.

Ororo shook her head to clear her thoughts. The identity of her visitor back then didn't really matter; he was probably just one of the many Imperial bureaucrats working for Victor. There were so many of the annoying little drones—constantly hovering around the White House, eager to please their master—that one face just seemed to blur into another.

"In a way," she said to Paterson, shrugging into a floor-length silk robe that was draped over a chair by the bed. "I have to stop letting my thoughts run away from me like that. After all, how can the people feel secure when their Empress has such trouble keeping her emotions in check?"

"It doesn't happen *that* often, Your Majesty, but you've got a point," Paterson said. "Then again, it *does* keep the weathermen on their toes. And it lets everybody know when it's a bad time to ask you for something."

Ororo laughed. "So, *that* is why the staff avoids me on rainy days." She tied the robe's belt tightly, then smoothed the flowing garment with the palms of her hands. "You can turn around now, Joseph."

Paterson hesitantly pivoted on one foot, momentarily staring down at his feet before working up the nerve to look at her. When he at last saw the robe, he breathed a sigh of relief.

"I apologize for making you feel uncomfortable, Joseph," Ororo said, smiling warmly. "It will not happen again." Paterson smiled

27

sheepishly, and glanced back at the painting of von Doom. Being the wife of the most powerful man on the planet, Ororo knew what *that* look meant. "And don't worry. This is the only room in the house that *isn't* monitored by Security, so no one will have to know of my . . . indiscretion. I *certainly* would not think of ever mentioning this to Victor."

Paterson visibly relaxed, a smile lighting his face. "Thank you, Ma'am. You have *no* idea how much I appreciate that."

Ororo nodded benignly. She also knew what *that* comment meant. For all the good things he had brought to the world—the abolishment of crime, an end to homelessness and hunger and war—still was Victor von Doom a man to be, not just respected, but feared . . . even, sometimes, by his own wife and children. His rage could be a terrible thing to see when unleashed—a roiling, thunderous darkness that rivaled the most powerful storm she could create; to be caught in its fury was an experience few survived. And not even a former S.H.I.E.L.D. agent would be foolish enough to tempt fate by openly gazing at the undraped form of the wife of such a man.

"Leave me now, Joseph," Ororo said. "I have much to do for my people today, and I need time to prepare. I will summon you when I am ready to depart for my first appointment."

"Yes, Ma'am," Paterson said, clearly grateful for the dismissal. Bowing sharply, he marched backward to the hallway, exited the room, and closed the door.

Chuckling softly, the image of her bodyguard's shocked expression still fresh in her mind, Ororo I slipped out of her robe and headed for the shower.

Outside, Joe Paterson drew the thumb of a gauntleted hand across his brow, wiping away the sweat that had accumulated there. He felt drenched inside his armor, and his left eye had suddenly developed a nervous twitch—a tic that hadn't bothered him since he'd left behind the world of international espionage for what he'd always thought would be far less strenuous palace duties.

"More thought, less reaction, moron," he said, quietly admonishing himself. "That'll teach you to go barging in to the Royal Chamber." He tightly squeezed his eyes shut and gently rapped his forehead with a metal-encased fist, trying to force the vision of the breathtakingly beautiful woman in the next room from his thoughts. The Psi Division could be making one of its periodic mental sweeps of the grounds for possible intruders at any moment; it would only end in tragedy if one of the "mentos" happened to detect any impure images playing on the projection screen of his mind.

What the Empress probably had not realized was that it wasn't his own life for which he had been concerned; rather, it was for the lives of his wife, Maria, and their son, Gregory. Joe had heard the stories over the years—stories of what had happened to some of the unfortunate souls punished by von Doom for perceived transgressions: their children abducted, never to be seen again; wives or husbands forced to watch helplessly as their spouses were killed before their eyes; entire families slaughtered. He had the feeling that the Empress was aware of the severity of some of the punishments her husband meted out, but chose not to question them; after all, any doubt shown by the royal family toward its monarch's decisions would be seen as a sign of weakness—and neither von Doom nor Ororo could ever be described as "weak."

But as terrible a man as Magneto might be—and based on his actions in Paris, "terrible" was a mild description for the international terrorist—his most savage reprisals paled in comparison to those inflicted by Victor von Doom upon his enemies. If anyone doubted that was so, they had only to ask of the fates of the Thing, or the Human Torch. Or Captain America.

Or Susan Storm-Richards.

The Invisible Woman. Joe felt a shiver run along his spine. He'd heard that her husband lost his mind when he saw what von Doom had done to her.

And the Emperor had laughed.

Rumor had it that Reed Richards was locked away in a nuthouse back in Latveria, scribbling jagged 4s on the walls and floor of his cell—and on himself—with a broken blue crayon all day long; his nights were spent screaming his wife's name over and over until he finally cried himself to sleep.

Could something like that be his own fate, for such a harmless mistake as seeing the Empress unclad?

Yes . . . if the Emperor were ever to find out.

For a moment—one that seemed to last an eternity—Joe formed a mental picture of arriving home at the end of the day, only to find his modest apartment in Georgetown wrecked, his family missing.

And one of Maria's severed fingers on the kitchen table; the blood seeping from the digit was still warm.

Joe violently shook his head, trying to dispel the nauseating image. Where had *that* come from?

And then he felt it—an itching at the back of his mind, like a spider crawling along the base of his skull. An involuntary tremor ran through his body, and he listened in horror as a small, sinister voice quietly echoed in his mind.

It "said" only two words, but they were enough to make him fall to his knees and weep, body hitching uncontrollably as tears streamed down his cheeks. Two words that let him know he should never have allowed his thoughts to wander, as his Empress had done before. Two words that made it clear that, even if he abandoned his post now and raced for home, he would still be far too late.

Two words—that heralded the end of his world.

*We know.*

It was a good day to be king.

Strolling through what had once been known as the Jacqueline Kennedy Garden, located on the east side of the White House, Victor von Doom paused long enough to feel the warmth of the sun upon his bare face—a rare moment of pleasure for a man whose days were normally spent constantly tinkering with the smallest parts of his near-perfect world, trying to smooth over the imperfections, few though they were. Dressed in a dark, pin-striped business suit—o, to at last be free of that damnable armor!—the purple silk sash of royalty draped from his right shoulder down to his left hip, he looked every part the strong leader that he was; after all, it was more than a mere suit of metal that made the man—it was the strength of his character, his sheer determination to overcome adversity, his constant drive for perfection . . . and the satisfaction of knowing he could thoroughly destroy his enemies.

A slight breeze ruffled his dark-brown hair; he smoothed it back into place with a well-manicured hand. Each finger of that hand contained a ring, as did the other; ten baubles in all, possessing an amazing variety of powers, despite their outward gaudiness—prizes recovered from the corpse of the Chinese warlord called The Mandarin after von Doom had stripped the flesh from his bones with an earthshaking blast of cosmic energy collected from the spent bodies of alien creatures like Annihilus, the self-proclaimed ruler of the anti-matter universe called The Negative Zone, and the brutish Blaastar, "the Living Bomb Blast." In the early days of von Doom's regime, a great many of Earth's so-called "super-villains" had made various bids to depose this modern-day Alexander the Great; all had failed, their rotting corpses raised high for all to see. Matters had quieted down quite a bit after that, though every now and then some misguided fool had to be reminded of his or her place in this brave, new world.

More often than not, that place was a grave.

Dispelling the pleasant but utterly useless memory of his many victories with a slight wave of his hand—for only the weak-minded lived in the past—von Doom turned his attention to the work that his wife had done on the garden in just a few short months: rose and oleander bushes were bursting with color, the sweet fragrances of their blooms mingling with those of hyacinth and hibiscus and gladiola; and somehow, despite the severity of Washington's summers and winters, Ororo had even found a way to maintain a row of megaflora normally found only in the hothouse-like environment of the Savage Land, that bizarre world beneath the snow and ice of Antarctica where native tribes still fought for survival each day, and all manner of dinosaurs still roamed, apparently unaware that they were supposed to be long extinct.

The Emperor nodded, pleased with what he saw. It was an orderly garden, one that quietly reflected the world around it.

His order. His world.

"Master?"

Von Doom turned. Just inside the doorway of the Garden Room stood a skittish, unassuming little man in a charcoal-gray suit. Of average height and build, thinning brown hair plastered across the top of his egg-shaped skull, he had about him the look of a frightened animal normally accustomed to hiding from the predators of the world—a nonentity destined to forever remain in the shadows. The Emperor made no attempt to recall his name.

"What is it, lackey?" he demanded. "Who are you, to disturb Doom in his hour of contemplation?"

"I-I m-meant no disrespect, Master," the man stuttered. Head bowed, eyes lowered, beads of sweat started to form across his brow, but he made no move to wipe them away. "I-It's just that your military advisers have arrived."

"Excellent," the Emperor said. "Tell them Doom will meet with them in the war room."

"Very good, Master." With a quick bow, clearly overjoyed that he had been given permission to leave, the aide backed away until he had stepped from sight.

Off to one side, an auburn-haired young woman dressed in a black leather bodysuit—one of a half dozen similarly garbed men and women who skirted the edge of the garden, ever alert for any sign of trouble—touched a hand to a small receiver tucked into her left ear, listened for a few moments, then nodded.

"Speak, Lancer," von Doom said.

Lancer—who normally went by the less dramatic name of Samantha Dunbar—turned to face her liege. "It's Phillips. They've responded to the tip from the Psi Division, and they want to know what they should do now."

Von Doom paused, considering his options. "Have the child taken to the Academy. He'll make a passable future soldier for Ms. Frost to shape."

Lancer fell silent. From the corner of his eye, von Doom watched her nervously chew on her bottom lip for a moment.

"The wife?" she finally asked.

"She is of no use to Doom," the monarch replied immediately. "Kill her."

Lancer winced, as though she had been struck. It annoyed von Doom that, after all her years of service, this woman, whom he had taken from the Earth of an alternate reality, to whom he had gifted incredible powers, in whom he had given a modicum of trust, could still be so weak. So . . . imperfect.

He might have to do something about that situation one day. . . .

"And Paterson?"

A half smile came to the Emperor's lips; a contortion of facial muscles that seemed as uncomfortable for him to assume as it was for an observer to look upon. There was no warmth in the expression—only a burning malignancy. "He has seen the elegance and beauty of his Empress—a magnificent sight reserved for Doom, and Doom alone. Let that be the *last* thing he ever sees."

Lancer swallowed, hard. "You want him killed, as well?"

Von Doom shook his head. "Not at all. He is to be released, unharmed—" he slowly opened the palm of his hand "—*after* his eyes have been presented to me."

Without waiting for an acknowledgment of his commands, the Emperor strode from the garden, knowing that not even Lancer would be foolish enough to consider defying him.

Truly, it *was* a good day to be king.

When Ororo exited the master bedroom—dressed in a flowing burgundy gown that swirled around her long legs, an ornate, black metal tiara holding back her hair—she was surprised to discover that Paterson was absent from his post outside her door; in his place was another armored guard, one who smartly snapped to attention at her approach. Ororo could immediately tell that it wasn't her constant companion—the new man's body language was too stiff, too formal, and his powerfully-built upper torso looked as though it had been crammed into the emerald-hued metal suit.

Another S.H.I.E.L.D. agent? Perhaps, but more likely than not he was a former "super hero" or "super-villain"—the kind of gaudily-attired individual whose practices had been outlawed by Victor a year after he came into power. The smart ones had registered their powers with the government and joined the Imperial armed forces; the rebellious ones had been eliminated by their own kind, per von Doom's mandates. As for the majority, most had gone into early "retirement," never to be seen again. It all worked out in the end, though—no longer would cities be transformed into battlefields by testosterone-driven egotists bent on flexing their overly-developed muscles for all to see, nor would the people of the world live in fear that some madman might one day destroy the planet as an act of revenge for some perceived slight. Nowadays, the only costumed men and women on display for the public were those featured in movies, like the one that had premiered in New York the night before.

"Your Majesty," the guard said, equally as stiff, through the speaker in his helmet. There was a heavy Japanese accent to his voice.

"I do not see Agent Paterson," Ororo said. "Can you tell me why he is not at his post, Agent . . . ?"

Eyes front, back ramrod straight, the guard hesitated for a brief moment before responding. "Kenuichio Harada, Your Majesty. Agent Paterson was . . . called away."

"By whom?"

Again, a hesitation. "By the Emperor, Your Majesty."

Ororo frowned. She didn't know which she found more annoying: the fact that Victor would call away her personal bodyguard without telling her, or the way in which this new guard seemed to be hiding something.

"And why was that?" she pressed.

"I-I do not know, Your Majesty," Harada replied. Ororo could almost see the sweat pouring down his face inside the helmet as he fought to remain composed. "I was merely told to take his place until further notice . . . and to notify you that the members of the Emperor's council have arrived. They will be meeting with him in the war room."

Ororo arched an eyebrow. All right, then—if she was going to learn anything, she would have to ask Victor directly . . . but later.

She turned on her heel. "Very well, Agent Harada, come along. I have duties of my own to which I must attend today. I shall speak with my husband when he next makes himself available." Head held high, Ororo strode down the hallway, bound for the private elevator that would take her to the ground floor.

Like a well-trained dog, the metal-garbed bodyguard hurried from his post and fell into step behind his mistress.

As the Empress made her way downstairs, her husband's war council was already convening.

Constructed in a sub-sub-basement of the mansion, the war room was a two-level, block-long bunker constructed of adamantium, the hardest, strongest metal on Earth. The lighting was intentionally kept low, so that the dozens of technicians and systems operators working there could concentrate solely on the monitors and computer stations at which they sat, processing data collected by the Langley, Virginia-based Psi Division—formerly the headquarters of the Central Intelligence Agency—and the hundreds of international agents around the world who kept the peace established by the Emperor a decade ago. There was no camaraderie here, no gentle buzz of office chatter, no personal items adorning the work areas; the only buzzing came from the banks of computers that lined the walls of the upper level, the only personal item belonged to the Emperor: a large, round, marble table adorned with the coat-of-arms of Latveria, sitting in the center of the lower level.

Seated around this table were two men and three women of widely diverse backgrounds—so diverse, in fact, that it would normally have been impossible to imagine them gathered in the same room, had it not been for the man who had brought them together.

First, there was Dorma, the Minister of Defense. A blue-skinned, red-haired amazon clad in green-and-gold battle armor that revealed far more of her body than it concealed, she was the former queen of Atlantis, hailing from the same parallel Earth on which von Doom had found Lancer. As a denizen of the ocean, Dorma could not survive long above water, so a clear plastic mask covered her nose and mouth, constantly recycling the sea water contained in her lungs. Her strength was as impressive as her temper was short—each fearful to behold, especially in the heat of battle, when her bloodlust would often build to such levels that she would become possessed by what in Norse legend was called a "berserker rage": a mindless, relentless, savage attack that would not end until the last of her enemies had been eliminated, and her desire for blood had at last been sated. Though there were times when she thought of von Doom as a weak man—why create alliances with former enemies when it was far easier to kill them and then take possession of what they had owned?—she respected him . . . and his power. The Emperor, she knew, was not afraid to dirty his hands by personally slaying anyone foolish enough to challenge his rule, as the Wizard, and Attuma, and the Master had learned. And his Psi Division allowed him to know of any future attacks before they developed beyond the planning stage, as so many others had discovered over the years—before they died.

Dorma was also well aware that, should the day come when she might attempt to cross swords with von Doom, there was no certainty that she would be the victor, for though she might find a way to best the Emperor, there was still his wife to contend with . . . and *she* commanded the elements. A difficult problem to consider, but Dorma had always enjoyed a challenge....

Possessing the ability to absorb kinetic energy—thus making him virtually indestructible in any fight—Sebastian Shaw was the Emperor's expert on Earth's mutant population ... not that he thought of himself as just another child of the atom, though. Born into a poor family in Pittsburgh, Pennsylvania, Shaw was the Horatio Alger of mutantkind, pulling himself up by his bootstraps from the depths of poverty to become a millionaire by age twenty, then parlaying that fortune into the creation of Shaw Industries, a multinational corporation contracted by the pre-von Doom U.S. government for the development of cutting-edge weaponry. Though there was no real need for a munitions designer—for, after all, who could create weapons superior to those built by Doom himself?—it was Shaw's contacts in the mutant communities scattered around the globe that made him invaluable to the Emperor. Often, they had provided better information about any superpowered dissenters among them than that gathered by S.H.I.E.L.D., especially when it came to the doings of the man who called himself Magneto; over the years, they had tipped off Shaw to the fugitive's various plots to strike against the government, which were then nipped in the bud by the Avengers, or even by von Doom himself.

Except for that one instance, in Paris, of course.

Strangely, though, there had been no reports about the "Master of Magnetism" for some time now....

Industrialist Anthony Stark originally made a name for himself as a weapons manufacturer for the United States government long before von Doom had taken power, or Shaw Industries had signed its first contract with the military. Unlike Shaw or the Emperor, though, he had been born into money, which seemed to naturally result in Stark's eventual transformation into a millionaire playboy, jetting around the world, dining at the finest restaurants, dating the most beautiful women. These days, when he wasn't overseeing the work performed by his company, Stark Solutions, he was von Doom's expert on the super hero community, having overseen the formation of the Avengers just before the Emperor's rise to power; he had even gone so far as to donate the Stark family mansion on New York's Fifth Avenue to the group as their headquarters. Because of his involvement with this team of "Earth's Mightiest Heroes," it was the millionaire industrialist's job to keep the Emperor apprised of all government-sanctioned super hero activities, and to make him aware of any new superpowered individuals who might pop up; in a world in which radioactivity seemed to trigger a recessive gene in some unsuspecting man or woman every other day of the week—and who knew what even sitting too close to a TV set might do?—it was only a matter of time before that person got up the nerve to sew together a form-fitting costume of some eye-catching hue and parade around in public to demonstrate their powers—illegally, of course.

Oddly enough, though it was the kind of work one would expect to see performed by a flunky, interviewing these new "Marvels" was a job that Stark actually enjoyed. Then again, considering his handsome, Errol Flynn-like features, and the fact that nine out of every ten new "super heroines" were young, pretty, and had the kind of perfect figure made for skintight spandex, there was no doubt in anyone's mind that "growing up" to become the CEO of a worldwide corporation had done nothing to affect the playboy's charm ... or his libido.

And speaking of sexual drives ...

As the director of S.H.I.E.L.D., Viper was the expert on international espionage, having been the leader of Hydra for a few years before switching her loyalties to von Doom—and then helping him to destroy the organization. A combination of femme fatale and superspy, she was the living embodiment of the type of woman Hollywood movies once referred to as "the bad girl": clad in an emerald-hued latex jumpsuit and opera-length gloves that seemed spray painted on her, she was tall and sleek, with flowing, jet-black tresses that cascaded over her right eye in a Veronica Lake coiffure, and the kind of smoldering, high-cheekboned Asian features that one would expect to find on the cover of a fashion magazine. It was widely known that if Viper couldn't use her "feminine wiles" to obtain information, she wouldn't hesitate to kill to get what she wanted. No one trusted her, not even von Doom, for anyone willing to switch sides so quickly in order to rise to a higher position of power could only be biding their time until their next upwardly mobile strike. The downside to such a situation, though, was that von Doom could have her killed at any time once he no longer needed her services, either by his own hand—the Mandarin's rings weren't just for show, after all—or by ordering her own agents to do the deed. She could easily name a dozen men and women under her direct command who wouldn't hesitate to complete that assignment, though none had been stupid enough to move against her . . . yet.

Still, she counted herself lucky whenever she thought about that ugly encounter with von Doom six months ago, when she had to report to him that her best agents had lost track of Magneto just outside of Marrakesh. Then, he had merely settled for crippling her, using just a fraction of the power contained in his armor to shatter every bone in her right hand.

Even after it was surgically repaired, she would never have full use of the hand again, and she was constantly reminded of that fact—and the penalty for failing the Emperor—every time a cold spell swept through the capital. There never seemed to be enough painkillers to dull the ache in her bones . . . or her mind.

Finally, there was Wanda Maximoff. Although born a mutant, gifted with a probability-altering ability that gave the appearance that she could perform incredible feats of magic—at least, that had been her initial understanding of her powers—she was not one of Shaw's subordinates. Instead, having studied various forms of magic under the tutelage of an ancient witch named Agatha Harkness, Wanda had been appointed von Doom's adviser on all things supernatural. Not to be overlooked, of course, was the fact that she was the daughter of the Emperor's longtime enemy, Magneto, which meant that she could always provide some insight into her father's habits ... and weaknesses. Though she was just as attractive as the S.H.I.E.L.D. director, with a bounty of curly, reddish-brown hair framing somewhat angular features, Wanda preferred to dress far more conservatively than the other women, opting for a dark-blue jacket and matching full-length dress. A dozen charm bracelets encircled her left wrist, each gold chain adorned with trinkets of various shapes and sizes—astrological signs, mystical symbols, even a tiny toy animal or three—and a pair of gold hoops hung from her ears. Though she and her brother, Pietro, were essentially gypsies like von Doom, born in the mountains of eastern Europe, Wanda carried herself with the air of a noblewoman, tending more often than not to look down her nose at the savage Dorma and the over-sexed Viper. Clearly, she felt superior to them both ... and, perhaps, to Stark and Shaw, as well.

Five individuals. Brought together once more at the Emperor's command, they sat and waited for their monarch to appear.

And waited.

And waited.

Arms held above her head, Viper yawned and arched her back, stretching with an almost feline grace over the top of the plush leather chair in which she sat. It was an unnecessary, overly dramatic gesture to smooth out a kink in her back, but it had the desired effect she'd wanted, causing both Stark and Shaw to openly stare at the way the low lighting of the war room played off the colorful rubber material of her jumpsuit.

Dorma grunted, annoyed by the men's idiotic gaping. "Children ..." she huffed.

Across from her, Wanda frowned and rolled her eyes, disgusted more by Viper's sex kitten act than the attention it was getting. "Oh, please ..." she muttered.

Viper eased back to a more natural sitting position and, rolling her head to one side, turned to look at Wanda. The director sneered, bright white teeth forming a shark-like smile; it looked even more disturbing set against the bright green of her lipstick.

"Feeling a bit outclassed, Wanda?" she purred, with a haughtiness that women always found downright infuriating, but men found incredibly sexy. "Maybe if you dressed less like a peasant and more like you did in the old days, you'd have men reacting to *you* the same way." The smile widened. "I've seen the pictures of you back when you were Daddy's Little Girl, you and big brother Pietro helping him with his plans to take over the world. Did he *really* approve of that whole swimsuit-and-body stocking look, or was that just a simple case of a teenaged girl rebelling against her father by dressing provocatively?"

"If it were, at least I grew out of that phase," Wanda replied evenly.

Viper laughed—a sharp, mocking sound without any trace of warmth. "I'm certain Daddy must be very pleased . . . wherever he may be."

Wanda glared heatedly at the raven-tressed woman, then glanced at her left hand, which was suddenly aglow; unconsciously, she had formed one of her "hex-spheres." She stared for a few moments at the chaos energy dancing around the tips of her fingers, then casually waved her hand in a dismissive motion.

Without warning, the base of Viper's seat collapsed as its metal supports suddenly twisted out of shape and snapped. Unable to react in time, the S.H.I.E.L.D. director yelped loudly as the chair fell backward, tossing her to the floor. In an instant, she was back on her feet, assuming a combat-ready position.

Wanda, however, remained seated. Picking off an imaginary piece of lint from the sleeve of her jacket, she looked up at the "unfortunate" recipient of her hex-bolt.

"I am *so* sorry, Viper," she said, smiling sweetly. "That's the problem with a power like mine: who knew that the odds of you making me angry enough to cause your seat to fall apart could be so great?"

Viper hissed through clenched teeth. "I'm going to *enjoy* breaking you, little girl . . ."

"Enough!" Shaw bellowed, slamming his fist down on the table. A powerful vibration ran through the marble, immediately bringing everyone's attention to bear on him. "If the two of you want to engage in a catfight, I'd be more than happy to arrange the event at my Hellfire Club in New York. I'm certain the members would find it ... stimulating. But for now—"' he glared at each woman, almost daring them to challenge him "—try acting like the professionals you are."

"Well said, Sebastian," said a voice from the upper level of the bunker. The quintet looked up to find von Doom, accompanied by Lancer, standing on the platform above them—but for how long? The four seated councilors jumped to their feet.

Gripping the railing, the Emperor lowered his gaze to lock eyes with his espionage expert.

"Viper," he said, voice rumbling with barely controlled anger, "there are times when you test the limits of my patience. Do you need *another* reminder of what happens to those who anger Doom?"

Glancing from the corner of her eye, Wanda was startled to see the instantaneous change that came over Viper: one moment, she was a confident, powerful woman skilled in a hundred different ways of destroying a man's very soul; the next, her one visible eye had widened in horror, and an uncontrollable tremor ran through her body.

"N-no, Y-your Majesty," Viper said, quickly lowering her gaze to the floor. She clutched her right hand with her left, holding it close to her chest, then winced slightly, as though more from recalling an unwanted memory than from any actual pain. Around her, the other war councilors did their best to avoid looking at her ... or von Doom.

"Excellent," the Emperor said. Signaling Lancer to remain where she was, he stepped over to the end of the platform; the part on which he stood quietly detached itself from the main section and floated down to the main level. Once it touched the floor, von Doom stepped off and walked over to join his advisers. One of the guards seemed to suddenly materialize near him, just in time to pull back the chair reserved for the Emperor. Von Doom eased into the seat, then motioned for the others to join him. And, as quickly as he had arrived, the guard moved back to his position.

"What news?" Von Doom asked.

The advisers glanced at one another, then Stark turned to face the monarch. "I gather from the way we're all staring back and forth across the table that the situation remains the same: there's now been no sign of Magneto for a year. The Avengers, the Thunderbolts, even Excalibur—none of the super heroes who are still active have seen hide or hair of him, not since the destruction of Paris." He frowned, clearly upset by the memory. "We've sent search teams into the Mole Man's realm, even worked with Prince Namor of Atlantis—" Dorma emitted a sharp, short laugh at the mention of the sovereign's name "—and Lord Plunder to plumb the depths of the oceans and the Savage Land, respectively. Nothing."

"He also hasn't used his powers in all this time," Viper added, regaining her composure. "If he had, we would have detected it with the network of satellites we have orbiting the globe. And he can't be off-world—there have been no recent signs of extraterrestrial vehicles in our solar system to allow him the possibility of hitching a ride, and no unauthorized spacecraft have been launched—at least, none that haven't been shot down within minutes of liftoff. His body wasn't in any of the wreckage."

The Emperor waved a hand in a dismissive manner. "Nor would I have expected you to find it, Director. Lensherr is a bold, clever man, in his own way . . . though still a child in comparison to Doom. Escape might be his plan, but he would not go about it in such a way that he would face the possibility of capture or death." He shook his head. "No, he would find some other means of avoiding the punishment due him . . ."

Von Doom's eyes narrowed as he turned to Wanda.

"Ms. Maximoff?" he asked.

Wanda drew a deep breath, held it for a moment, then slowly released it. Though she had cut all ties with her father years ago, and had been horrified by the destruction of Paris—how could even

Magneto have brought himself to crash a nuclear-powered space station onto the City of Lights, killing millions of innocent people?—she was still hesitant to respond whenever she was asked to provide information about him. A case of blood being thicker than water, she often surmised; even though he was now a mass-murderer, on the run from the citizenry of an entire planet, she was still his daughter, and a small piece of her—one she constantly fought to ignore, often failing—continued to love him for the gentle man he had once been, continued to hope for the day when they might be reunited as a family.

A futile hope, Wanda knew. She had been drifting away from her father even before his most infamous act against the Empire, growing increasingly disenchanted by his continuous plans for striking out at von Doom, in some misguided bid to seize power for himself. Eventually, she just walked away, fearing that, if she did not put distance between herself and her father's obsessions, the madness would overtake her as well.

To her surprise, Magneto had allowed her to go. She had never looked back.

On the day he wiped out one of the most cherished cities in the world, though, he died in her heart for all time. Now, for Wanda, he truly *was* the monster von Doom had once proclaimed him—an uncaring, remorseless brute who had to be put down like a rabid animal before more people were harmed.

Still, he *was* her father . . .

Wanda shook her head to clear her thoughts, then looked to von Doom.

"He's not dead," she finally said. "His . . ." She paused, licked her lips, which had suddenly become dry. "His spirit has not passed on to the astral plane, nor have any of my spies in the higher dimensions detected his presence, which eliminates the possibility that he might have employed someone with magical abilities to escape *this* dimension."

Von Doom sat back from the table, slouching regally in his chair. Frowning, he rested his chin in his left hand and stared off into space, deep in thought. His advisers sat quietly, glancing at one another while they waited.

"Not dead," he muttered, "yet not active, either." The hint of a malevolent smile played at the corners of his mouth, and his eyes sparkled with mischief. "What are you up to, my old enemy? What dark thoughts run wildly through your mind each time you are reminded that Doom is master of all, and there is nothing you can do to make it otherwise?" The smile broadened. "Had I the opportunity to look into your eyes, to see what such knowledge can do to a man's soul . . ." Von Doom chuckled softly, then straightened in his chair, eyes clearing. He fixed each of his advisers with a steely gaze.

*"Find him,"* he commanded. "Lensherr *is* clever, but not so clever that he can eliminate *all* traces of his movements. I will tolerate his existence not a moment longer, nor will I tolerate failure from any of you. On the night that all the world celebrates the glory and majesty that is Doom, I have every intention of presenting to my beautiful wife a gift that no other but Doom could give to her on such a momentous occasion:

"The head of the Empire's most infamous villain, resting on a silver platter for the world to see."

Von Doom smiled then, and to Wanda Maximoff, it was an expression that she found disturbingly familiar—one she had often seen etched on the features of her father many times.

It was the face of madness.

# 3

ALF A world away, the target of the Emperor's ire shivered uncontrollably—an unconscious reaction to, as the old saying went, the feeling that someone had just walked across his grave.

An odd sensation, considering he was standing at the edge of a desert.

Body wrapped in a thin, coarse blanket, head covered by the red-and-purple-hued, metal, gladiator-style helmet that was his trademark, Erik Magnus Lensherr—the man more infamously known to the citizens of the Empire as Magneto—pulled the makeshift cloak tighter around his shoulders and gazed at the world around him. He stood on the outskirts of a village called Araouane, in the West African state of Mali—less a proper village, really, then a scattered collection of rough, mud-brick buildings now worn smooth and half-obscured by the constant ebb and flow of the dune sea around them as it washed against the decades-old constructs. Beyond the village was the vast wasteland called the Sahara—nothing but miles of sand stretching off to the horizon, the monotony of the less-than-impressive view occasionally broken by a blast of hot, dry air that created dust devils that danced and swayed across the landscape as though moving in time to a beat

47

that only they could hear. If any spot in the world could truly be considered the last place in which one would expect to find the Empire's greatest enemy, it was here, in this former oasis 160 miles north of Timbuktu.

And yet here he stood, and it was here that he had lived for the past year.

*But it hasn't* really *been a year,* Magneto thought. *At least, I do not think it has* . . . He frowned. Time in the desert was mean-ingless—the sun rose in the morning and set in the evening; what you did in between was pass the hours not so much living as merely surviving. But could enough days have passed to equal an entire year? Magneto shook his head. *No, it's* less *than that—I'm sure of it. But how long, then?* Seeking some sort of proof for his belief, he opened the blanket and looked down at his body, and wasn't pleased at all with what he saw: the chiseled, weightlifter's form he once possessed had grown soft with disuse, and he had lost some weight. The washboard-like abdominal muscles and rock-hard pectorals that once had looked so striking coated in red spandex had lost their well-defined edges to a diet of coarse meats and rice, and a lack of exercise brought about by the fact that there was really nothing to *do* here.

"Perhaps it *has* been a year, then," he muttered softly, then sighed.

He turned his gaze to the oasis, if only to take his mind off his current state of decay; it was in no better shape. The village was a far cry from the elegant splendor he had once enjoyed when he had been headquartered aboard an asteroid that he had forced into geosynchronous orbit around the Earth with his awesome powers. Christened "Asteroid M" in honor of its owner—for Magneto was never known for his humility—the hollowed-out rock had served as a space station of sorts . . . as well as a launching point for some of his most ingenious plots to seize control of the planet. Floating high above the Earth also had its defensive advantages, as his enemies had learned, since it was next to impossible to launch a counterattack when the mutant overlord could clearly see it coming and take measures to stop it. Sadly, though, that sense of luxury and security had come to an end the day the asteroid fell from orbit.

Lensherr shook his head. *How the mighty have fallen, indeed* . . . he thought ruefully.

He wiped away rivulets of perspiration that trickled down his face from beneath his helmet, reached up to remove it so he could run a hand through his matted, shoulder-length white hair, then stopped. No matter how uncomfortable it was to wear in the constant heat, the helmet was probably the only protection he had against von Doom's much feared Psionics Division, its delicate micro-circuitry creating a "barrier" that shielded his thoughts from any unwanted mental probes. An ironic situation, he had come to realize, since he had originally created the circuitry to subjugate the minds of his own enemies, wiping hatred and bigotry from their subconscious as part of his ongoing efforts to make the mutant race the dominant species on the planet. He'd managed to create similar circuitry for the small bedroom of his house, which allowed him to remove the helmet so he could sleep with some sense of security, but he had run out of supplies before he could extend the barrier to encompass the entirety of the building.

A sharp wind from the east suddenly ripped through the village, threatening to tear the blanket from his grip. Lensherr tilted his head and body into the superheated gale, fighting for possession of his meager cloak—his only protection from the airborne grains of sand that punished his exposed skin with what felt like the sharp pricks of a million needles.

Gritting his teeth—a movement that afforded the desert sand yet another opportunity to try and pour into his mouth like an ocean rushing to fill a pitcher—the Master of Magnetism once more fought down the urge to use his powers to create some sort of barrier that would separate him from the granules that coated him in ever-thickening layers, even if only for a short time. Tempting as it might be—just to be able to breathe clearly for a few minutes!—he knew that *any* use of his mutant-spawned abilities would result in death; he was well aware of the satellites that orbited the globe, waiting for him to slip up and provide von Doom with his precise location. And once the "Emperor" had that, it wouldn't be long before S.H.I.E.L.D. and the Avengers and the other countless lapdogs who served von Doom would be sweeping across the dunes, like hounds bearing down on the lonely fox.

But this fox, as Magneto had been more than happy to demonstrate in the past, was a most dangerous animal when cornered . . .

Nevertheless, as frustrating as the wind and sand and oppressive heat were, he was willing to tolerate them, if such resignation meant that he would have one more day to survive, if only to spite his enemy.

One more day, he thought darkly, to plot his revenge.

As suddenly as it had sprung up, the wind abated, and Lensherr was at last able to relax, the muscles in his arms now twitching uncontrollably and burning like fire after their battle with the elements.

*I really* do *need to get back into shape* . . . he thought wearily, rubbing his limbs to alleviate the spasms.

A scraping sound from just behind him caught his attention, and he glanced over his shoulder. As he had expected to see, the source of the small noise was no villain or Guardsman creeping up to attack, but a dark-skinned woman in her thirties, using an oversized bowl to dig away at a pile of windblown sand that had accumulated on her doorstep. She was wrapped in a flowing, colorful blanket of yellow, blue, and green patterns set on a red field. Wordlessly, the woman lifted her filled bowl, walked a dozen paces from her home to dump the load, then walked back to start the process again; this would continue until she had cleared the entrance to her satisfaction, then she would head over to one of the other houses to do the same. She was one of the village's three "sand women" who labored from dawn to dusk, clearing the doorways and courtyards of the thirty buildings that had not yet been swallowed by the desert, as more than a hundred other homes—plus a mosque—had been over the years. It was a never-ending battle, and one they were ultimately destined to lose, but that knowledge did nothing to dampen their spirits, nor did it deter them from their task—not when the payment for such work was a small bag of rice or sugar. Enough food to go on working for another day; to keep their families alive for one more day.

Just past the woman, her daughter—a girl of three or four years—stood in the open doorway, sucking on a piece of raw lamb fat and doing her best to shield it from the grainy particles that still swirled in the air. Like her mother, the girl looked older than her actual age, eyes bright but somber, body as worn down by the elements as the building in which they lived. It was a sobering sight, this child with the eyes of an adult, and one that forced even the mighty lord of magnetism to turn his gaze elsewhere. He focused on the mother.

"Good day, Abena Metou," Lensherr said pleasantly.

The woman looked up from her labors and smiled warmly. "A good day to you, as well, John Smith. The Bright Lady must smile upon us, for two things have now occurred: the wind has stopped so that I may work, and I see that you have begun to master our language."

Lensherr shrugged. "Not as much as I would like, good lady," he admitted. "But enough to hold a . . . um . . . a . . ." He paused, suddenly unable to recall the right word for—

"A conversation," Abena said.

Lensherr smiled lopsidedly. "Yes. That."

Abena nodded in understanding and raised the sand-filled bowl, turning her attention back to the work; one never knew when the next gust of wind might race through the village and force her to start the cycle all over again, so she tried to move as quickly as the heat would allow. Lensherr watched in silence as she carried the pile from one spot to another, making no offer to help, for this was how the woman made her living and, as meager as the pay was, it still provided some comfort for her family. To interfere would have been akin to taking the food from her daughter's mouth.

*At least it would provide some exercise,* he thought, his gaze drifting down toward his softened body. Grunting harshly in disgust, he pulled the blanket tighter around himself.

Besides, he reminded himself, performing such menial labor was beneath the great Magneto, a man who could move entire *buildings* with the merest application of his powers, let alone a mere pile of dust. A man who dreamed of the day when all *Homo sapiens* were down on their hands and knees like this sand woman—though, under his rule, such a submissive position would be a sign that humanity had at last recognized him as their undisputed ruler, and that they had acknowledged the fact that they were an inferior race.

But as he observed Abena's struggles against the desert, Erik Lensherr couldn't help but wonder if his own efforts—to wrest power from von Doom, to establish *Homo superior* as the dominant species—might also be ultimately doomed to fail.

Lensherr grunted. It did no good to think that way—a man who had survived the Nazi death camps, who had eluded capture for years despite the best efforts of the Empire, should have no place in his mind for dwelling on negative thoughts; they merely wasted precious time better spent formulating a plan of attack. Now angry with himself, he shook his head to clear his mind and tried to focus on more important matters.

Like the dark form taking shape on the horizon, its features distorted by the waves of heat rising from the sands.

"Visitors," Lensherr muttered, eyes narrowing. "Perhaps I might get some exercise today, after all . . ."

It took another two hours for the phantom-like shape to solidify into something far more recognizable: a silver-and-white-robed man—shoulders hunched, turbaned head resting against his chest—seated upon a camel. Even from the doorway of his home, Lensherr could see that the rider was dozing, more than likely lulled to sleep by the swaying motion of the beast as it lurched over the dunes.

Of course, it could be a trick—an apparently harmless wanderer on his way, perhaps, to the salt mines of Taoudenni, nine miles to the north, who feigns sleep in order to close in on his intended mutant prey before finally revealing himself to be one of von Doom's superpowered hounds, come to run an equally-superpowered international terrorist to ground. It wouldn't be the first time such a deception had been attempted.

Then again, it just *might* be a harmless wanderer seeking a brief reprieve from the searing heat. After all, Araouane had once been a regular rest stop for the trans-Saharan camel caravans that had moved through the area, before the desert began to extend its boundaries and consume everything in its path.

A grim smile etched itself across Lensherr's weather-beaten features as an old joke flitted through his mind: "Just because I'm paranoid, that doesn't mean they *aren't* out to get me." He'd never figured out exactly who "they" were supposed to be—he'd always had trouble understanding humor—but after years of dealing with Victor von Doom and his government, he had a good idea of who "they" *might* be . . . at least, in his case.

As the camel and its charge drew nearer, Lensherr stepped from his home, intending to meet it before it entered the village proper; though the oasis's inhabitants were not of his own kind, the mutant terrorist had grown somewhat attached to them . . . despite their inferiority. They had given him shelter, shared their food, treated him with respect, and had accepted him for the person he appeared to be—John Smith, a wanderer in search of a peaceful existence—never questioning him about why he had come to Araoune, or why he had remained.

In Magneto's case, however, that sense of attachment was more along the lines of the feeling an owner would have for a loyal, obedient pet.

They *were* just humans, after all.

Truth be told, it was not for any fear of destroying the crumbling houses around him or accidentally wiping out the village's small population that caused the master of magnetism to approach the new arrival—casualties and property damage were just small parts of the larger game being played between the mutant terrorist and the Emperor he sought to overthrow, and Magneto had long ago stopped being concerned with the consequences caused by each roll of the dice; the winning of the game mattered far more than broken homes or shattered bodies. Paris was a prime example of *that* philosophy. Nor was it some misguided belief that he could reason with the man before matters turned ugly. What drew him out was a desire to avoid any prolonged battle that would force him to use his powers and give von Doom's forces time to zero-in on him.

Of course, as Lensherr had come to realize long before the Emperor had come to power, it was that the use of his magnetic abilities should always be a last resort when it became necessary to eliminate an enemy; using common weapons, or even his bare hands, made tracing his movements around the globe far more difficult. And if there was one thing he had learned from the guards and staff at Auschwitz—as he had watched each member of his family slowly starve to death, or march into the infamous "showers," or scream in agony and terror as they were used as part of some horrific eugenic experiment—it was the variety of ways available to kill another person without resorting to superpowers. The Nazis had been excellent tutors, and the boy who had become a man behind the guard towers and barbed wire fences of the camp had been most eager to demonstrate all that he had learned after the war . . . on each and every one of them that he could find. Over fifty years later, some of those "lessons" still stuck in his mind.

The rider was closer now, and Lensherr quickened his pace. If he could get close enough before the man made his move, dismount him from the camel and slice his throat with the dirk concealed within the folds of his robes . . .

The man suddenly raised his head, and stared at him. Lensherr stopped, eyes narrowing as he tried to imagine who it was he was facing. It was impossible to figure out, though; the man's features were covered by a pair of dark-lensed goggles, and a strip of cloth that concealed the lower half of his face.

The camel continued its slow pace, now angling toward the mutant fugitive. Acting nonchalantly, Lensherr raised a hand to wave to the rider, as though in greeting; the gesture concealed the movement of his other hand, which had slipped to the back of his robes, and the dagger that lay sheathed there.

As the beast finally drew alongside him, Lensherr's hand closed around the blade's handle. He smiled pleasantly at the man, who was now within striking distance. The fugitive's hand started to come around with the dirk as he crouched, preparing to leap at the mysterious visitor—

And then the man was suddenly standing at his side, the dagger now in *his* hand.

Caught by surprise, Lensherr could not help but stand agape as the rider removed his headgear to reveal a younger version of the mutant criminal—or so it would seem to the casual observer: the same white hair, but cut short and spiky; the same angular features, but less lined, and pale in skin color, as opposed to the older man's sun-darkened complexion. But this was no android built by von Doom to look like him, no laboratory-created clone dispatched to eliminate him and take his place.

This was Lensherr's own flesh and blood—a son known by the more colorful codename "Quicksilver," gifted, not with his sire's magnetically-based abilities, but with the power of moving at incredible speeds; so fast, in fact, that Magneto's attempt to attack him had seemed, to his eyes, to play out in slow motion. Dismounting from the camel and removing the weapon from Lensherr's hand had all taken place in a fraction of a second—no challenge at all for someone capable of breaking the sound barrier, or performing a dozen or so tasks at the same time.

"Hello, Father," the visitor said evenly. He held up the dirk. "Still lacking the basic social skills necessary for greeting a guest properly, I see."

Slowly, Lensherr's shocked expression dissolved into a broad, friendly grin.

"Pietro . . ." he said.

Night fell on the Sahara, and, after a veritable banquet of delicacies from around the world provided by Pietro—Lensherr had almost forgotten what knishes and caviar tasted like—father and son at last sat down in the psionics-protected bedroom to talk.

"So, Pietro," Lensherr began, easing himself into a wicker chair, a glass of merlot in one hand, "how is your family?"

Pietro flopped down onto an assortment of oversized pillows piled near the door and stretched his legs. "My family? It's only been six months since my last visit—not all that much has changed. Aren't you more interested in what your Emperor is up to these days?"

Lensherr grunted. " 'My' Emperor. Bah." He waved a hand in a dismissive gesture. "There's time enough to talk of that tinheaded despot. For now, I'd rather hear about more pleasant matters." The look of anger carved into his features softened to a small smile. "So—how is my granddaughter?"

Pietro smiled, clearly beaming with pride. "As pretty as her mother, and growing more beautiful with each day. She misses her grandfather, you know."

Lensherr's eyes sparkled with joy. "Misses her grandfather . . . or the presents he brings her?"

Pietro laughed. "Well, she *is* a child. Sometimes choosing between the two can be difficult—especially when one considers the number of gifts you've showered her with over the years." He shook his head disapprovingly. "You *do* have a tendency to spoil her."

"As is my right as a grandparent," Lensherr said firmly. He paused and stared into space for a moment, picturing Luna's smiling face, then sipped at his wine before continuing. "And Wanda? Any word on her?"

The white-haired speedster's gentle expression suddenly transformed into a look of disgust. "Wanda is still one of von Doom's lapdogs, from what my contact in Washington has told me," he said with a sneer. "She's become quite the authority on you, Father—von Doom has come to rely on her knowledge of your motivations, your probable hiding places, the people to whom you might turn for help . . . although the information *has* become dated over the past year." A mischievous smile played at the corners of his mouth. "They don't know *what* to make of your prolonged absence. They'd like to believe that you're dead, but with no physical evidence . . ."

Lensherr chuckled. "It must drive von Doom to the point of distraction, knowing that I must be out there somewhere, keeping to the shadows, avoiding the probes of even his most powerful telepaths, biding my time until the slightest opportunity presents itself to—what? Destroy another city? An entire country, perhaps?"

Pietro snorted. "You could start with his homeland. I doubt anyone would even notice the loss of such an insignificant spot on the map."

The mutant terrorist smiled wickedly. "I can almost imagine how that armored buffoon must have spent the past year, waiting for the moment when I might tip my hand and allow him the opportunity to strike me down and at last claim victory—only to realize with mounting frustration *that that day has never come.*"

"Which is why he's gathered together Wanda and his other advisers," Pietro added. "With the anniversary of his rise to power being celebrated next week, I think it's safe to assume that the entire world—von Doom included—is holding its collective breath, wondering if that is the time when the dreaded Magneto will at last reappear and resume his campaign of terror."

Lensherr raised an eyebrow. "His anniversary, you say?"

Pietro nodded. "It will be ten years next Wednesday."

"Ten years . . ." Lensherr frowned. "Ten years of attack and withdrawal; of hiding from superpowered dolts, prying telepaths, and armored buffoons wielding plasma weapons; of having my name made synonymous with the kind of atrocities perpetrated on my people by the Nazis." His lips peeled back in a feral snarl. "All because of *him*."

The mutant overlord rose from his seat and began pacing the room. "Well," he mused aloud, "if von Doom is so certain that I will try to eliminate him at his celebration, who am I to disappoint him . . . ?"

"Are you *mad*, Father?" Pietro angrily snapped, leaping to his feet. "Do you think you can just step off a plane in America—let alone try to enter any airport around the world—and *not* expect to be assassinated the moment your identity is revealed?"

Lensherr nodded. "You are right, my son. I am all too aware of the dangers involved in this desire to confront the spider in the center of its web." He sneered. "But I have had my *fill* of Victor von Doom and his much-lauded empire, and wish to bring a swift end to both. And now that you are here, I can proceed with the plans I have been formulating over these long twelve months." He gestured toward the doorway. "Go forth this very evening and start contacting those mutants who are still loyal to the cause. Tell them I have said the time has come to excise the cancerous growth that sits upon the throne; that they must join me to at last bring to reality the dream we have held onto for so long."

"And if they refuse to sacrifice themselves for the 'dream'?" Pietro asked, a slightly sarcastic tone to his voice.

Lensherr eyed him warily. "If I did not know you better, my son, I would start to think that you were not raising that question as though you were playing devil's advocate, but as an excuse to avoid joining your father on his—" he smiled "—quixotic crusade."

Pietro said nothing.

"It *is* true, though," Lensherr continued. "Not all of them will be willing to put their lives on the line, no matter how important the prize; that is to be expected. Regardless, there must be someone out there willing to join us in opposing that pompous, steel-faced egotist. Other members of our race who know that what von Doom has done to this planet is wrong, and are as eager as I to remove him from power." He clapped Pietro on the shoulder, certain in his beliefs. "They *are* out there, my son, and they *will* answer the call to arms."

"We shall see, Father..." Pietro replied, clearly unconvinced.

"Tell your contact in Washington to make the necessary arrangements for my entry to America," Lensherr said decisively. "The time has come for Magneto, Master of Magnetism, to step from exile and finally put an end to the tyranny of Victor von Doom.

"And this I swear," he continued, his voice rising with a fanatical fervor. "Before the last hour of his 'anniversary' has passed into history, before the last drop of his blood has seeped into the ground, there will be a new order to the world, and humanity shall at last bow before the superiority of mutantkind, and acknowledge us as their true masters!"

Not even Pietro could question *that* statement.

# 4

I T WAS like looking out on an alien world.

Actually, it was more a case of looking out at the nexus of all reality—a point where Time and Space swirled and eddied like two streams merging to form a mighty river—and realizing how small and insignificant you were, compared to the awe-inspiring majesty of Creation.

Humbling, to say the least.

Not that such a realization bothered the yellow-and-blue-costumed man who gazed at the roiling forces from one of the observation suites of the Starlight Citadel, that magnificent, city-sized construct that was home to the Supreme Guardian of the Omniverse. Arms folded across his broad chest, the man known only as Logan—who more often than not preferred being addressed by his codename of Wolverine—watched the perpetual clash of temporal and spatial energies with all the interest of someone who had visited a familiar tourist site they'd been to before, had seen all there was to see the first time, and was now eager to move on.

And since he was a member of the international group of super heroic mutants called the X-Men, it was a safe bet to assume that he *had* seen far more interesting sights.

Logan reached up and pulled back the mask that covered the

upper half of his head to reveal sharp, weather-beaten features seemingly etched into a permanent scowl, and an unusual hairstyle that started as a widow's peak above his furrowed brow and then expanded out to form a pair of immense tufts that stood up from the sides of his head, each tapering to a fine point; the mask had been constructed to fit around those tufts. It was a distinctive look, one as distinctive as the man himself. Standing just over five feet tall, in what appeared to be his mid-forties—although some people thought his real age might well be over a hundred, since he could recount tales of his world-spanning adventures that went at least as far back as World War II—Logan was a born scrapper: the kind of man who would start a fight at the drop of a hat... or in retaliation to someone calling him "Shorty." And he'd win every time, no matter how many opponents he faced, or how many beers he'd downed beforehand. As he often liked to say, "I'm the best there is at what I do," and if what he did was brawl with a savagery unparalleled in the Great White North, then the owners and patrons of a vast number of roughneck bars and tumble-down saloons across his native Canada could attest to that fact.

Now, though, he was as far from the familiar streets of Vancouver and Montreal as one could possibly imagine; not just beyond the rim of the Milky Way, but beyond the boundaries of Time itself. A spot where an infinite number of alternate dimensions coalesced, all monitored by the Guardian who was also acting as host to Wolverine and the other members of his troupe.

*And in* one o' those *alternate dimensions,* Logan considered darkly, *some* other *Canucklehead's gettin' the beer an' stogie I oughtta be havin'* ...

Slowly, Logan's eyes narrowed as he suddenly felt something intrude upon his thoughts, like a gentle tickle in the back of his mind. Tilting his head back slightly, he sniffed the reconstituted air that circulated throughout the citadel, then grunted softly in recognition of a familiar scent.

A few moments later, the door behind him irised open, and a tall, red-haired woman in her twenties entered the suite. She was clad in a form-fitting, green spandex bodystocking and gold opera-length gloves and thigh-high boots; a golden sash—its ends trailing around her ankles—was tied around her waist and held together with a bird-shaped clasp. Completing the outfit, set against a deep-blue triangle of cloth attached to the upper half of her costume, was a golden bird-shape, similar in design to the clasp, its wings spread across her chest, along the length of her collarbone. The stylized avian symbol was meant to be a representation of an Egyptian mythological bird known for its ability to live for five or six hundred years and then consume itself through the ritual of fire in order to start the cycle anew; a creature so powerful that not even death itself could hold sway over it for very long.

The Phoenix.

An appropriate codename for the woman—whose real name was Jean Grey—considering the many times she had cheated death, either on her own or while standing beside her teammates in battle.

"Mornin', Jeannie," Logan rasped, his voice made husky from a lifetime of cheap alcohol and even cheaper cigars.

"I hope I'm not interrupting, Logan," Jean said.

Logan shrugged. "Just contemplatin' my navel . . . which you already knew."

Jean nodded in agreement, though his back was still turned to her. As a telepath, she had the ability to scan the minds of others, even from a distance—a talent she had possessed since turning fourteen. And after years of dealing with power-mad super-villains, renegade mutants, hate-filled humans, and a race of insectoid monsters that made the creatures in *Aliens* look tame in comparison, she always mentally probed any room she was about to enter; such precautions often spared her the painful experience of having a hidden enemy bring a metal pipe crashing down on her head, or being surprised by a psi-powered individual like herself.

Occasionally, though, it meant that she might accidentally stumble into her friends' most private thoughts.

"I'm sorry about that, Logan," Jean said. "Force of habit."

"No big deal," he replied. "Even without you rappin' on my

chamber door proper, I picked up the smell o' yer perfume while you were still comin' down the hall." He sniffed again. "Wings?"

Jean smiled. "It's Scott's favorite."

Logan nodded, then turned to face her. "We 'bout done here, Red? I ain't had a beer in a month—" he waved a hand at the room around them "—and this place don't even have a minibar."

Jean laughed softly. The sound sent a pleasant shiver up Logan's back. He'd fallen in love with that laugh when they'd first met at Xavier's School for Gifted Mutants. Back then, he was the rough-and-tumble Canadian spy that the school's director, Charles Xavier, had recruited to join his academy; she was one of the original students, using the less attractive name "Marvel Girl" during her exploits with her four fellow students—Scott Summers, Henry McCoy, Bobby Drake, and Warren Worthington III. It had been a long time since he'd felt like a nervous schoolboy around a pretty girl, but Jean Grey had had that effect on him, almost from the moment he laid eyes on her. And like any man who suddenly finds himself tongue-tied by the sight of someone so beautiful that he can't bring himself to speak for fear of looking foolish and forever ruining the moment, Logan was never able to work up the nerve to tell Jean how he really felt for her; in fact, he made the situation even worse by eventually cutting himself off from the other X-Men, keeping to his own company, often leaving the school for long periods of time without telling anyone where he was going, or when he'd be back.

It was better that way, he often told himself. In his eyes, Jean was an unreachable goal; a woman who shone with the brightness of a sun. And he? He was Icarus, forever reaching for that shining star, basking in its warmth, only to be violently hurled to the ground, his once-lofty wings no longer able to support his weight.

Or his dreams.

An almost laughable situation, considering Logan had never been so hesitant—or outright smitten—during a lifetime of fighting and loving and, when the moment required it, killing.

The final, fatal blow to his heart had come on the day that he

had found himself unable to hold back the truth—the hurt—any longer. It had been a brief conversation, for Logan had always been a man of few words, but the outcome had been as he'd always known it would be: she cherished his friendship, but her heart belonged to another.

To Scott Summers, in fact.

It had come as no surprise to Logan. Summers was the team leader, a twentysomething mutant with an ability to project powerful, destructive beams of force from his eyes. It had been determined through years of testing that he was actually drawing upon the energy of a "non-Einsteinian universe," whatever the blazes that meant; Logan had never done well with science courses. Whether the power was a gift or a curse could only be determined by Summers, who had no control over it—merely opening his eyes when he awoke each morning would be enough to unleash an explosive force strong enough to level a good-sized hill . . . if he hadn't trained himself to keep his eyes closed in such situations. The only way to harness the wild energy, he had learned early in life, was through the use of ruby quartz, which was why he wore specially-designed sunglasses wherever he went, day or night, and why, when he was dressed in his flamboyant costume of blue and yellow, his eyes were covered by a slitted visor—one that had thus provided him with an appropriate codename: Cyclops. Tall and handsome, soft-spoken yet confident, with an air of tragedy that seemed to constantly hang over his shoulders like a stifling cloak, Summers hadn't pursued Jean—like Logan, he considered himself beneath her—but that hadn't stopped her from going after him. They'd been through too much together through the years, she'd insisted, had shared too many secrets to treat their relationship as nothing more than a by-product of a lengthy working environment. Slowly, she reached the poetic soul that lay hidden beneath the stoic exterior he had always projected, cracked the shell of professionalism he had used as a barrier to protect himself from an often cruel world.

But, with Jean's help, the walls around his heart eventually crumbled. Love followed soon after.

Logan never had a chance.

He'd gotten over the hurt, eventually. Showed up for their wedding day—though he'd kept to the shadows, away from the ceremony—even went so far as to pull her aside one day and utter "The Oath," that dreaded special occasions' pledge that has gotten more men into trouble over the centuries than any build-up to a war: wherever she was, he told her, whatever fix she might find herself in, all she had to do was call him, and he'd come running to her side. And being a man of his word, he'd meant every syllable of that promise.

Then he'd left to drown his sorrows.

After that, he'd given up any thoughts of trying to take Jean away from Scott—honor demanded it. But the ache was still there, sometimes, when he looked into her bright green eyes and saw the lively sparkle that had won his heart.

Or when she laughed that throaty little laugh of hers . . .

"Penny for your thoughts, Logan?" Jean asked.

"Huh?" Logan started, then shook his head to clear it. "Nothin' special, Red—my mind's just wanderin'." He glanced around the room. "Must be this smoke-free environment; all this clean air is messin' with my head."

A small smile played at the corners of Jean's mouth. "Then I guess it's even *more* important that we start heading for home. I wouldn't want you passing out before you've had the chance to refill your lungs with the nauseating smoke of those carcinogenic materials you love so much."

"That's the beauty of havin' a healin' factor, Jeannie," Logan replied, referring to his mutant ability to recover quickly from any illness or injury. "Can't get sick from tobacco, can't get too drunk from alcohol." His facial muscles twitched into an approximation of a smile. "All the vices, none o' the consequences."

"I'll keep that in mind the next time I see you praying at the porcelain altar after one of your more . . . self-indulgent evenings," Jean said sarcastically. She gestured over her shoulder, toward the hallway outside. "Right now, however, we're needed in the throne room. Roma wants to speak with us one last time before she sends us back to Earth."

"If it's so flamin' important, how come you just didn't beam that message into everybody's noggins, like you and Charlie usually do when you want our attention?"

"Because I didn't want to come blaring into everyone's minds like some overactive clock radio with the volume cranked to ten," Jean replied. "Even though we're outside the time stream, our bodies are still attuned to Daylight Savings—it's about seven A.M. back home. Rogue and Gambit are still fast asleep, Scott was lightly dozing when I left our room, and the Professor was just sitting down to breakfast. But knowing *your* habits, I figured you'd already be up and about."

"Where's the elf?" Logan asked—his nickname for their blue-skinned, pointy-eared teammate, Nightcrawler.

"Kurt's been up for hours; actually, I'm not even sure he went to bed. He found a screening room on one of the citadel's lower levels, and a collection of first-generation movie prints. He's been holding his own, private classic film festival." She shook her head in mild disapproval. "If he doesn't wind up gorging himself on hot, buttered popcorn, it's a certainty he'll still get sick from all the jujubees."

Logan grunted. "Let 'im have his fun. After all the fightin' we've had to do against that crazy fascist broad, Opul Lun Sat-yr-nin, ever since we got here, catchin' some downtime ain't a bad thing. If the elf wants t'eat like a five-year-old an' stay up all night watchin' movies, that's his prerogative . . . long as he don't wind up gettin' sick all over my boots."

Jean wrinkled her nose and grimaced, clearly imagining what that scene might look like. "*Any*way . . ." she said, quickly changing the subject, "I told him to save me a seat if he comes across a copy of *Casablanca*—especially one with Ronald Reagan as Rick. I've always wanted to see how his performance might stack up against Humphrey Bogart's, since Reagan had been the original choice for the part back on our world." She smiled. "One advantage of having access to the omniverse, wouldn't you say? You can check out all the alternate versions of your favorite films." She pinched her chin between thumb and forefinger, an idea obviously springing into her mind. "I wonder if there's a lending library here? I've never seen Buddy Ebsen's performance as the Tin Man in *The Wizard of Oz*. Jack Haley might never have gotten the chance to play the part in the final version if Ebsen hadn't been allergic to the silver makeup..." Her voice trailed off, and she gazed at Logan. "I'm babbling, aren't I?"

Logan shrugged. "I don't mind. Never knew you were such a big movie trivia buff, though."

"One of my few vices that Scott has learned to put up with. Sit me down on a couch with a bag of nacho-flavored corn chips and a TV tuned to American Movie Classics, and I won't even realize the world might have come to an end until the cable signal goes out." Jean shook her head, a few scarlet strands of hair drifting down between her eyes. "Oh, well—there are more important things to deal with for the moment. We'd better wake the others and get to the throne room before Roma thinks we're taking advantage of her hospitality."

"Then, let's not keep the lady waitin', darlin'," Logan said. "You know how cross these goddess-types can get if us 'mere mortals' don't come runnin' at their beck an' call."

"Logan, you're...you're incorrigible." Jean wagged a disapproving finger at her teammate, but her broadening smile belied any hint of anger she might have been trying to show.

"That's one'a my better qualities, Red," Logan replied. "You oughtta know that by now." He bowed slightly, and dramatically waved a hand toward the open door. "After you, darlin'."

Jean politely curtsied, fingers delicately holding up the hem of an imaginary skirt, then turned to go. Instantly, the smile faded from Logan's features as he mentally kicked himself. Letting his mind wander like it had in the presence of a telepath was a rookie mistake—one that would have cost him an advantage—or his life—had they been engaged in battle, and not in polite conversation.

And considering the fact that the telepath in this case was Jean Grey, who was all too aware of how strongly he still felt for her, allowing his thoughts to bubble to the surface where she could easily detect them was almost certain to result in her avoiding any social contact with him for a couple of days.

It wouldn't be the first time it happened; nor, probably, the last.

Jean, however, had acted as though she *hadn't* "heard" them, for which Logan had been grateful. But, he now wondered, was that because she had consciously tuned down her power before his mental slip, so as not to intrude on his thoughts again . . . or had they come streaming into her mind, and she was trying to avoid discussing them, in order to keep from having to revisit the whole messy issue of the emotional triangle that had once existed among the two of them and Scott? He'd never know for certain, unless Jean mentioned it, but she was far too sweet a person to do that and possibly run the risk of embarrassing him.

Slipping his mask back over his head, Logan stomped out of the observation suite after Jean, hoping that an opportunity would eventually present itself so that he could unleash his self-directed anger on the nearest handy object.

Or person.


Located on the uppermost level of the Starlight Citadel, the throne room of the Supreme Guardian of the Omniverse was as opulent as it was immense. Containing sweeping stone arches and two-foot-thick marble columns that stretched so high that the ceiling could not be seen, the room seemed less like a seat of multiversal power and more like a vast gothic cathedral whose nave ran the length of two football fields, and whose transepts were as wide as a city block. On closer observation, visitors to this awe-inspiring place often wondered aloud how a room so huge could exist in such a finite area as the citadel; the answer they were given was that the citadel was, in scientific terms, "dimensionally transcendental," which, roughly translated into English, meant that it was bigger on the inside than the outside. Truth be told, it was really built that way because Roma—like her father, Merlyn, before her—liked having a lot of space in which to think.

At the moment, Roma was doing a *lot* of thinking.

By human standards, she was an attractive woman in her early twenties, with an oval face and large, dark eyes. Her waist-length black hair was tied into a ponytail with a golden band, the better to display delicately-formed ears that tapered to small points at their tips. But referring to the Guardian in human terms would have been as insulting to her as someone making a vulgar comment about a friend's mother. Roma was, in fact, an immortal, an inhabitant of the higher dimensional plane called Otherworld, from which her father also hailed. As immortals go, Merlyn was the grandest of manipulators, often going so far as to fake his own death in order to bring his plans to fruition, as he had done centuries ago, when it appeared he had been slain at the hands of the dreaded sorceress Morgana Le Fay, as the legends of King Arthur and his Knights of the Round Table have depicted. The strategy worked again hundreds of years later, when he put into play his greatest scheme: to turn an unassuming man named Brian Braddock into Captain Britain, the superpowered champion of the omniverse, and, in turn, influence Braddock to create a superteam called Excalibur—comprised of British heroes like himself, as well as former members of the X-Men—in preparation for the day when the omniverse would be threatened by a powerful sorcerer called Necrom. The plan had ultimately proved successful, and Merlyn had departed for other realms, leaving his daughter in charge of the Starlight Citadel as the new Supreme Guardian of the Omniverse.

It also left Roma as the focus of Braddock's anger when he finally learned the truth about his role in Merlyn's plans, and about his own real identity: that his late father, James, Sr., had actually been an inhabitant of Otherworld—had, in fact, been one of Merlyn's chosen guard, sent to a specific Earth to set the Master Plan in motion. That Brian—like his sister, Elisabeth—was really *half*-human, born with a genetic makeup that, in his case, provided him with tremendous strength and the power of flight.

The best that Roma could do when Brian and Betsy eventually confronted her with this information was to shrug and say that it had all been for the greater good of the omniverse.

Not quite "I'm sorry"; not quite "You're welcome."

But enough of a reply for an immortal.

Now, lounging in a corner of one of the throne room's transepts, in a small, rock-lined pool that was constantly replenished by a quiet little waterfall that descended from the inky blackness high above, Roma stared intensely at an elaborate chessboard that floated in front of her, six inches above the churning, pale-green liquid. Its squares were made of ivory and black onyx, and scattered across them were a number of objects made of the same materials—not the traditional pieces of kings and queens, knights and pawns, but startlingly accurate representations of various individuals—both superhuman and nonpowered—from the world designated as "Earth 616." The X-Men who were here as her guests were included in the collection; they comprised the set of white pieces on one side of the board. On the other side were half-a-dozen black figurines: scaled-down versions of Victor von Doom—*with* armor—Magneto, Quicksilver, Wanda Maximoff, Sebastian Shaw . . . and Ororo.

And in the center of the board stood a very odd piece. From a foot away, it appeared to be a representation of Betsy Braddock, dressed in a dark-blue swimsuit and matching thigh-high stockings, a Japanese sword—a *katana*—gripped in one hand; a garish red mark—possibly makeup, possibly a scar of some sort—glowed hotly under her left eye. On closer inspection, though, Roma could see the figure flicker and fade and change appearance, from lethal femme fatale to cabaret singer, the swimsuit changing into a full-length evening gown, the sword becoming a microphone. Then it would shift again, constantly in a state of flux, moving back and forth from one version to the other.

"This is not right," Roma mused aloud, eyes narrowing to slits as she stared at the morphing game piece. *"None* of this is right . . ."

Rising from the water, she stepped from the pool and shrugged into a full-length, white silk robe; the chessboard automatically moved to remain in front of her, floating to a halt at chest-level. A deep frown creasing her flawless face, Roma quickly strode across the transept toward a platform near the apse which contained her throne. The board kept pace with her.

Sweeping up a short flight of steps to the platform, Roma stopped before a pulpit-like stand, into which was set an assortment of long, oddly-shaped white crystals. It was one piece of quartz in particular that immediately caught her attention—and sent a slight chill racing up her spine.

There was a spot of black in its center.

Roma's eyes widened in surprise. Each crystal contained the life-force of an entire dimensional plane—millions of worlds, billions of lifeforms, all condensed to a single, six-inch-wide sliver of quartz. As such, the clarity of each piece reflected the fact that that segment of the omniverse was in complete working order—no flaws, no chips, no worn edges, so to speak. To have an imperfect crystal—especially one possessing such a disturbing bit of discoloration—was unacceptable.

One last thing to check.

Leaving the platform, Roma moved over to an immense, clear globe that floated above the highly-polished floor nearby. It was a scrying glass of sorts, used to peer into the events of any world, any dimension that Roma wished to observe. Waving a hand before its surface to activate the device, the dark-haired woman waited for an image of Earth 616 to appear and, possibly, confirm her worst suspicions.

But no image was forthcoming; in fact, the glass turned completely dark, not even providing a general overview of the dimension.

Roma frowned again, a knot of concern taking form in her stomach. Blocked from observing a part of the omniverse? Such an occurrence should have been impossible, given the powers possessed by a Supreme Guardian.

She touched a small contact on her robes. "Saturnyne?"

"Yeeesss, m'lady?" muttered a sleepy female voice.

"There is a ... problem ..." Roma said slowly.

"I will be there immediately, m'lady," the woman responded, all traces of weariness quickly wiped from her speech by the call to duty.

Roma broke the connection, then glanced at the scrying glass once more. After all the X-Men had just done for her, how was she going to break the news that their world faced possible destruction ... again?

"You wished to speak with us, Your Majesty?" asked a deep, male voice from behind her, the sound echoing and reechoing in the vast chamber.

Roma turned. Standing at the crossing—the part of the throne room where the nave and transepts met—was an odd collection of costumed men and women, grouped around a baldheaded man wearing a conservative business suit: Professor Charles Xavier, teacher and spiritual guide in their ongoing quest to create peace and understanding between mutantkind and humanity. He was seated in a machine that resembled a wheelchair; it silently floated a good foot and a half above the floor, supported by a series of small, but powerful, anti-gravity beams projected from the underside of the seat. Among the group were Wolverine and Jean Grey; her hand was lightly resting on the arm of Scott Summers, the tall, sandy-haired man beside her, whose eyes were hidden from view by a gold-colored visor that partially wrapped around his head. Just behind Jean and Scott was another twentysomething couple: a ruggedly handsome man with scraggly brown hair, and an easy smile; and an attractive woman with waist-length hair, its dark-brown color offset by a large patch of white that started just above her forehead and ran down the center, giving the flowing locks an almost skunk-like appearance. His codename was Gambit—real name Remy LeBeau, a former member of the Thieves Guild, back in his native home of New Orleans, Louisiana—and he was dressed in a black-and-maroon costume, over which was worn an ankle-length leather coat, its wide collar turned up. She was Rogue—whether or not that was her real name had never been determined—and she wore a form-fitting yellow-and-green bodysuit—an "X" emblazoned over its left breast, as well as on the buckle of the leather belt that hung loosely around her waist—with bright yellow leather boots and matching kid gloves; a brown leather bomber jacket, its sleeves rolled back to her elbows, completed the colorful ensemble.

"Yes, I did," Roma replied to Xavier's query. "I *had* wanted to thank you once again for providing Captain U.K. with assistance in bringing an end to the reign of terror perpetrated on Earth 794 by Mastrex Opul Lun Sat-yr-nin—" she glanced toward the chessboard "—but far more troubling matters have arisen of late. Matters that involve your world—and, quite possibly, the omniverse."

"Somethin' dat needs de X-Men to set right?" Gambit asked in his Cajun drawl. "Well, just point us in de right direction an' let's get to fixin'. Dat's what we specialize in, y'know." He grinned broadly. "Just ask yer ol' pal, Opul."

A trace of a smile whispered across Roma's face. "I wish it were as simple as that, my friend." She gestured toward a set of chairs that had suddenly appeared at the foot of the steps leading to her throne. "Please, be seated, and I shall explain the situation as best I understand it."

As one, the group moved forward to take their seats, an intense look of concern shared by them all.

Well . . . all but one.

With an explosion of air and a burst of brimstone-laced smoke—a peculiar sound that registered to the eardrum as a loud *BAMF!*—the final member of the X-Men made his appearance. Tall and lean, with an acrobat's physicality, Kurt Wagner was the most unusual member of the team . . . and an almost perfect, living definition of the word "mutant": his hair and skin were a deep blue, the sclera and irises of his eyes a bright yellow, and he sported a set of sharp, white fangs in his mouth; his hands and feet each contained but three digits, and a prehensile tail—like those found in certain species of monkey—had grown to a three-foot length from a spot just above his buttocks. From a quick glance, a casual observer might mistake him for a demon straight out of a devout Roman Catholic's nightmares of hell; in reality, though, he was a kind, loving man, and a well-respected member of the group.

When he didn't show up late for an important meeting, that is.

"Nice'a you t'join us, elf," Wolverine grumbled.

Nightcrawler bowed deeply, then straightened. "I apologize for my tardiness, my friends," he said in his clipped, German accent, "but it is extremely difficult to tear oneself away from the radiant beauty that is Hedy Lamarr to attend a farewell party." He glanced at his teammates, and immediately noticed their somber expressions. "Or is something far more sinister in the works . . . ?"

"You got *that* right, sugah," Rogue said in her husky, Southern voice. "Pull up a chair—we were just about to get the lowdown from Roma."

Nightcrawler quickly joined the others, and turned to face their host.

Roma looked at each of them in turn, saw their bodies already tensing as though they were preparing for battle.

"I have detected an . . . abnormality in your home dimension," she began.

Gambit, who had been using his feet to rock his seat back and forth, groaned loudly and set the chair down with a sharp *clang* that reverberated across the throne room. Everyone turned to look at him, especially Xavier, who glared at him with an intensity that could melt steel.

Clearly wishing to avoid eye contact with his mentor, Gambit quickly lowered his gaze to the floor and shrugged. "Sorry," he muttered. "It's just annoyin' as hell that, after de mess we done finished cleanin' up here, we don' even get a chance to just go home an' relax a spell."

"I understand your frustrations, Remy," Xavier said, his rich baritone voice seeming to fill the vast space around them. "We all do. But our duties as X-Men often require that we put aside our disappointments, our grievances, and concentrate on far more important matters."

"In other words, Cajun," Wolverine harshly translated, " 'Stuff Happens.' *Live* with it."

Gambit sighed and turned to Rogue, who sat beside him. "So much for dat Harry Connick, Jr. concert tonight, *chere.*"

"You can make it up to me another time, Remy," Rogue said, and gently patted him on the arm.

Xavier turned back to Roma. "Please, Your Majesty—continue."

The dark-haired woman nodded. "As I was saying, something has occurred with Earth 616 that I am at a loss to explain." She gestured toward the chessboard, which hovered within arm's reach. "It is the custom of the Supreme Guardian—my father before me, and now I—to use this board in our work. It is set with pieces representing those mortals from across the multitude of dimensions with whom we are currently dealing."

"Manipulating, you mean," Logan grumbled softly.

"When your work was completed on Earth 794," Roma continued, choosing to ignore him, "the board automatically reset itself to begin the next . . . game. New pieces then appeared, replacing the previous set. All was as it had been for countless millennia.

"But then I noticed *this.*" She pointed to the Betsy Braddock piece, which was still shifting between its torch singer and female ninja forms.

The X-Men rose from their seats and moved to gather around the board. Jean leaned forward to stare at the morphing figurine.

"It's Betsy!" she said in astonishment. "But why is it doing that? Is something wrong with her back on Earth?"

"I do not know," Roma replied. "I have attempted to determine the cause of the abnormality—and the reason for the unusual effect it has had upon the board—but for reasons I cannot fathom, I have been unable to look upon Earth 616. Nor can I determine the length of time the abnormality has existed, since I have been more concerned with events on other worlds as of late."

"So, you have no idea what might be happening back home," Cyclops said.

"None," Roma admitted.

"Has this ever happened before?"

"It has *never* happened before, Scott Summers. Despite the increasing number of omniverse-threatening events that have taken place on your world since the first appearance of superbeings like yourselves, *never* have I, nor my father, Merlyn, been prevented from gazing upon it when we desired to do so."

She paused, letting her words sink in. The X-Men looked at one another uneasily.

"Okay, so we know the questions," Wolverine said finally. "How do we go about gettin' some answers?"

Roma pursed her lips and silently gazed at the chessboard for a few moments. Even though she was an immortal—someone who had lived a lifetime even before Dimension 616 had been born, and would continue to exist long after the X-Men had turned to dust—she suddenly felt the first disturbing twinges of fear. It was a sensation she had not felt in . . . well, a very long time.

The Supreme Guardian studied the expectant faces of the X-Men. They were all looking to her for answers, but she had none to give. The only comforting thought she had was that Merlyn almost certainly would have been stymied by the same predicament, though he would likely have settled for a more direct solution, like unleashing the full complement of the multidimensional Captain Britain Corps on Earth 616 and letting them tear the planet apart until they found the cause of the disruption.

Not very practical, but such a plan *did* have its charms . . .

"If I may be so bold, m'lady," said a female voice from the shadows of the nave, "I *do* know of a solution to the problem." As the group turned to face her, the speaker stepped into the light.

Dressed in flowing robes that were as white as her shoulder-length hair, Opal Luna Saturnyne was a stunning figure to behold—a flawless combination of icy professionalism and red-hot sensuality. Her official title was Omniversal Majestrix, which meant that she was responsible for maintaining order and reality throughout all dimensional planes . . . under the direction of Roma, of course. It was one of the many alternate versions of Her Why-ness that the X-Men had been recruited to battle, and Saturnyne had been pleased by the outcome.

It cut down on any possible competition for her job.

"If I may remind the Supreme Guardian," Saturnyne said, "you have at your disposal the means to end this . . . imperfection before it can spread across the entirety of that reality, and thereby threaten the omniverse." She gestured toward the black-tinged quartz on the dais. "All it would take is to shatter the crystal containing that dimension's life-force; remove the entire plane from existence—"

"You mean *destroy* our reality?" Jean interjected, barely con-trolling the anger in her voice. "Isn't that like killing a patient in order to stop a cancerous growth from spreading throughout their body?" She shook her head emphatically. "No. There *has* to be another way."

"I agree, Jean Grey," Roma said. "But there are few options. I *could* isolate the plane of Earth 616, let the 'infection' run its course; it would ultimately result in your dimension collapsing in upon itself, eons before its natural end. Or I could set into motion forces that would destroy your world without harming the rest of reality; using your medical analogy, that would be akin to am-putating a diseased limb to save an otherwise healthy patient."

"But think of the billions of lives lost!" Jean insisted.

"Think of the countless billions more *saved*," Saturnyne coun-tered.

"An' what would happen to *us*, Roma?" Rogue asked, her voice strained. "Would *we* just up an' disappear when any of that hap-pened?"

Roma shook her head. "No, friend Rogue. The state of temporal grace generated by the citadel ensures that no harm would come to any of you, should either your world or dimension cease to exist."

"And then?" Nightcrawler asked. "Not to sound ungrateful, but where does one go, Your Majesty, when one no longer has a home to go to?"

"You could work for me," Saturnyne replied. "The responsibilities of my office often require me to use superpowered agents, like the Captain Britain Corps, or the mercenary band Technet, to handle the more—" her nose wrinkled with obvious distaste "—*physical* solutions often required to readjust the inconsistencies that tend to pop up throughout reality. And you've already proven your effectiveness against one of my more ... embarrassing counterparts."

"Sure you don' want a couple ref'rences t' check before givin' us de job?" Gambit muttered. Rogue playfully punched him in the upper arm to silence him. She *just* managed to avoid breaking the humerus with her incredible strength.

Nightcrawler frowned. "I appreciate the offer, Saturnyne, but after the brief run-ins the two of us have had during my time with Excalibur, I find it a bit difficult to trust you—you work far too hard at manipulating people to make me all that comfortable in your presence." He flashed a brief smile. "No offense."

Her Whyness said nothing, a mischievous gleam in her eye. Clearly, she considered his words to be more complimentary than critical.

"There's *another* solution, Roma," Cyclops said. "You could send us in to find out what happened. With your help, and a bit of luck, it shouldn't take long to track down the source of the disturbance and find a way to correct it."

"It makes sense, Your Majesty," Xavier said. "If the trouble our world is experiencing is, in a manner of speaking, some sort of disease, then the logical course of action is to fight that disease from within—like antibodies rallying to overcome an infection."

Roma paused to consider this option, then slowly nodded in agreement. "You are right, Charles Xavier, but I can offer no aid. Since I am blocked from viewing the events taking place in your dimension, I cannot determine the point of origin for the disturbance. The most assistance that I can provide is to open the gateway that will send you back to your world." She smiled thinly. "After that, you shall have to rely on your 'bit of luck.' " The smile quickly faded. "I am sorry."

"No need to apologize, Yer Highness," Wolverine said. "We've been in tougher scraps 'n this. We'll make do."

"I would expect no less of you, my friends," Roma said.

"Then the matter is settled," Xavier stated. He looked to Cyclops. "Scott, you will lead the mission. Start at the mansion; see what information you can gather using Cerebro. Try to discover the locations of the other X-Men if they are not there—I imagine they're already working on their own to find the source of the disturbance. If they're not . . ."

Cyclops nodded. "Then we're on our own." He flashed a brief smile. "We'll get the job done, Professor. Don't worry."

"Sure you don't wanna come along fer the ride, Charlie?" Wolverine asked, a trace of a wicked smile splitting his rugged features.

Xavier shook his head. "No, Logan; my presence is not required." He gestured down toward his high-tech wheelchair. "Besides, since a certain degree of stealth may be required, it will be far easier for all of you to move about without having to see to my needs." He smiled broadly as he gazed at Wolverine. "I imagine, though, Logan, that you in particular will have difficulty staying out of trouble without my guidance."

"That's what I'm *countin'* on, Charlie," Wolverine replied with a wink.

"A final warning, X-Men," Roma said. "Given the severity of the situation, and the effect it will soon have upon the omniverse if it is not checked, I can only allow you a limited amount of time in which to resolve the matter."

"Here it comes . . ." Gambit mumbled. "I was *waitin'* for de other shoe to drop."

"*How* limited?" Cyclops asked.

"One week, by your standards of time," Roma answered.

"And if we haven't made things right by then?" Jean asked,

though it was clear from her expression that she already knew the answer.

"Then," Roma said slowly, "I shall have no choice but to shatter the crystal and remove your reality from the omniverse." She smiled warmly, reassuringly, pausing to gaze at each of them.

"Move swiftly, my friends," she said. "There are forces at work here beyond even my ken, and they cannot be allowed to extend their influence to other worlds. The safety of the omniverse rests squarely on your shoulders."

Nightcrawler raised an expressive eyebrow, then looked to Jean.

"No pressure, eh, *mein freund?*" he asked, with more than a hint of sarcasm.

Jean smiled uneasily. "No pressure, Kurt," she replied. Her gaze drifted toward the ever-changing game piece that represented one of her closest friends, and her smile faded. "No pressure at all . . ."

# Interlude

**T**HE MAN in the Moon was angry.

It could be considered a certainty that, in an age of tele-communications, superpowered men and women, extraterrestrial visitors the size of mountains, and time travel, not many people still remembered the classic fable; knew that he did, indeed, exist on that airless satellite that constantly circles the Earth like an eternal dance partner; or that he was an actual man. Nor were they aware that he did not really spend his time moving about *in* the moon, but on its surface, in an area of what is referred to as its "dark side," because it cannot be seen from Earth. And, contrary to fanciful beliefs, he lived, not in some brick-and-mortar castle with flying buttresses and colorfully-draped minarets, but within the metal walls of a half-dozen drab, nondescript buildings. Oblong in shape, their surfaces pitted and scored by hundreds of microscopic meteorites pushed along by the solar winds, they were linked by a series of long metal tubes, the top halves of which protruded from the gray, barren ground; seen from space, the over-all shape of the grouping was somewhat akin to that of a starfish, the extended "arms" connected to a central hub.

This was—as one could readily determine upon seeing it—a man-made installation; a military base, built by human hands at the peak of one man's overwhelming desire to conquer first his own planet, then the trackless void, laying claim to worlds beyond number in his mad dream to create a star-spanning empire. That dream had never come to fruition, of course—not yet, anyway—but the base still had a full complement of workers, well-paid to work in such an inhospitable place and perform the duties assigned to them without question.

And, just to prove that he was prepared to greet any potential interlopers from Earth, or one of the many celestial visitors who tended to see the people of this magnificent blue-and-white planet as either guinea pigs for scientific experiments or appetizing hot lunches, the installation also had a full complement of weapons, from conventional handguns to laser projectors—so-called "death beams" powerful enough to annihilate large sections of the planet even from this great a distance. At the moment, every single one of those projectors was trained on a different location around the globe, their targeting systems automatically recalibrating to zero-in on new strike zones with each rotation of the planet.

The Man in the Moon hated unexpected guests.

Far more important than the potential offensive uses of the installation, however, was the fact that it was located two hundred and fifty thousand miles from the world ruled by Victor von Doom—and therefore unaffected, for the moment, by whatever forces had transformed Earth 616 into the hazard it now presented to the continued well-being of the omniverse.

The Man in the Moon, of course, knew nothing of the danger presented by these very same forces that now threatened to destroy an entire dimensional plane, but he *was* very much aware of the current status of the world that was oh so far away, yet tantalizingly still within striking distance.

Truth be told, he was not even the beloved figure depicted in the children's fairytales, but he had lived on this cold, barren planetoid for so long, plotting his nefarious plans and continually stoking the boilers of his undying hatred for all those he considered lesser beings, that he often felt as though that *had* become his true identity. He half expected to see a cow leaping above him some day.

He found such thoughts troubling—a sign of weakness that could not be tolerated. He would have to do something to counteract this feeling of complacency that threatened to wash over him and pull him down into the depths of despair.

Not yet, though. Not yet.

But soon. When he did, at last, move to strike down his enemies, it would be a killing blow—one that would leave no doubt as to the identity of the final victor in this cosmic game of chess. And once victory was his, once he again held the reigns of absolute power, then the world would truly come to know the level of strength he possessed . . . and come to fear it.

An approximation of a smile twisted his grotesque features with that consoling thought.

His spirits now buoyed by the mental image of his enemies laying beaten and bloodied, life flowing from their shattered bodies to momentarily quench the eternal thirst of the ground beneath them, the man known only as "The Controller" gazed at his surroundings. He was seated on a plush leather chair in his private office, which was located in the command center, the largest—and connecting point—of the six linked buildings; not exactly a spot from which one would expect to launch an empire, but it was a start. The lively strings of Mozart's *Eine Kleine Nachtmusik* softly issued from the speakers of a small entertainment center, providing a touch of Old World civility amid the New World Order's sterile technology and artificial environments. The music did wonders for him, soothing his tensions as he forced himself to heatedly glare at the wall-sized viewing screen across from his desk; the crisp, almost three-dimensional image being broadcast on it was of the Earth, provided by cameras on the side of the moon closest to the planet.

*Von Doom's* planet, the Controller reminded himself with a snarl.

"But not for much longer," he whispered. "Soon. Very soon . . ."

A knock on the door harshly shook him from his reverie.

"Enter!" the Controller barked.

The door opened, and a young man hesitantly stepped inside the office. Garbed in a dark green uniform, black leather jackboots polished to a glaringly bright shine, he was in his early twenties, tall and athletically built, square-jawed and straight-backed, his blond hair cut short and stylish—all in all, the very model of a proper Generation-X toady. Under one arm he carried a large stack of papers.

"What is it, Lawrence?" the Controller asked.

"I have the latest intelligence reports, sir," his assistant replied, eyes fixed straight ahead.

"Let me see them," the Controller said. He waved Lawrence over, and his assistant placed the stack of printouts on his desk. Red-rimmed eyes studied each page, scanning the pages of information that had been compiled by his computer experts—men and women of Lawrence's age, who had hacked, first into the Empire's vast satellite network, then into the very heart of S.H.I.E.L.D.'s top secret files and defensive systems. With such limitless knowledge at his disposal, there was *nothing* that the Controller did not know about the world of Victor von Doom.

"Fascinating," the Controller said, glancing at one report in particular. "I had no idea the mongrel could maintain this level of influence over the planet for such a lengthy period of time. It cannot last, though, for he is a weak man, and like all weak men, he is destined to fail." He grinned, lips pulled back in a feral snarl. "I, however, am *not* a weak man; I am his better, as von Doom well knows. *That* is why he has feared me all these years, why that gypsy pig has never been able to truly defeat me in battle, though he would never admit to it. But he *will*, in time . . . just before I end his worthless life." The Controller nodded, as though in agreement with himself. "What a sight that will be, eh, Lawrence? The oh-so-mighty von Doom, brought to his knees by a true warrior, forced to call him 'master' and beg for his life, only to choke on his own blood, his pleas for mercy unheard, as my sword slices through the pale skin of his throat."

"Yes, Controller," Lawrence agreed. He gestured toward the reports on his superior's desk. "Your orders?"

"All in good time, Lawrence. All in good time." The Controller eased back in his seat, placing his elbows on the padded armrests and steepling his fingers in front of his face. Closing his eyes, he listened as the CD player replaced Mozart's soul-stirring violins with even sweeter, though far more melancholy, strains. The music seemed to flow through him, and a faint smile split his thin lips.

"Do you know what this is, Leonard?" he asked, eyes still closed.

"Umm . . . no, I don't, Controller," the young man admitted. A faint sheen of sweat suddenly appeared on his brow.

The Controller chuckled—a dry, mirthless note that sounded like swatches of sandpaper being rubbed together. "I imagine they did not teach 'Music Appreciation' in whatever backward *Englischer* school you attended in your youth."

"No, Controller," Leonard responded.

"It is called *Kol Nideri, for Violoncello and Orchestra, Opus No. 47*, by a composer named Max Bruch. You did not *know* that, did you?" The Controller's eyes suddenly opened, and he stared coldly at his assistant.

"N-no, C-controller. I d-did not," Leonard stammered, unconsciously taking a step back. His gaze shifted to the office door; he appeared to be measuring the distance from his superior's desk, as though contemplating the possibility that he might need to move quickly in the next few seconds.

The Controller ignored Leonard's panicked expression and slowly shook his head. "That is the trouble with your generation— no desire in your meaningless, pathetic lives to try and appreciate the finer things: Art. Music. Dance." His eyes sparkled. "And finer still: The chill that runs up the spine as you feel the life slipping away from an enemy, your fingers clamped tightly about his throat; feel his last breath whistle softly through stilled lips to brush your cheek like a shy lover's kiss. The sight of freshly-spilled blood on virgin snow, its warmth spiraling like a fine mist in the cold, mountain air.

"But, no; your generation has no time for such pleasures. Always flitting about from place to place like hummingbirds, never taking the time to slow down long enough and discover what it is to truly *live*. It is these moments, these sensations, these testaments to man's creativity and destructive powers that keep us from falling to the level of the beasts; and it is these very things that we must strive to preserve, after we have destroyed our enemies, and I have taken my rightful place as master of the world.

"For now, though," the Controller continued, "we shall wait and see what develops in the days ahead. Patience, it is said, is a virtue; and it is the patient man who learns to spot his enemies' weaknesses, and know the right moment to exploit them." He raised a quizzical eyebrow. "Do you understand what I am saying?"

"Yes, Controller. You're right," Leonard said quickly, nodding his head.

The Controller gazed at his assistant for a few moments, and knew that he had been wasting his time talking to this cipher. Like the other men and women of his generation, sage advice gathered from a lifetime of experiences did not seem to interest him. All the young fool understood were his own pathetic yearnings to attain power of any kind. No, that was not entirely true; he also understood that his superior possessed power in abundance—so much, in fact, that he could declare unquestioned mastery over even life and death themselves. The Controller nodded silently. He had been like that once, ages ago—an intellectual midget, destined for a lifetime of menial labor and mindless toil—until his eyes had been opened to the world around him by a man of seemingly infinite power.

Such comparisons, though, meant little to the Controller. Unlike his own mentor, he had no time to waste on trembling lackeys. The fool wasn't even worth wasting a bullet on to put a quick end to his meaningless existence.

"Continue to monitor the situation," the Controller replied

gruffly. He waved a hand in a dismissive gesture. "Now go. Do not disturb me unless you have something *important* to tell me."

"Yes, Controller," Leonard said, clearly pleased for the opportunity to exit the office under his own power. "Thank you."

The Controller watched his assistant scurry from the office, and a look of unbridled disgust contorted his already twisted features.

"Bah," he muttered. "Idiots. Everywhere I go, I am constantly burdened with idiots." With a contemptuous sneer, he swiveled his chair around to gaze at the wall-sized projection of the Earth. His eyes narrowed to slits as he studied the contours of a world that should belong to him, and would ... in the end.

"Soon, von Doom," the Controller said softly. "Soon, the dreamer must awaken, and it shall be *I* who takes the greatest pleasure in rousing him from his slumbers—before sending him to his *final* rest...."

# 5

LOCATED IN New York's Westchester County, about an hour's drive from Manhattan, Salem Center had always been a quiet, suburban village—the kind of place Norman Rockwell immortalized in paintings of small town America, and Ray Bradbury waxed poetic about in short stories that spoke of the magic of childhood, and the wonders that could be found right outside one's front door. Its greatest appeal was that it was close to the hustle and bustle of New York City for stockbrokers, fashion models, and housewives wanting to spend a day shopping in "The City," yet it was far enough away so that the Big Apple's perceived "bad influences"—crime, drug trafficking, a proliferation of trendy coffee houses—were kept at arm's length by miles of wilderness and quaint, two-lane roads that seemed to lead everywhere but the center of town.

But, as was true with most small, populated areas—like Arkham, Massachusetts, and Blackstone, New Hampshire, and Castle Rock, Maine—Salem Center had its fair share of secrets, and they were not the typical, two-old-biddies-gabbing-over-a-picket-fence kind of hushed whispers that involved penny-ante scandals about who was sleeping with whom, or what kind of double life that charming—but strange—young man who lived alone in the corner house might be leading when he pulled down the shades at night.

*These* secrets were as black as the heart of Satan himself, and as chilling as the grave.

And their roots all led back to what lay along Graymalkin Drive, that winding country road just outside of the village proper.

No one ever talked about what was on the Drive, or about the black trucks that rumbled along it in the dead of night, or about the inhuman wails that drifted into the otherwise quiet hamlet when the wind was blowing in the right direction. It was best to leave things be, the older folk often said; some things were just better left not knowing about. Such logic seemed perfectly agreeable to the rest of the populace, so they decided it was, in the end, less stressful for them all if they just let the whole matter drop. Thus, their minds eased, the people of Salem Center continued to live their lives and raise their families and make their daily trips to "The City."

And did their best to ignore the evil that lay draped over their quaint little village like a burial shroud.

Unfortunately for the people of Salem Center, that ignorance was not going to last much longer.

A mile outside of town, a tiny pin-prick of light suddenly formed in the air above the dreaded Graymalkin Drive, just as the Salem Center town hall clock struck midnight; the chimes echoed clearly across the quiet countryside. The spot of light wasn't much to look at—merely the smallest of disruptions in the Space/Time continuum—but it shone like a beacon in the darkness. Barely a second after it had formed, the pin-prick widened to a hole, then to a large, oval-shaped portal from which light poured, pushing aside the surrounding blackness.

And through this portal walked Cyclops, then Phoenix, then the rest of the X-Men. A split second after Nightcrawler stepped from it, close on Wolverine's heels, the portal quickly closed with a soft rush of air, leaving them standing beneath a breathtaking, velvet-lined canopy of millions of stars.

For what it was worth, the X-Men had finally come home.

"Dis ain't de school," Gambit commented, looking around. They were standing in the middle of the road. "Somebody screwed up on de directions."

Beside him, Nightcrawler was nearly invisible in the darkness, his dark coloration acting as a natural camouflage. "That's the problem with celestial beings, *mein freund*," he quipped. "They're not nearly as infallible as they'd like to think."

"Want me to take a gander from up top, see where we are?" Rogue asked. Slowly rising in the air, she was about to soar higher when Cyclops waved her down.

"Hold up, Rogue," Cyclops said. "I *know* where we are." He pointed to a nearby sign that stood beneath a lamppost. The sign was wood, painted a bright green and trimmed in gold leaf:

WELCOME TO THE VILLAGE OF
SALEM CENTER, N.Y.
POPULATION: 500
DRIVE SAFELY!

"We're on Graymalkin Drive," Cyclops continued. "The school's just around the next bend. There's no need for aerial reconnaissance— not yet, anyway. Besides, until we find out what exactly is wrong with the world, I don't want us attracting any undue attention."

"Dat means no flyin', *chere*," Gambit pointed out.

Pouting slightly, Rogue floated down to stand beside the handsome Cajun.

"Is that a fact?" she asked sarcastically. Clasping her gloved hands against the side of one cheek, she batted her eyelashes. "Why, suh," she cooed in a saccharine-sweet imitation of a stereotypical Southern Belle, "I simply don't know *what* I'd do if a big, strong man like yuhself wasn't around to explain such complicated terms to little old me." She lowered her hands and frowned.

"Knock it off, you two," Cyclops ordered. "Everyone spread out. Wolverine, you've got the point."

Logan nodded and moved forward, crouching low and stepping lightly along the edge of the road, relying on the stealth techniques taught to him ages ago by ninja masters in Japan. Behind him, the X-Men took their positions, creating a triangular formation as they followed him.

Wolverine tilted his head back and sniffed the cool night air.

"Hold up," he said, raising a warning hand. "Somethin' ain't right."

The team stopped immediately and assumed combat-ready positions, their eyes sweeping across their moonlit surroundings, alert for the slightest indication that they might be about to face an attack at any moment.

"Trouble?" Cyclops asked.

Wolverine shook his head. "Worse'n that."

"What is it then, Logan?" Phoenix asked. "What do you smell?"

Wolverine eyed her somberly. "Death, Jeannie. The stench is everywhere."

The X-Men looked at each other, as though hoping that one amongst them might have some idea as to what could have happened to the world they had departed from just a month past. But no answers were forthcoming.

"Betsy . . ." Phoenix whispered, her thoughts immediately flashing on the image of the shapeshifting chess piece back in Roma's sanctuary.

"All right, people," Cyclops said calmly. "Let's not get ahead of ourselves." He looked to his wife. "Jean, scan the area. The school is just around the bend in the road—see if you can pick up any stray thoughts that might allow us to get a handle on the situation." Phoenix nodded, and he turned to face the others. "I want this played by the numbers, all right? The last thing we need to do is go charging in half-cocked because we're concerned for our friends' safety, only to do someone a favor by conveniently walking into any traps that might have been laid for us. Agreed?"

Slowly, the remaining team members nodded; Wolverine, however, still looked ready for a fight—head lowered, body tensing like a spring about to be released.

"Oh—oh my God . . ." Phoenix suddenly wailed softly.

Cyclops was at his wife's side in a split-second, steadying her trembling body as she clutched the sides of her head in agony.

"Jean!" he yelled, unable to keep a note of panic from creeping into his voice. "Jean! Let it go! Whatever you're picking up, just let it go!"

"They're dying . . ." Phoenix cried, her eyes brimming with tears. "They're all dying . . ." Her voice trailed off, but her lips continued to move silently as she mouthed the word "dying" over and over again. She blankly stared straight ahead, clearly unaware of Scott's gentle grip on her shoulders, or even the worried expressions etched on the faces of her teammates, who clustered around her. Whatever thoughts she was tapping into, though, seemed to be providing her with a vivid display of what it might be like to stare into the pits of hell.

Tenderly, Cyclops pushed aside Jean's fiery locks and placed his mouth beside her ear.

"Jean," he whispered. "Please. Let it go." He reached out to stroke her cheek, then turned her head so that he could look into her eyes. "Come back to me. Please, Jean . . ."

It took an agonizing moment or two, but, slowly, Phoenix's numbed expression softened; her trembling muscles relaxed.

But the haunted look in her eyes remained.

"Scott . . ." she whispered. She reached up to wipe away the tear that had slid down his cheek from under the golden visor.

Cyclops smiled warmly. "Welcome back."

Jean's eyes sparkled. "It's good to *be* back." Gathering her strength, she straightened and stepped back from her husband, letting her hand slip down to hold his.

"You all right, Jean?" Rogue asked. "Y'all had us worried there for a minute."

"I'm fine," Phoenix replied, though the strain in her voice said otherwise. "I just wasn't prepared . . . so much sorrow . . ."

"You said, 'They're all dying,' " Cyclops said. "Who did you mean? Is it the other X-Men?" It was apparent from his expression that he regretted having to press Jean for information so soon after she had recovered from her ordeal, but it had to be done.

"I didn't detect *any* of our friends," Phoenix replied. "Ororo, Betsy, Warren, Hank—either they've left the area, or . . ." She paused, then shook her head, pushing the unpleasant alternative from her mind. "They're not there."

"Then who—?" Nightcrawler began.

"I don't know, Kurt. When I scanned the area, I ran into . . . I can only describe it as a 'psychic tidal wave.' A culmination of powerful emotions—anger, fear, despair—created by a large group of minds nearby. It was like opening a door and finding a wall of water bearing down on me. I wasn't able to erect a stronger mental shield fast enough to block it before it struck."

"And it was coming from the school?" Cyclops asked.

Phoenix nodded. "Or some place very close to it."

"All right, then," Cyclops said. He glanced at each of the men and women under his command. "Same positions as before, but let's double-time it. And be ready for anything."

As before, the X-Men spread out as they moved down the road, but now there was a nervous energy that seemed to hang in the air around them—an electricity formed of worry, and anger, and, yes, even fear.

Cyclops frowned. Fear had its uses in battle; it kept the edge on, kept you moving, as long as you didn't allow it to overwhelm your thinking. But fear could also be a deadly distraction, especially considering the amount of danger involved in their line of work. He risked a quick glance at his wife. Phoenix was trying to appear stoic, doing her best to focus on her job, but from the way she was chewing on her lower lip, it was clear that she was still haunted by the mental images left by the psychic assault.

*We'll get through this, honey,* Cyclops thought. *I promise.*

Phoenix looked to him and smiled—she'd "heard" him. Two words suddenly formed in his mind, projected by Jean for him alone: *Love you.*

"Cyke," Wolverine said, interrupting their silent conversation. "You better come see this." The Canadian was standing just a few yards ahead, where the road curved toward the gravel driveway that led to the school. Cyclops smiled reassuringly at Phoenix, then jogged up to join his point man—

—and stopped dead in his tracks.

"What in God's name . . . ?" Cyclops whispered. Behind the ruby quartz of his visor, his eyes widened in shock.

The mansion—the home for these colorfully-garbed students of the Xavier Institute for Higher Learning—was gone.

In its place, spread across the acreage that once contained a wide, two-story building, Japanese gardens, a small airfield, and an Olympic-sized swimming pool, was a collection of wooden bunkhouses—about two dozen or so—surrounded by twenty-foot-high chain link fencing, the top of which was wrapped in lethal razor-wire. Thirty-foot-tall guard towers were spaced ten yards apart, their searchlights continually sweeping across the muddy grounds, their uniformed occupants walking a slow circuit around the steel-and-cement parapets, formidable-looking rifles clutched tightly in gauntleted hands.

"Oh, no . . ." Phoenix moaned softly.

Rogue gasped, clearly stunned by the unexpected sight. Beside her, Gambit said nothing, any sarcastic remark he might have been about to make lodging in his throat.

"*Mein Gott* . . ." Nightcrawler muttered, yellow eyes flashing brightly in the moonlight.

As for Wolverine . . . well, Logan had seen something like this decades ago, in Europe; it was the type of nauseating sight that one could never completely wipe away from the mind's eye after witnessing it, no matter how much time passed. He growled softly.

"What's goin' on here?" Gambit finally asked. "Dat looks like some kinda mil'tary installation."

"That ain't no soldier base, Cajun," Wolverine said, his lips pulled back in a savage snarl. "It's a death camp."

* * *

If there was one truism about being an inmate in Detainee Camp #1879, it was this: Life was cruel, life was harsh, life was what you tried to hang onto as long as possible in those rare moments between beatings, and only the dead were the lucky ones.

Lucky enough to have escaped their torment.

Carol Danvers had learned that lesson a long time ago, at the end of a guard's truncheon, or the boot heel of a matron, or from the fist of one of the savage prisoners who were allowed to mix with—and terrorize—a general population consisting mainly of writers, musicians, and an odd politician or two. Some of the brutes she recognized as former second- and third-class "super-villains" who had been swept up by von Doom's growing reserve of super heroes during the early days of the Empire; she had spotted the Trapster, Electro, and Titania her first day in the camp. Sentenced to life imprisonment, their powers negated by neural inhibitors that "rewired" their brains' synapses so they were unable to use the mental "on-switch" that activated their powers, they were more than willing to vent their frustrations on the "normals" who cowered in their presence. Carol had tried to do something about the situation when she first arrived, but that selfless dedication to helping others had soon been beaten out of her, along with two teeth and a pint or two of blood. And for each day she spent here—she'd lost count of the exact number—there was always someone more than eager enough to take advantage of any opportunity to provide her with a refresher course on the perils of getting involved in other people's business.

After all, it's often been said that one teaches by repetition.

Life hadn't always been this bad for Carol Danvers, though. By the time she turned twenty-five, she seemed to have had it all: an Air Force captaincy, a modest apartment in Manhattan, even her first stable relationship in years.

But then, one day, she made the mistake of questioning the government's policy of imprisoning political radicals in what appeared to be work camps—a policy enacted by Emperor von Doom soon after taking power. She couldn't understand how a man who seemed so benevolent to his subjects could be so willing to recreate the gulags of Stalinist Russia, just to silence his more outspoken detractors.

Her fall from grace didn't take long after that, for only a fool questioned the orders of the Emperor—a suicidal fool, in fact. In the span of two days, Carol lost her rank, her apartment, her short-time boyfriend . . . and her freedom. It still horrified her, knowing how quickly, how easily, the foundations of her life had been shaken apart: One minute, she was a decorated officer, a respected member of her community, a woman deeply in love; the next, she was just another nameless victim—attacked on the street by a half-dozen black-suited men, drugged, tossed into the back of a non-descript van, and presented with the unwelcomed opportunity to experience first-hand just what life was like in one of the camps. Her family, she later learned, had been told that she had committed suicide, choosing to hang herself rather than face up to the shame she had brought them by her dishonorable discharge.

Her "ashes" had been left on her parents' doorstep in the middle of the night, so they'd be sure to find them when they went to retrieve the morning paper.

Carol still shuddered whenever her thoughts flashed back to those first few days following her abduction: the crippling beatings, the maggot-infested food, the psychological torture. But, thankfully, when enough new "guests" had arrived at the camp to momentarily sate a seemingly endless hunger for doling out abuse, the guards and the once-powered prisoners eventually grew tired of using her as a punching bag and went hunting for fresher game. She knew that wouldn't last forever, of course—even a grown child would go back and play with an old toy just for the sake of nostalgia—but she considered each day that they left her alone a blessing.

Now, one year later, she was twenty-six but looked forty-six, her smooth complexion and bright attitude replaced by callused skin and a bitter cynicism. There were streaks of gray in her blond hair, and her pale blue eyes always seemed to be bloodshot—brought on by a severe lack of sleep, no doubt. But that was to be expected in a place where death could come swiftly, silently, as a dagger in the belly, or a thin piece of wire pulled tightly across a frail windpipe if one slept too soundly.

Such was the glamorous life at Detainee Camp #1879.

Lying on her bunk in one of the "girls' dormitories," as they were known—as though anyone would mistake the drafty, wooden structures for some kind of college campus apartment complex—Carol tossed fitfully, unable to sleep. Her stomach ached fiercely, her bladder felt like it was going to explode, and she was starting to run a fever; more than likely, there had been some kind of bacteria in the water—possibly as part of a government experiment, if the rumors she heard whispered around the camp were true—and her body was demanding that she do something *now* to purge it from her system. Carol gritted her teeth and tried to ignore the pain coursing through her, but the fetal position into which she had drawn herself was as tight as it was ever going to be, and that had brought no relief.

There was no way around it: she *had* to go to the bathroom.

Slowly uncoiling her aching body, Carol slid out from under the coarse blanket that covered her bed and unsteadily rose to her feet. A wave of nausea threatened to overwhelm her—she could taste the bile burning its way up her throat—but she fought the sensation and ordered her body to move forward; it responded, to a small degree, and she quietly shuffled across the rough, wooden floor in threadbare slippers. She glanced around the darkened room, but none of the other female prisoners seemed to have heard her movements, nor did any of them appear to be exhibiting any signs of the illness that now forced her to walk doubled-over. Carol swore under her breath; she'd probably been used as an unwitting test case—*again*—for some new strain of virus with which the government was experimenting. That would make three in the last year for her alone. Not for the first time, she wondered if there were any real uses for the bugs, or whether her jailers were just trying to discover what it would take to finally kill her.

"Better men than you have tried, jerkface..." she muttered to an imaginary scientist, just before another river of bile tried to force itself through her lips.

Moving to the front door of the bunkhouse, Carol paused to look around. Prisoners were not allowed out of the dormitories after "lights-out," no matter the reason. If she were caught by one of the guards now, an upset stomach would be the least of her worries. The burning lava flow that seemed to be rolling around in her gut, however, insisted that she had to take the chance. The women's bathroom was only twenty yards away, so even with her shambling gait, she should be able to reach it in under a minute.

Carol scanned the area from the dorm to the bathroom once more to make certain that no one was around, then set off for her porcelain salvation.

Unfortunately, she neglected to check around the corner of the bunkhouse....

"Get outta my way, Summers..." Wolverine growled. Teeth bared, he glared menacingly at Cyclops, who was standing between him and the camp.

"*No*, Logan," Cyclops said. Arms folded across his chest, he stared down at the feral scrapper, never breaking eye contact. "When I said we weren't going to just charge into a situation without a plan, I *wasn't* just saying that because I like the sound of my own voice. It would be bad enough for the team if you tipped our hand too soon by rushing in there, but what do you think might happen to the *people* in that camp if you started a fight with the *heavily-armed* guards who are protecting it? Do you *really* want to put that many lives at risk?"

Wolverine said nothing. His teammates watched silently, breaths held in anticipation, waiting for Logan to make the next move.

"All right," he finally said. "Point taken." He pointed a warning finger at Cyclops. "But quiet or loud, with or without yer permission, I *am* goin' in there."

"Agreed," Cyclops said. "We *all* are—but working together, as a team. Understand?"

Wolverine grunted.

"So, what's the plan?" Rogue asked.

"First, we need information," Cyclops replied. He pointed to Nightcrawler and Wolverine. "Kurt, Logan—you're our stealth experts. Get inside the camp, get a lay of the land, then *come right back*. Once we've got a handle on the situation, we can form a strategy."

"I'll maintain a telepathic link with the two of you," Phoenix said. "If there's any trouble, give a shout."

Cyclops glanced at Wolverine. "Hopefully, that won't be necessary."

"Don't worry, Scott," Nightcrawler said cheerfully. "We'll be as quiet as church mice." He stepped beside Wolverine and placed his hands on the shorter man's shoulders. "Ready, *mein freund?*"

"Do it," Wolverine said gruffly.

And with a burst of brimstone-laced smoke and an implosion of air, they were gone.

"What now, Cyclops?" Gambit asked.

Cyclops glanced at the wry Cajun, and frowned. "Now, Gambit," he said, "we wait . . ."

Seconds later, their fellow X-Men reappeared within the grounds of the camp, just beyond the chain link fence. Wolverine immediately dropped into a crouch—presenting the smallest target possible for any rifle scopes that might be trained their way—and surveyed the area. Nightcrawler, however, staggered back a few steps, into the shadows cast by one of the bunkhouses. Against the inky blackness, he was virtually invisible, but his labored breathing gave away his position.

"You all right, elf?" Wolverine muttered softly.

Nightcrawler nodded. "I'll be fine. It's just the strain of tele-porting two bodies over such a great distance..." He glanced at Wolverine. "Have you put on weight?"

"Funny," Wolverine said. "Real funny." He pointed an accu-satory finger at his teammate. "Little more time trainin' in the Danger Room, little less time bein' a couch potato watchin' movies, bub." He raised his head to sniff the air, then grunted in surprise.

"Something?" Nightcrawler asked.

"Familiar scent," Wolverine replied. "Can't get a good read on it yet—" he jerked a thumb over his shoulder, toward the center of the camp "—but it's comin' from this way."

"Then, let's go see what it is," Nightcrawler said.

Moving quietly, staying in the shadows, the two heroes began making their way through the camp.

Carol Danvers was just stepping from the lavatory, grateful for having regained the ability to stand erect again, when a callused hand clamped over her mouth; before she could pull away, a pow-erful arm wrapped around her waist, pinning her arms to her sides.

*"Don't make a sound,"* a coarse, male voice whispered into her ear. Carol recoiled from the stench of cheap alcohol that seemed to explode from his mouth. Twisting her head to one side, she caught a glimpse of dark-green material and shiny brass buttons.

It was one of the guards.

"You're a pretty one," the man continued. "A lot better lookin' than some of the others they bring in here. Don't know how I missed you before, but we can always make up for lost time..."

Carol's eyes widened in fear. As the guard started to pull her back into the lavatory, she twisted violently, trying to pull away, digging her heels into the muddy soil to slow their progress, but the burning fever and her roiling stomach had drained away most of her strength. In desperation, legs flailing wildly, she raised one foot, then drove her heel into the top of his booted foot, just below the ankle, with all her might. Thankfully, it had the desired effect: the guard yelped in pain and loosened his grip, enough for her to tear herself away from him. Carol spun around quickly and lashed out with her hands clasped together, throwing her strongest punch. She was lucky; the blow caught him across the nose—his low moaning caused by the injured foot leapt a few notches in volume to a high-pitched shrieking amid the sound of delicate bones breaking.

Carol turned and started to run, but the man was still quick enough to lash out with the injured foot, catching her just below the right knee with the steel toe of his boot. She cried out in agony and crashed to the ground.

The pain was blinding; multicolored spots of light danced before her eyes, making it difficult to focus on the guard as he hobbled toward her. Teeth bared, the lower half of his face smeared with blood and snot, he reached down and grabbed a handful of her hair and savagely yanked her to her knees.

"Forget about gettin' to know each other better, baby," he hissed. "I'm just gonna *kill* you." His free hand dropped to the wide, brown utility belt around his waist. Moonlight glinted along the serrated edge of a foot-long knife as it was pulled from its leather sheath.

Carol closed her eyes. She knew that, even if one of the other guards, or even another prisoner, should happen to stumble upon this scene, no one would try to help her. That's just how things were done here: every person for themselves. Trembling, she waited for the end.

But, surprisingly, the killing stroke never came.

And then a new sound reached her ears: a noise not unlike that caused by a sword being drawn from a scabbard—that sharp, clear *snikt!* of metal on metal.

The guard moaned, and warm blood spattered Carol's face like a gentle rain. She started, not knowing what to make of this, yet afraid to look to find out. Curiosity, however, soon got the best of her; slowly, she opened her eyes.

Her attacker was still in front of her, but his head was now tilted back, as though he were looking at the night sky instead of his intended victim. He also seemed to standing off-balance, like he was about to collapse.

Carol didn't know what to make of it.

But then she saw the reason for his unusual posture, and shivered, despite the warm temperature of this June night.

Three sharp, metal spikes were protruding from the guard's chest, their pointed tips coated with blood. Not only had they skewered the man, but they also seemed to be the only things holding him up, for it was plain to see that the man was dead.

Suddenly, the spikes retracted—*back through his chest*—and the guard collapsed, face first, onto the muddy field. His eyes, eternally frozen in surprise, stared blankly at Carol.

"You okay, darlin'?" a gruff voice asked.

Carol's gaze shifted from the corpse to another man, who had been standing behind the guard; his killer, obviously. He was short and hairy, and dressed in the kind of colorful costume she might have ordinarily expected to see in a circus. To her surprise, there was no trace of whatever weapon he had used to dispose of the human trash now lying beside her.

"Who—" she began to say.

*"Mein Gott*, Wolverine," interjected a voice from the darkness. "Was killing that man really necessary?"

The man called "Wolverine" turned to someone she couldn't see and frowned.

"Yeah," he said simply.

His companion stepped from the shadows, then, and Carol had to fight the overwhelming urge to run and hide—he looked like some kind of blue-skinned demon!

"W-who are you people?" she whispered.

Wolverine turned to face her, and tilted his head in a quizzical fashion. "What're you talkin' about?" he asked.

Carol started; she hadn't been expecting *that* kind of reaction. From his tone of voice, and the way he was staring at her in total confusion, it seemed evident that the man had expected her to recognize him. How that might be so, she hadn't the faintest idea, but if she could just talk her way out of this situation...

She glanced toward the women's barracks; its door was so tantalizingly close. If she somehow managed to get a good head start on running for it, and if her stomach would hold off from making any serious efforts to double her over with an unexpected wave of cramps as she made her escape, there was a chance these two lunatics would leave her alone once she got inside—a slim chance, granted, but one she was willing to accept. Slowly, she rose to her feet, trying to avoid making any sudden moves that might upset these newcomers—and considering the dangers she had often faced during her time in the camp, it wouldn't come as any surprise to find herself going from a bad situation to an even worse one.

"What's the matter, Ace?" Wolverine asked, flashing what appeared to be his idea of a friendly smile. "I ain't been gone all *that* long fer ya t'go fergettin' me."

"I... wish I could help you," Carol said slowly, doing her best to keep her rescuers calm. "It's just that I don't remember meeting any... umm... circus performers since I was a little girl." She tried to smile politely—an ultimately futile effort, since it came out looking more like a sickly grimace—while keeping her hands away from her body to show she posed no threat. "Not that, you know, there's anything *wrong* with being in the circus," she added quickly.

"We mean you no harm, *fraulein*," the demon said.

"I'm sure you don't," Carol replied in a gentle, soothing tone of voice—the kind one would normally use when speaking to a child... or a dangerous criminal. "Look, it's not that I'm ungrateful for what you've done for me—" she nodded toward the dead guard "—but it's not gonna be too long before one of the other guards stumbles across him, and I *really* don't want to be standing right next to a corpse when it hap—"

Wolverine took a step forward; Carol immediately moved backward. He looked surprised by her behavior.

"Carol, it's *me*," he said, hands held palms up to show he meant no harm.

"Me *who?*" Carol replied. "Look, friend, a lot of things have happened to me in my life—*especially* more than my fair share of bad stuff ever since the day I got thrown into this pit—but I don't *ever* recall meeting you—" she pointed to his companion "—or your running buddy over there, either in this dump, or in the real world. *Trust* me—I'd remember."

Wolverine and his blue-skinned companion looked at one another for a moment. The demon frowned.

"First, the school disappears," he said. "Now, an old friend doesn't recognize us . . ." His voice trailed off, and the two men stood silently, as though they were listening to a conversation that only they could hear.

Carol slowly began to step back, preparing to make a dash for the bunkhouse. If these two clowns could just stay zoned-out for a few more seconds . . .

"Ahh, this is *nuts*," Wolverine finally said. Carol froze as he pulled back his mask. "Look, Ace, it's *Logan*. Yer old drinkin' buddy? The guy who used t'work with you in Intelligence, back when I was workin' outta Department H in Canada? The guy who's saved yer bacon more'n once? *Now* do you remember me?"

Carol shook her head. "I'm sorry. I really am."

His sidekick sighed. "Well, this *is* bad," he commented.

Wolverine sniffed the air, his body suddenly tensing. He slipped his mask back on as he stared at the center of the camp. "It's about t'get a whole flamin' lot worse . . ."

Following the direction of Wolverine's steely gaze, Carol looked over her shoulder, in time to see a pair of armed guards—one male, one female, both with rifles slung over their shoulders—turning the corner of the bunkhouse. The duo came to an abrupt halt, startled by the unexpected appearance of a prisoner breaking curfew, a blue-skinned demon, and a circus midget.

*"DON'T MOVE!"* the male guard ordered. The female guard quickly unslung her weapon, bringing it to bear on them.

Carol turned back to the costumed men, to see what they were going to do about *this* problem, and her jaw dropped in shock as she saw *a half-dozen foot-long spikes come shooting out of the backs of Wolverine's hands.*

Now, at last, she knew how he'd killed the guard.

The realization that such weapons had to be sheathed within the skin of his bare arms, however, only made her stomach problems resurface.

In the woods on the far side of Graymalkin Drive, Phoenix turned to Cyclops, her face full of worry.

"Trouble," she said simply.

"Pull them back," Cyclops ordered. "Tell them to grab Carol and get out of there right now!"

Phoenix nodded, and her brow knitted as she telepathically conveyed the message. She knew, though, that it was too late for their teammates to escape without a fight.

"No!" Nightcrawler said. "No more killing, Wolverine!"

With that, he disappeared in a puff of smoke, to reappear an instant later beside the male guard, who looked more than a little surprised. A three-fingered, white-gloved fist lashed out, catching the man across the left temple. Knocked senseless, the guard stumbled back, into his partner. Out of reflex, the woman's finger tightened on the trigger of her rifle; the gun barked three times, the shots ricocheting off the lavatory's outer walls.

The reaction to the gunfire was immediate.

Around the camp, an ear-piercing alarm began to wail. Searchlights that had originally been sweeping the camp as part of their computerized programming now started swiveling in the direction of the altercation. Before Carol and the costumed men could seek cover, they found themselves awash in beams of the purest, whitest light.

"Oh, *great*," Carol muttered sarcastically. "That's just ...

# 6

**D**AMN IT . . ." Cyclops murmured.

Pinching his lower lip between thumb and forefinger, he watched as the camp came to life—dogs began barking, armored soldiers poured from barracks, and every light in the compound snapped on, illuminating the camp with the intensity of daylight.

*Once*, Cyclops thought. *Just once I'd like something to go without a hitch . . .*

He turned to his team. "All right, people," he said somberly. "It's a little ahead of schedule, but we have a camp to liberate—the quicker, the better."

Nightcrawler quickly knocked out the female guard before she could make any more trouble, and tossed her rifle onto the roof of the bunkhouse. Carol and Wolverine raced to join him.

"Nice work, elf," Wolverine said sarcastically.

"Er . . . yes," Nightcrawler conceded. "That *could* have gone better."

"What now?" Carol asked.

"First order of business is t'get you outta here," Wolverine replied. He pushed her into Nightcrawler's arms.

"But, what about you?" Carol asked.

"I'll wait for the next bus," Logan said. He looked at Nightcrawler. *"Go."*

The blue-skinned X-Man nodded. "I'll be right back."

A burst of smoke, and he and Carol were gone.

"Take yer time, bub," Wolverine muttered, as the sound of heavy boots striking the ground reached his ears. "I got *other* things t'occupy my time till ya get back . . ."

Logan smiled grimly and raised his foot-long, adamantium-sheathed claws as a half-dozen armored soldiers came charging at him from across the main yard.

"Step right up, boys an' girls!" Wolverine called out. "I got plenty o' hurtin' fer everybody!"

And with a roar like a wild beast, he ran to meet them.

Nightcrawler and Carol reappeared on the edge of Graymalkin Drive. Taking the point, Cyclops led the other X-Men across the road to meet them. The blue-skinned X-Man was bent forward, hands resting on his knees as he sucked in lungfuls of air. Standing beside him, Carol looked slightly confused—not just by the growing number of costumed characters suddenly appearing in her life, but by the fact that she was actually outside the camp.

"Wolverine . . ." Kurt gasped between breaths. "I had to . . ."

"I know," Cyclops said, reaching his side.

"Give me another minute . . ." Kurt wheezed.

The night air suddenly filled with the sounds of gunfire bursts, the clash of metal on metal, and the pitiful screams of the dying and injured.

"We don't *have* a minute," Cyclops said. He turned to his teammates. "Rogue, Gambit—get in there. Take out the guard towers first—I want their high-ground advantages eliminated. Kill the spotlights and the radio transmitter, too."

"What about Wolverine?" Gambit asked.

"Logan can take care of himself for the moment," Cyclops replied. "Now, go!"

"You got it, Cyke!" Rogue said. Grabbing Gambit around the chest from behind, she shot into the air and zoomed toward the camp.

Cyclops turned back to Phoenix. "Jean, you're with me." He looked to Nightcrawler. "Kurt?"

"Ready to go, Scott," the blue-skinned mutant replied. He was standing erect again, having finally caught his breath.

"Go back and give Logan a hand," Cyclops ordered. *"Try* to keep him from getting out of control."

Nightcrawler nodded. "Easier said than done, but I'll do my best." He teleported away.

Cyclops looked to Jean. "Let's go."

"Hey, what about me?" Carol asked.

Cyclops stared at her for a moment, as though he had just focused on the fact that she was standing there.

*"You* stay here," he said, and gestured toward her emaciated frame. "You're in no shape to help out."

"The hell I am. You think that, just because I don't have a flashy costume, I'm gonna miss out on the opportunity to pay those animals back for everything they've done to me?" Carol asked, cheeks glowing red with anger. "Not a chance, pal."

Cyclops considered his possible choices—they weren't many: he could have Carol join them and help in some limited capacity in liberating the camp, and try to keep her out of harm's way; or he could leave her behind, which more than likely meant that she'd go back to the camp on her own anyway and run the risk of getting killed.

"All right," he said. "But stay close."

Carol nodded in agreement. Cyclops looked to Phoenix, who flashed a brief, warm smile.

" 'Once more unto the breach, dear friends,' " she murmured. " 'Once more . . .' "

And with that, the trio began heading toward the battlefield.

* * *

High above the camp, Rogue made a quick circuit of the facility, holding tightly to Gambit as she zigged and zagged through the air, evading the gunfire that was now being directed at them from the towers.

"You plan on doin' something *soon*, Remy?" Rogue asked. "Or should I just throw you at them an' see what happens?"

"Don' you worry, *chere*," Gambit said casually. "I got de situation under control."

Reaching into one of the voluminous pockets of his duster, Gambit pulled out a deck of ordinary playing cards and fanned it out as though he were about to perform a magic trick. Selecting two cards at random, he concentrated for a moment, and the pieces of wax-coated white paper suddenly turned a pinkish-red, glowing brighter with each passing moment as a haze of crackling energy formed around them. Gambit had just brought his unusual mutant ability into play: the power to charge any inanimate object with kinetic energy—in other words, he could turn just about *anything* into a bomb. Being a thief and gambler, he naturally opted to use playing cards as his means of delivering an explosive payload.

"De man wan' de high ground taken away," Gambit said, a sinister smile playing at his lips. "Den dat's exactly what he gon' get." And with that, he flung the cards at the nearest tower.

The results were staggering: as the cards struck the metal walkway, they exploded with all the force of a howitzer shell, disintegrating the tower and flinging its occupants high into the air. Small bits of twisted metal rained down on the camp.

"Nice goin', sugah," Rogue commented, watching the guards tumble to the ground. Though the impact produced some broken bones, and a lot of pain and suffering, she was still glad to see that none of them had been killed by either the explosion or the fall. "You ready for another one?" she asked her teammate.

"Let's get *to* it, Rogue," Gambit said. He fanned the cards out again. "I still got most'a a full deck."

"That's *your* opinion . . ." the Southern Belle said dryly.

Before Gambit could think of a witty comeback, she headed for their next target.

The first impression that Nightcrawler had upon his return to the camp was that he had just stepped into the middle of some updated version of a *Conan the Barbarian* movie.

Amid the sounds of adamantium claws clashing against—and then slicing through—rifle barrels and body armor, Wolverine was standing on a mound of bodies ten or twelve feet high, the upper half of his costume torn to shreds, exposing his hirsute—and blood-spattered—chest. He was bleeding from a dozen or more entry wounds—high caliber bullets, judging from the look of the holes in his body, as well as knife thrusts—but his mutant healing factor allowed him to continue fighting without missing a beat. His mask was gone, making it easy to see the wild, chilling look of bloodlust in his eyes. Lips pulled back in a feral snarl, he was more animal than man now—a shark revelling in the throes of a feeding frenzy. Below him, a quintet of guards, their rifles sliced in half by Logan's far deadlier weapons, tried to get at him with bayonets, but the thin steel of the blades was no match against claws fashioned from the strongest metal on Earth—or their owner.

*"Mein Gott,"* Nightcrawler whispered, eyes widened in shock. "All the blood . . ."

From the corner of his eye, Logan spotted his teammate standing off to the side. "Jump right in, elf!" he called. "Wouldn't want ya t'miss out on all the fun!"

And with that, he leapt off the pile of bodies, throwing himself at the guards, who now looked like they were more interested in running for their lives than defending their place of employment. Not they had a choice, though; Wolverine wasn't about to let any of them escape.

That didn't mean, however, that Nightcrawler was about to just stand there and watch as his fellow X-Man slaughtered five people, no matter how cruel their actions might have been in the past. Teleporting himself across the short distance, he caught Wolverine in mid-leap, then 'ported again, despite the strain it was putting on his body. They landed in a heap five yards from Logan's intended victims. The guards immediately lost no time in vacating the scene.

With a howl like that of a lost soul consigned to the pits, Wolverine leapt to his feet and prepared to go tearing after his quarry.

"Logan, stop!" Nightcrawler said, stepping into his path. He looked winded, but not enough that it would keep him from preventing another murder. "The killing must end. I know how you feel about all this, but you *must* find another way to handle the situation."

"*You* don't know how I feel, elf." Wolverine retracted his claws—the metal-sheathed bones quickly sliding back into his arms—and pointed a gloved finger in Kurt's face. "Why don't ya wake up an' take a look around you, bub?" he growled. "We ain't mixin' it up with the Acolytes or the flamin' Brood. We're bustin' up a *death camp*, like the kind that used to exist back in the bad ol' days o' your country. Remember those? I bet you read all about 'em in school, right? Well, I was *there*, bub, an' I've had my fill o' malnourished bodies an' mass graves. I'll be *damned* if I'm lettin' any o' these monkey-suited sadists escape the punishment they got comin' to 'em." He glared up at Nightcrawler. "You ain't got the stones to do a job that needs doin', then stay outta my way an' go help the people that *need* helpin'." He snarled. "An' I *don't* mean the flamin' guards."

Not bothering to wait for a response from his stunned teammate, Wolverine pushed past him and, extending his claws once more, went hunting for fresh game.

All hell was breaking loose.

Guard towers were exploding—courtesy of Gambit and his deck of kinetically-charged cards. Armored troops tore across the compound, some of the soldiers still struggling to put on boots or cram shoulder-length hair into battle helmets. In their pens, German

shepherds were barking wildly, eager to attack the enemy, but in the confusion, no one had the sense to release them. Somewhere deep on the grounds, gunfire erupted, only to be silenced moments later.

And in the midst of all this chaos, the inmates began to stream from the bunkhouses; some joined the battle, attacking whatever guard was handy. Most, though, stampeded in the opposite direction, only to be brought to an abrupt halt by the high fencing designed to keep them in.

*Scott, we've got to get the prisoners out!* Jean's thoughts were brimming with concern, yet she kept her emotions in check.

*I'm on it,* Cyclops replied. He turned to the chain link fence and the wave of humanity that was surging against it. If he didn't act now, the people in front would be crushed against the links by those in the back who were too panicked to realize that they weren't going anywhere.

"*STAND BACK!*" Cyclops shouted above the din. But either no one heard him, or they weren't paying attention to his plea.

Raising his hands, he touched two small contacts on each side of his visor. Immediately, the ruby quartz lens rolled back, into the upper half of the metal shell, exposing his eyes—just for a second.

But it was time enough for two beams of bright red energy to lance forward from his pupils, to strike the ground in front of the fence with all the force of an exploding missile.

*That* got the inmates' attention. They froze, clearly uncertain of what to make of what had just transpired. As one, they stared, wide-eyed, at the blue-and-gold-garbed X-Man standing before them.

"Move back from the fence!" Cyclops yelled. "I'll have you out in a second!"

They did as they were told this time, and the mutant's visor flashed again. Instantly, an entire section of the fencing came crashing down. Before the broken metal had even touched the ground, though, the prisoners began pouring through the hole, frantically climbing over one another in their haste to be free.

"Single file, people!" Carol barked. "Plenty of fresh air and freedom to go around!"

The joyous occasion, however, was soon disrupted by screams of terror from the back of the line. Using her amazing mental powers, Phoenix pushed off from the ground and gently floated into the night sky. Her eyes narrowed in anger as she spotted a dozen armored soldiers stomping across the yard, in the direction of the crush of prisoners. The air filled with the sound of laser weapons cycling to full power.

"This one's *mine*," Phoenix said. Her bright green eyes flashed a deep crimson color and, with but a thought, she telekinetically grabbed hold of the collapsed fencing and flung it at the guards. In seconds, they were securely pinned to the ground, and no longer a threat.

Cyclops turned to Carol. "Help the other prisoners as they come through. Jean and I have to get inside." Carol opened her mouth, probably to argue about being left behind, but Scott gently placed a hand on her shoulder before she could say anything. "Please," he said.

Carol seemed to consider this for a moment, then nodded.

Cyclops smiled briefly. "Thank you." He glanced at Jean, who was still floating above them. Her eyes flashed again, and he rose up to join her. Together, they flew over the inmates and into the camp, as Carol struggled to create some sense of order in the midst of hysteria.

*Now*, I *get to have some fun*, Rogue thought, a malicious smile spreading across her face.

Having completed her bombing run with Gambit, she had dropped the wily Cajun onto the roof of one of the barracks to help out Wolverine—and Nightcrawler, who was probably back in the thick of things—and then had taken to the air again. Below her, the camp was in chaos as fires burned, shots rang out, and the prisoners turned against their captors, attacking them with whatever weapons they could find—table legs, metal folding chairs, their bare hands.

And speaking of captors . . .

From what appeared to be the commandant's office, a group of armed men and women came running out, followed by someone who was more than likely the man in charge. Considering the conditions of the camp and its prisoners, Rogue had expected someone who looked like the devil himself to be in charge—dark and sinister-looking, powerfully-built, with neatly coiffed hair and a pointed goatee, his uniform crackling with each confident step that he took. What she saw instead was a man with all the physique of a scarecrow, possessing bulging eyes, unkempt, thinning hair combed across a sunburned scalp, and a uniform that was badly in need of pressing.

*Guess there must've been some pretty slim pickin's down at the employment agency . . .* Rogue thought.

Forming a double-line across the main yard, the guards raised their rifles and pistols and took aim on the inmates, clearly intent on using deadly force to stop the riot.

*Not if I can help it,* Rogue thought grimly. With a burst of speed, she bore down on the firing squad.

*"FIRE!"* yelled the commandant.

Twenty-five fingers squeezed back on twenty-five triggers to begin the massacre—

—only to close on empty air.

Nonplussed, both guards and commanding officer stared at their hands, obviously wondering what had become of the weapons they had just been holding.

"Y'all lookin' for these?" Rogue asked. She serenely floated twenty feet above them, a Chesire Cat-like grin lighting her attractive features. As they watched in astonishment, the skunk-haired mutant crumpled the guns into a ball with her gloved hands, and then, like a major league pitcher delivering a fastball to home plate, wound up and threw the oversized paperweight into the middle of nearby Breakstone Lake.

"Lemme ask y'all somethin'," Rogue asked, standing in midair with her hands on her hips. "Without those peashooters, how y'all think you'd do in a *fair* fight?"

"Against a freak like *you*, who can do something like what we just saw?" the commandant replied with a sneer. "How is *that* a fair fight?"

Rogue wagged a disapproving finger at the annoying little man. "Now, there's no need for name-callin', sugah. Y'all don't see *me* climbin' up on my high horse an' callin' *you* a wall-eyed, turd-sniffin' polecat with delusions of bein' a *man*, do ya? 'Course not." Her grin widened. " 'Sides, I wasn't talkin' about *me*." She pointed over her shoulder. "I was talkin' about *them*."

The commandant and his men looked past her to see the very prisoners they had been targeting now rushing toward them. Before the little man could bark an order, the inmates were upon them, knocking them to the ground and giving them a not-so-healthy dose of their own brutal medicine.

Rogue chuckled as she saw the commandant scramble to his feet and run screaming, a group of inmates hot on his tail.

"I love this job . . ." she said with a sigh.

Her work, however, was far from complete.

A flash of moonlight on green metal off to one side caught her attention, just before a powerful laser beam struck her below the collarbone, knocking her out of the sky. Semi-conscious, Rogue soared across the yard and slammed hard into a black-painted truck parked near the main entrance, crashing through its roof with her indestructible body and collapsing in a heap on the cold, metal flooring of its container. Dazed but unhurt, she groaned and slowly sat up, in time to see a quartet of airborne soldiers in what seemed to be modified Guardsman armor—at least that's what it looked like, based on the pictures she'd once seen on the Xavier Institute's computer files . . . when the institute had been on these grounds, that is—hovering a few yards away.

"Blast that freak!" one of the soldiers yelled. As one, the Guardsmen raised their hands, palms held forward. Rogue saw flashes of light erupt from the center of each hand as the laser generators built into the armor released their deadly energies.

And then the truck exploded around her.

Nightcrawler had lost sight of Wolverine in the middle of the fray.

The last glimpse he'd had of the hotheaded Canadian came just before a green-armored soldier had swooped down from out of the night sky to backhand Kurt into the side of a bunkhouse. An exploding playing card that connected with the soldier's boot-jets—courtesy of Gambit—had shorted out the man's flight systems and sent him wildly careening over the fence and into the lake. Then, side by side, the blue-skinned teleporter and the dark-haired thief had joined forces with the hordes of angry prisoners to finally turn the tide of battle against the seemingly endless swarms of armed guards who opposed them.

Now, the ground suddenly trembled as a new explosion rocked the camp. Flames and thick, black smoke shot up from a transport truck standing near the camp entrance. Gambit frantically looked up into the night sky, then gazed at the burning vehicle and the armored figures swarming around it.

"Rogue?!" he yelled.

"She'll be fine, *mein fruend*," Nightcrawler assured him. "Rogue is quite resilient, you know. It will take more than an explosion to knock her out of the game. For the moment, however, we must concentrate on the matter at hand."

"I guess . . ." Remy said, though it was clear from his tone that he was distracted by his concern for his beautiful teammate. That didn't mean he wasn't still capable of fighting, though. Pulling three cards from his ever-present deck, he tossed them at a trio of guards clad in body armor; the cards detonated on impact with the steel plating, the force of the released charges throwing the now-unconscious men across the yard.

Gaining a small respite, Gambit stole a quick glance at the burning vehicle.

"Come on, *chere*," he whispered. "Don' let ol' Gambit down now . . ."

At the main entrance, the Guardsmen touched down on the muddy field, forming a rough semicircle around the truck; the smoke was thickening, fueled by the melting rubber tires, making it difficult to see the wreckage. One of the armored figures turned to the others.

"Okay, that's one down," she said. "Fan out and eliminate the rest of her bud—"

Her order was cut short, however, by the scream of metal scraping against metal.

As the Guardsmen watched, the pile of debris shifted, then fell to one side, and Rogue staggered out. Her hair was in complete disarray, her costume was in tatters, her ears were ringing like school bells from the explosion, and she was covered from head to toe with oily smut, but she was very much alive.

And very, very angry.

"Now," she said, glaring at her attackers, "it's *my* turn."

Creeping around the corner of a bunkhouse on the far end of the camp, the commandant pressed up against the rotted, wooden slats of the wall and tried to become as one with the shadows. He'd managed to evade the prisoners who had bolted after him, though it had taken a masterful series of twists and turns to finally put some distance between himself and his pursuers. The window-shattering explosion from the front of the compound had also helped to buy him time enough to hide. For the moment, he was safe.

That moment, unfortunately, ended all too soon—shattered by the vise-like grip of the hand that now closed around his throat from behind.

"If I ain't mistaken, based on how popular you are with the inmates," Wolverine growled, "then *you* must be the piece o' trash runnin' this hellhole. Am I right?"

The commandant opened his mouth to cry out for help, but Logan's grip viciously tightened, thumb and forefinger pressing down on the man's Adam's apple. A low gurgling sound issued from between the commandant's lips, and he began turning an unhealthy shade of blue.

"The *last* thing you wanna do is get me *really* honked off by makin' any trouble, bub," the feral X-Man warned. "The only reason you're still breathin' is 'cause you still got a use or two. But you try *anything* guaranteed t'raise my blood pressure even a *little*, an' you'll be wishin' I'd let yer 'guests' work ya over instead. You understand?"

Though his eyes were starting to glaze over, the commandant frantically nodded his head.

"Good."

Wolverine released his grip, and the commandant fell to the ground. The little man alternately coughed and gasped for air as a copious amount of drool poured from his mouth. When his breathing seemed to have stabilized, and his skin tone had returned to a more natural color, Logan grabbed him by the collar of his uniform and hauled him to his feet. Eyes wide with fear, chin slick with lines of spittle, the commandant stared, open-mouthed, at the X-Man, clearly afraid of what might happen next.

"Here's the deal," Wolverine said. "You're gonna order yer men to stop fightin' an' lay down their weapons. If they don't, I'll *kill* ya."

"A-all r-right," the commandant stammered.

"Then yer gonna free the rest o' the prisoners. I know you mighta gotten confused an' all, with everybody runnin' around like chickens in a barnyard, but I'm sure you got some folks locked up in solitary, or a punishment box, or whatever you sick freaks use to break a man or woman down. If ya *don't* set 'em loose, I'll *kill* ya."

"Y-yes. Im-immediately."

"Then, you're gonna burn this place t'the ground."

The commandant's eyes widened even further. *"B-burn* the camp—?"

*"Shut up,"* Wolverine snapped. "Yeah—burn this whole stinkin' hellhole. Don't leave a beam standin'. Burn the armor an' the uniforms, too. If I see one trace o' those goosesteppin' monkey-suits after tonight—"

"You'll k-kill me."

Wolverine nodded. "Smart boy. Now, get t'work."

And with that, he shoved the commandant forward, directing him back to the center of the camp.

Phoenix and Cyclops touched down in the main yard just in time to avoid a collision with a Guardsman who was *not* flying under his own power. His armor riddled with fist-shaped dents, flight systems rendered inoperative, he soared across the camp and crashed head first into what was once a mess hall. The structure collapsed on top of him.

"That would be Rogue's doing . . ." Phoenix said, watching as the mess hall roof buckled, seemed to hang in the air for a moment, then dropped onto the rest of the wreckage.

"That would be *my* guess, too," Cyclops replied.

They turned to look in the direction from which the soldier had been sent flying. Looking worse than she probably felt, Rogue was happily cracking Guardsman armor like lobster tails, then reaching in to scoop out their contents; men and women clad only in camouflage-hued skivvies were roughly yanked from their protective shells and deposited on the ground, deprived of their weapons and their dignity.

"The situation seems to be under control," Cyclops mused aloud.

Phoenix didn't respond, pausing instead to lightly touch the tips of her fingers to her temples. "Kurt and Remy could use a hand, though," she said, having picked up their mental call for assistance.

"Let's not keep them waiting, then," Cyclops said.

"You'd think with all that's going on, these *verdammt* guards would have surrendered by now," Nightcrawler commented between gritted teeth.

The strain of fighting without pause was beginning to tell on both X-Men, as well as the prisoners standing beside them. Kurt had pushed himself to the limits of his powers, 'porting to and fro around the compound, throwing a punch to the jaw here, a kick to the groin there, but finally he had to give it up; his body felt like it would tear itself apart if he tried one more spatial jump. Gambit had run out of playing cards a while ago, and had to settle for basic fighting skills until he could get his hands on something that he could use as a weapon.

Unfortunately, there seemed to be no end to the guards. Apparently having conceded the loss of the camp, they had put all their effort into taking their frustrations out on whomever had been left behind during the mad dash for freedom, thus forcing the remaining prisoners back toward the chain link fence enclosing the eastern side of the camp, near the lake. Luckily, though, either the guards were out of bullets, or they'd crazily decided to settle the matter with knives and bare hands; either way, it would account for why no one had started firing into the crowd.

A mixed blessing, to be sure.

"Don' you worry none, Kurt," Gambit said, cheerfully breaking the nose of a guard who had gotten within striking distance. "You heard Jeannie—de cavalry's on its way."

"I do not hear anyone blowing a 'charge' on a bugle," Nightcrawler said sarcastically.

*That's because my parents paid for piano lessons, friend. I could knock out a quick "Mapleleaf Rag" for you later, if you'd like.*

Kurt broke into a huge grin as he spotted the redhead. *Jean!*

he replied telepathically. *Nice of you and Scott to join us! Cutting it a little close, wouldn't you say?*

*I thought you liked it that way, Nightcrawler.* It was Cyclops; Phoenix had linked their minds for easier communication. *A last-minute save is more in line with those movie serials you like to watch on Saturday mornings, isn't it?*

*Not when it comes to real life,* Nightcrawler replied. *I prefer to restrict my cliffhangers to the small screen.* He gestured toward the guards, who were pressing their attack. *Would the two of you mind . . . ?*

*Just like a man,* Phoenix replied. *Always expecting a woman to clean up his mess.*

Green eyes flashed, and the guards in the back of the horde suddenly found themselves airborne, bound for Breakstone Lake. Their indignant cries of protest were soon drowned out by the loud splash they made when they hit the water.

*If that's how you feel about things,* Cyclops pondered, *I'll start picking up my socks when we get back home.* He glanced around quickly, and frowned. *After we've managed to restore our home, that is.*

Raising the lens of his visor, Cyclops fired a series of short, powerful bursts of energy that scattered the guards like tenpins, tossing them high into the air so that Phoenix could telekinetically grab them on the fly and send them to join their compatriots in the chilly waters. Soon enough, they had cleared a path all the way up to the beleaguered Nightcrawler and Gambit.

"You two all right?" Cyclops asked.

"Better, now dat we seen a friendly face," Gambit replied, smiling as he looked at Phoenix.

"Hey, that's my *wife*, mister," Cyclops said. Though he didn't smile, the trace of humor in his voice was quite apparent.

Gambit shrugged. "I'll keep dat in mind."

Around the X-Men, the few guards who hadn't been sent to the showers moaned as they lay on the ground, some dazed, most semi-conscious. Arms folded across her chest, Phoenix gazed down at them.

"If any of you are planning to get up to try this again," she said coolly, *"don't."*

Wisely, they heeded her advice.

"Looks like I missed out on last call," said a gruff voice from nearby. The X-Men turned in its direction.

Still pushing the commandant ahead of him, Wolverine entered the main yard. "I didn't even get to throw any o' the bums out," he said, glancing toward the lake.

Phoenix gazed at the scrappy X-Man's blood-streaked and tattered appearance and frowned. "It looks like you've done more than enough for one night, friend."

Logan smiled grimly. "Ya should see the *other* guys."

Phoenix grimaced. "Thanks, but I'll pass. I've already *had* my fair share of seeing the kind of stuff that runs around inside your head."

"Who's yo' friend, Wolverine?" Gambit asked.

Logan gave the commandant another shove. "This is the turd responsible fer runnin' this dump. We were just havin' a little heart-to-heart about some changes he's gonna be makin' around here." He glanced at the commandant. "Ain't that right?"

The commandant's nervous head-shaking seemed to be about the only answer he was capable of giving at the moment.

Logan gazed at Nightcrawler. "See, elf? I can be a reasonable guy . . . when I wanna be."

"For which I am always most grateful, Wolverine," Kurt replied, though his dark expression made it perfectly clear that he had not forgotten Logan's earlier actions—or his words.

"Could y'all gimme a hand here?" Rogue asked, as she walked over to join the group. "I'm feelin' a little . . . well . . ." She gestured toward the remains of her costume; most of it hung in tatters, though some parts, like her gloves and leather jacket, had survived more or less intact. Not exactly a scandalous appearance, given the costumes worn by some of her female peers in the superhuman community, but the fact that *any* of her skin had become exposed to the night air seemed to make her incredibly nervous as she approached the X-Men and their charges.

With Rogue, however, her concern didn't stem from any overwhelming sense of modesty—she'd worn bathing suits that involved far less material than she was wearing at the moment; no, her concern was for the other people around her—and herself. As strong as she was, as invulnerable as her body might be, Rogue's powers had one disturbing drawback: if her bare skin touched the flesh of any man, woman, or child, she automatically absorbed their thoughts, their memories, even their skills, whether they be as simple as bricklaying or as complicated as a mountain-leveling superpower. The absorption was an unconscious action over which she had absolutely no control, and one that had first manifested itself during her teenage years, while she was kissing a boy.

He was plunged into a coma as a result. The response to the accident had been immediate: Rogue was banished from her community, scorned by even the people who had been her closest friends.

The activation of her powers during such an innocent moment—and the unrelenting feeling of shame that resulted from it—left deep emotional scars on the young woman.

Not surprisingly, it had been a long time since Rogue had a real boyfriend.

She had tried various methods to counteract the unwanted power since that traumatic experience, but the only thing that seemed to negate the process was, simply and amazingly enough, clothing. Thus, always fearful that she might wind up harming someone with the slightest touch—tapping a shoulder, brushing against a bare arm on a busy street—Rogue tended to wrap herself in outfits that did wonders for complimenting her figure, yet nonetheless kept her leech-like abilities from inadvertently coming into play at inopportune moments.

Now, exposed as she was, and as nervous as she seemed—based on the small, furtive glances that she stole at the prisoners who stared at her from behind the other X-Men—it was painfully apparent that Rogue was afraid of the nightmarish memories she might have to "relive" if she came into contact with any of the poor unfortunates they had just rescued.

"Here y'go, *chere,*" Gambit said, stepping forward and removing his duster. He draped it over Rogue's shoulders. "Wouldn't want ya t'catch yo' death."

"Thanks, Remy," Rogue said, gratefully pulling the warm leather around her body.

Cyclops gazed around the smoldering camp and saw the fright that was evident in the eyes of the former prisoners; they didn't seem to know what to expect from these costumed men and women standing before them.

"Thank you," Cyclops said softly. "For all your help."

Some of the prisoners murmured responses, but most of them just stood quietly.

*Scott . . .* Jean's thoughts "sounded" clearly in his mind. *I ran a quick scan of these people, just to see if anyone knew why the school wasn't here.* He glanced at her with concern, and she shook her head slightly. *I'm fine.* Jean flashed a brief smile. *Don't worry—I'm not going to get caught flatfooted by another psi-wave. But we do need information, and what I found so unusual, though, is that it seems* none *of them recognize us.*

Cyclops turned to face his wife; behind his visor, an eyebrow rose in a quizzical fashion. *How could that be possible? I know we've always tried to keep a low profile, but considering some of the situations we've been involved in, and the way most people react to us just on principle, I'd think at least a few of the prisoners might have started backing away from us "muties."*

*I thought so, too,* Jean responded, *but that might explain why Carol didn't recognize us, either, despite her history with Logan.* She gestured toward the prisoners. *All I get from their thoughts are confusion and worry and an intense fear that the rescue might be some kind of trick to get their hopes up about finally escaping, and that any second now they'll be forced into trucks and transported to another camp.*

*Another?* Nightcrawler's thoughts interjected. *Mein Gott, how many of these godforsaken things are there? And who's responsible for them?*

Phoenix stared at each of her teammates, her features darkening with anger as she provided them with an answer:

"Doctor Doom," she said aloud.

Wolverine growled softly—a sound which automatically sent a new wave of panic coursing through the commandant. A small puddle formed around his feet.

"All right, we need answers," said Cyclops. He pointed at the commandant. "And *you're* going to provide them."

# 7

IT WAS a sobering history lesson, to be sure.

*"Ten years?"* Phoenix asked. "That's impossible!"

The first pink rays of dawn were just edging over Westchester County as the X-Men and Carol Danvers assembled on the shore of Breakstone Lake, where the soothing beauty of Professor Xavier's Japanese gardens had once flourished; with the construction of the camp, the ground had been turned into a graveyard for the prisoners who had died while under the care of their cruel hosts. Behind them, under the watchful eye of the now well-armed former inmates, the commandant, his guards, and his soldiers were standing in a circle in their undergarments, setting fire to their uniforms, per Wolverine's non-negotiable demands. Green-tinged smoke rose high into the early morning sky.

Phoenix looked at each of her teammates; they were all finding it difficult to accept what they had learned first from the commandant, and then from Carol, who had provided a more truthful explanation of how the world of Victor von Doom was run.

*"I'll* say it's impossible," Rogue said, agreeing with Jean. "We've only been away a *month,* an' Doom sure wasn't in charge of the place when we left. An' for ten years?" She grimaced and shook her head. "Ain't no way."

"Could Roma have made a mistake?" Nightcrawler mused aloud. "She *did* mention before we left that she had not been paying all that much attention to events on our Earth. Perhaps she sent us into a possible future timeline by mistake, or—"

"Or dropped us on an alternate Earth instead?" Cyclops said, completing Kurt's thought. Nightcrawler nodded in agreement. Scott paused for a moment to mull over the possibility, then shook his head. "I can't see that happening. Roma would *never* be that sloppy. And, given her powers, I doubt she's even *capable* of making such a monumental error. But, even considering the possibility that such a mistake might have occurred, there still exists a threat to the omniverse—one we already agreed to handle."

"No argument dere, boss," Gambit said. "A job's a job." He gazed at each of his friends. "I jus' t'ink we'd all rather know fo' sure if dis be our world—fo' peace o' mind, if nothin' else. 'Cause if dis *is* our Earth—" he looked over his shoulder at the camp, then turned back to Cyclops "—den I'd say it's a whole lot more screwed-up den e'en Roma was thinkin'. An' if Doc Doom's involved, it's fo' sure we gon' have some battle on our hands tryin' t'clean up his mess." He glanced at Rogue, flashed a brief smile. "He one big ol' puppy dog to be runnin' 'round loose wit' no proper paper trainin', y'know."

Rogue turned her head and raised a hand to her lips, to cover a smile that seemed so . . . disrespectful in such a tragic place. She knew Remy was trying to lighten the mood in the midst of a depressing situation—that was one of the charms that made him so damned appealing to her—but it just didn't feel right to be laughing when their world was suffering under the oppressive thumb of a madman like Doctor Doom. There'd be time enough for her and Remy to share a laugh or two later, when their work was done—she'd see to it. Suppressing her chuckle by clearing her throat, Rogue turned back to face the group.

"All right," Cyclops said, "our objectives are clear: we find Doom, discover the means by which he's transformed the world, and either destroy it or force him to tell us how to shut it down."

"And just how to you plan to convince him to do *that?*" Carol asked.

"Leave that t*'me,*" Wolverine said, a dangerous gleam in his eyes. For dramatic effect, he popped his claws. Carol's eyes widened as she stared, momentarily transfixed, by the way the morning sunlight played along the edges of Wolverine's bio-weapons. "By the time I'm done carvin' through that leftover Renaissance festival outfit o' his," Logan continued, "he's gonna be hopin' that *all* I'm lookin' for is the shut-off switch, an' not his heart."

Carol grimaced as she watched the metal-coated bones slide back into Logan's arms. "Ooookay," she croaked, looking a little pale. She quickly turned to Cyclops. "Well, you won't have to look hard to find him. He and the Queen are living in the White House."

"Yeah, an' that's somethin' else I don't understand," Rogue said. "How is it that Ororo'd be willin' to marry that tin-plated nut, let alone agree to go rulin' the world with 'im? I don't see the connection between 'em."

"Before yer time, darlin'," Wolverine replied. "First run-in the new team had with Doom, he invited her t'dinner at his castle upstate while the rest o' us were dukin' it out with his goons in the basement. Some foolish attempt t'rescue that grinnin' jackass, Arcade—the reasons *why* are too complicated t'get into right now. Least we *thought* it was a rescue mission; shoulda known better. Turned out to be a flamin' trap he set up for us with ol' metalhead."

Phoenix nodded. "Ororo confided in me about that once. She was . . . embarrassed by how she'd allowed herself to be drawn to Doom's power and . . . well, charisma, I guess, in the middle of a mission. And although he tried to kill her and our friends, she and Doom parted on civil terms—he even . . ." Jean paused, then shrugged. "Well, from the way Ororo described it, it sounded like Doom was hitting on her."

"*Hittin' on her?*" Rogue asked incredulously. "This *is* Doctor Doom y'all are talkin' 'bout, right?"

"Well, that's what it *sounded* like when Ororo told me," Jean replied. "He said he found her 'fascinating,' and wanted to get to know her better. And Ororo—for some reason—was actually open to the idea, though she never took him up on the offer."

"Jus' like a woman, eh?" Gambit quipped. "Say she gon' call de next day, den never does."

The icy stares directed his way by Jean, Rogue, and Carol did wonders for wiping the smile off his face.

Nightcrawler turned to Cyclops. "So, Scott, what is our next move?"

Cyclops pinched his lower lip between thumb and forefinger, then stood silently for a few moments, considering their options.

"Allies," he finally said. "We need to find out if there are any heroes in this world still opposed to Doom, and whether they'd be willing to throw in with our lot. Having to take on him *and* an entire planet under his rule without some back-up—well, let's just say I don't like the odds."

"Good luck to you, pal," Carol said sarcastically. "You're certainly gonna need it, considering most of the super-types are working for Doom, and the ones who don't aren't gonna want to get involved."

"We've got to try anyway," Cyclops insisted. "If nothing else, we need someone to create enough of a distraction that will allow us to get to Doom directly."

"Makes sense, if you can actually *find* someone nuts enough to run interference for you at the risk of having their own head blown off," Carol said. "I gotta tell you, though, when it comes to costumed types like you folks, the pickings are mighty slim among the ones that are still operating."

"Well, what about *you*, Carol?" Phoenix asked.

"What *about* me?" Carol replied.

"Why can't you help us? We know how powerful you are as Warbird—you'd certainly be able to help shift the balance in our favor."

Carol stared at Jean as though the X-Man was crazy. "What in God's name are you *talking* about? Don't you think that if I had some kind of powers like you people, I would've torn down this suburb of hell a long time ago?" She snorted and waved a hand toward Rogue. "What, are you telling me I can go around bench-pressing trucks like *her?*"

Rogue's cheeks flushed a deep red, and she quickly turned away from Carol. Although the blond-haired woman didn't recognize her now, Rogue was all too aware of the past they shared: of how Carol, in the pre-Doom-ruled world, had been a super heroine named Ms. Marvel, and Rogue had been a member of an organization called the Brotherhood of Evil Mutants; of how Rogue, following the orders of the Brotherhood's leader, Mystique, had ambushed Carol one night in San Francisco and used her powers to leech away not only her cosmic-spawned powers, but part of her psyche, leaving her body a nearly empty shell; and of how, after draining her enemy, Rogue had tossed her off the Golden Gate Bridge in an attempt to kill her. Though Carol had eventually recovered both her mind and her powers—a slow, painful process that took years—and changed her super heroic codename to the more aggressive Warbird, she had never forgiven Rogue for stealing away her individuality, and could barely stand to be within spitting distance of her former adversary to this day.

"Carol," Phoenix said softly, "I'd like to try something, with your permission. I'm a telepath—"

Carol's lips pulled back in a sneer. "You're a *mento?*"

Phoenix started. "A *what?*"

Nearby, Gambit turned to Rogue. "I t'ought dat was some kinda candy," he whispered.

"Sshh!" Rogue replied, her raised index finger pressed against her lips.

"One of Doom's mind readers," Carol said, practically spitting out the words. "He's got them stationed all over the world, running their little mental scans, taking leisurely strolls through the minds of every man, woman, and child on this planet, making sure no one's going to try and overthrow their fearless leader."

"The Thought Police," Nightcrawler murmured to Wolverine. "George Orwell would be proud."

Wolverine grunted. "Or Hitler."

"I understand how you feel, Carol," Phoenix said. "Believe me, you're not the first person to react so strongly to what people like I can do. But I swear to you that I'm nothing like Doom's enforcers—a polar opposite, you might say."

"Right." Carol snorted. "And your friend Ororo is really a kind, loving soul opposed to the dictatorial rule of her husband."

"Actually, she is," Phoenix replied. "But that's besides the point. What's important right now is getting to the bottom of this whole maddening situation."

"And you want to go rooting around in my head to find out why I don't know any of you—" Carol smiled slightly as she looked at the team's costumes "—colorful folks, or where these alleged superpowers of mine might have gone to. Right?"

"Yes," Phoenix replied. "And that's *all* I'll be looking for. I promise I'll avoid any part of your subconscious that you don't want me to see." She fell silent, then, not wanting to push her friend too hard for a decision.

Carol stuffed her callused hands into the pockets of her prison jumper and stared at the ground for a few moments. Even without reading her thoughts, Jean could tell how hard she was wrestling with the idea of someone sifting through her mind for information. Carol took a deep breath, released it slowly between gritted teeth, and kicked at a small rock by her feet; she watched it skip across the water three times before it sank with a small splash.

"All right," she finally said. She wearily ran her hands through her hair, then lifted her head to lock eyes with Jean. "But if you make me start clucking like a chicken, so help me, God, I'll rip your head off and punt it like a football."

Wolverine chuckled. "Now, *that's* the Carol Danvers I know."

Phoenix smiled at Carol. "Deal."

"Okay. So, what do you need me to do?"

"Just relax and try to clear your mind," Jean replied. "I'll do the rest. And I promise this won't hurt a bit."

Carol closed her eyes. "That's what my dentist used to say just as he started drilling a tooth. That was usually the exact moment when the shot of Novocain wore off." She opened one eye to gaze evenly at Phoenix. "Having a low pain threshold tends to mean whoever's handy gets to suffer right along with me."

"I'll keep that in, er, mind," Phoenix said.

Carol nodded and shut her eye again.

Reaching out with both hands, Jean lightly placed her fingertips on Carol's temples, then closed her own eyes as well.

"More waitin', eh, boss?" Gambit muttered.

"Yes, Remy," Scott said quietly. "More waiting . . ."

She was seated on a quilt-covered waterbed in a blue-walled, white carpeted bedroom, an issue of *Tiger Beat* laying open on her lap; she glanced at the article: "My Dream Date With Simon LeBon." Sitting next to her on the bed—keeping her company, it seemed—was a collection of stuffed animals: teddy bears of varying sizes and colors, wide-eyed yellow lions, a sky-blue porpoise, even a rainbow-hued unicorn. Across the room, in a corner, stood a large potted plant that looked like a miniature palm tree, but she knew that wasn't the actual species; unfortunately, unlike Ororo, she'd always been bad with plant names. On the walls and ceiling were posters of various rock stars from the 1980s—Rick Springfield, The Thompson Twins, Duran Duran, Culture Club. Beside the bed, a small clock-radio was softly broadcasting the Eurythmics' "Sweet Dreams (Are Made Of This)." Early morning sunlight streamed into the room through two windows across from the bed, and the pleasant chirping of birds from the trees outside seemed to fill the room.

As mental images went, Jean thought, it was a surprisingly original one—most people's psyches tended to create vast, desolate landscapes of blinding sandstorms or Salvador Dali-esque shapes, or a crossroads suspended in a void, its winding paths meeting at a nexus where a sign usually stood, its infinite number of arrows pointing in an infinite number of directions, leading the traveler to whatever memories were being sought.

The setting wasn't a complete surprise to Jean, however; she'd been in Carol's mind quite a few times during the course of their friendship, back when the world was sane. What always amazed Jean, though, was how well-ordered the woman kept her subconscious—no stray thoughts barging through like a bull in a china shop, no dark, menacing shapes standing just along the edge of your vision, no monsters from the id the size of mountains looking to destroy her sense of identity.

In terms of pop psychology, this was Carol's "happy place"— the spot she went to relax when the pressures of the world became overwhelming; in this case, happiness was found in the mental recreation of the bedroom owned by a teen-aged Carol Danvers, who had spent a good deal of her time hanging out in the real-world version while living with her parents. And considering the horrifying experiences she must have undergone while in the camp, it was a testament to the adult Carol's sheer force of will that she hadn't chosen to retreat into the bedroom for good and lock the door behind her.

Speaking of doors . . .

Jean looked up from the magazine as the bedroom door opened, and the grown-up Carol entered. She was dressed in black tights, white low-topped sneakers, and a gray sweatshirt with a frayed collar; it hung on her body at an angle, exposing her right shoulder.

Somebody's *seen* Flashdance *one too many times* . . . Jean thought.

Carol started when she realized Jean was sitting on the bed. "Hey, how did you . . . ?"

Jean smiled. "I've, um, been here before."

Carol gestured toward Jean's legs, which were stretched out on the comforter. "And you thought you'd make yourself at home?"

Jean's smile widened, and she raised a booted leg. "My feet were killing me." She chuckled as she caught her friend's confused expression. "I know: in this place, we're just psychic representations of our real selves. But right now, the real me is in a heck of a lot of pain from running around in high heels all night long."

Carol raised a quizzical eyebrow. "And I suppose in your profession, sensible shoes are frowned upon, right?"

Jean shrugged pleasantly. "It's the price one pays for looking good."

Carol snorted. "Thanks, but I don't need to look *that* good."

Jean smiled. "You say that now . . ."

"Oh, I get it," Carol said, slowly nodding her head. "That whole 'Super Carol' thing you were talking about before." Her brow furrowed. "You mean I actually dress up like a stiletto-heeled circus acrobat—no offense—and fight crime, like Wonder Man or She-Hulk?"

"None taken," Jean replied. "And yes, you do. Actually, you weren't off the mark when you mentioned being able to bench-press trucks—you have incredible strength. And that's just *one* of your abilities."

"You don't say . . ." Carol said, clearly intrigued.

"I do." Jean smiled wickedly. "And when it comes to dressing up like a 'circus acrobat,' honey, *your* heels are even higher than *mine.*"

Carol whistled through her teeth. "Where did *my* dignity go . . . ?"

"Care to see everything I've been talking about?" Jean asked. She patted the bed, beckoning Carol to join her. Her friend quickly complied.

Instantly, the room faded away, until only the bed remained. Carol gasped in surprise and bounced across the water-filled mattress toward the center of the bed, trying to get as far away as possible from the void that had suddenly appeared beneath them.

"Don't worry," Jean said soothingly. "I've got everything under control."

"Glad to hear it," Carol said. "Now what?"

Jean grinned. "You like movies?"

"I haven't seen one in a long time, considering my previous situation," Carol replied sourly. "But if you plan on showing me *Stalag 17* or *The Great Escape*, I'll have to hurt you."

Jean shook her head. "How about *The Carol Danvers Story*?"

Carol wrinkled her nose in mild reluctance. "I don't know . . . I hear parts of it are kind of depressing."

"Ah, but this is the special widescreen edition," Jean countered, "with never-before-seen footage and big-budget special effects." She paused. "Well, never-before-seen by *you*; I'm already quite familiar with it."

Carol shrugged. "So, let's see it, then."

Jean smiled and dramatically waved a hand. A movie theater-sized projection screen suddenly appeared before them.

"Not bad," Carol commented.

"It gets better," Jean said. "Watch."

From the darkness behind them, a light began flickering, casting indistinct images on the screen.

"Focus!" Carol yelled over her shoulder to the imaginary projectionist. Jean giggled.

Slowly, the images took solid shape, becoming a shot of up-close faces happily staring at the "camera." A handsome, dark-haired man in his twenties, eyes sparkling with tears, was beaming proudly. Beside him, propped up in what looked like a hospital bed, was an attractive—though exhausted—blond-haired woman, who was also crying. It was immediately clear to see where Carol had gotten her good looks.

"That's my mom and dad!" Carol said. She paused, and turned to Jean. "Hey, wait a minute—are you saying I can remember the day I was *born?*"

"Uh-huh," Jean replied. "It's long been theorized by psychologists that we can recall events that far back, though, like most memories, they tend to fade away as we get older. But the subconscious retains just about everything."

Carol shook her head. "That's just . . . freaky."

"I'll speed things up—get to the good parts," Jean said. "And I'll shift to . . . well, I guess you could call it an 'external camera'."

Carol nodded. "You mean a third-person point of view—like when I'm dreaming, and I'm watching myself doing something."

"Exactly."

The screen darkened for a moment, then was filled by an image of Carol, wearing a dark business suit, standing on New York's Fifth Avenue, across from Central Park. Behind her stood an impressive-looking building that Jean immediately recognized as Avengers Mansion, home and headquarters of what was regarded as Earth's greatest team of super heroes. Carol turned from the "camera" and started walking toward the building—

And then the image was abruptly replaced by *another* "scene": this one of Carol in her Air Force staff car as she drove to work one morning, happily singing off-key to Robert Palmer's "Addicted to Love" as it blared from the vehicle's radio.

Jean glanced at Carol, who was staring, transfixed, at the screen.

"Did you see that?" she asked.

"See what?" Carol replied. "Proof that I'm tone-deaf?"

"No. That—that jump-cut."

Carol shook her head. "No." She gestured toward the screen. "So, when do I get to see me changing the course of mighty rivers?"

"That's what *I'd* like to know . . ." Jean mumbled softly.

As movies go, this one was poorly edited, with frames deleted in a haphazard fashion, causing scenes to end abruptly and jump to the next segment of the reel: Here was Carol at her tenth birthday party, where Robbie McDowell gave her her first kiss; here she was graduating from the Air Force academy, throwing her cap high into the air alongside her classmates; and here she was as head of security at Cape Canaveral where, Jean knew, Carol was destined to meet the alien super hero Captain Marvel—a meeting that would forever change her life.

But *that* memory wasn't there. There was no denying it, then.

There were definitely gaps in Carol's memory. But, more surprisingly, *she didn't know they were there.*

"So, do I look good in spandex?" Carol asked.

Brow furrowed, Jean turned to face her. "Hmm? Oh. Well, yes, I suppose," she said, still distracted by what she *wasn't* seeing in her scans. "Black one-piece, opera gloves, and thigh-highs. Little domino mask. Red sash around your waist." She turned back to the screen. "The *guys* have always thought you looked good in it."

Carol giggled. "I didn't know I could be such a *tramp.*"

Jean nodded, not really paying attention to her friend's musings, and probed deeper. More images appeared on the screen, the speed at which they moved increasing as Jean flipped through them, in the manner of someone hurriedly thumbing through a book: a succession of lovers—some good, but most bad; vacations and spy missions and birthdays and holiday parties; Carol's rise to captaincy; then memories of her fall from grace, and her years in the camp.

But her experiences as Ms. Marvel? As Binary? As Warbird?

Gone—tossed aside like a bunch of discarded frames lying on a cutting room floor. What they were seeing now was some soulless movie studio executive's cut of *The Carol Danvers Story.* And its star seemed to be completely unaware of the hatchet job done to the last reel.

Jean gritted her teeth. This was unacceptable.

*All right,* she thought. *One last time. Let's try something* big . . .

As difficult as it was to force Carol to relive a traumatic experience, perhaps the shock of one might jolt her memories back into play. True, it was akin to trying to fix the reception on a television set by slapping it repeatedly with your hand until the picture settled, but Jean was running out of options. But which—

Rogue's attack.

Jean hated herself just for considering it. As traumatic experiences went, it was as bad as—possibly even worse than—anything Carol had had to endure during all her time in the death camp.

Jean knew that there were other bad memories lurking in the darkness behind them—a few that might even make a temporary loss of identity seem like a slap on the wrist—but not even she was willing to draw upon those.

So, Rogue's attack it was. Steeling herself, Jean started the "projector" again, and began searching for that bleak, rainswept night in San Francisco.

And found nothing.

It was a stunning revelation, to say the least. Anything that had to do with Carol's powers, her career as a super heroine, as a member of the Avengers, as a friend of the X-Men—all gone. Replaced with false memories of an armored madman rising to power without resistance, taking Jean's dearest friend as his wife, and lording it over the planet for an entire decade.

Sheer insanity.

It was as though Doom's dream of one day conquering the Earth had been stamped onto Carol's mind and carved into her subconscious as incontrovertible fact.

It was also one of the most horrifying examples of psychic butchery that Jean had ever witnessed. And if this had been done to Carol, she wondered with mounting horror, did that mean the same thing had happened, not just to the super hero community in general, but to all their friends?

To everyone on the planet?

Jean's eyed widened in shock. Where in heaven's name could Doom have gotten such power . . . ?

*"Well?"* Carol asked.

Jean started, roused from her musings, and, still wide-eyed, turned to face her friend. "W-what?"

"I'm still waiting for you to show me how I look in spandex," Carol replied. "So far, I've seen the stuff I already know, followed by a lot of nothing." She waved a hand toward the projection screen that floated in front of them. "If I want to stare at a blank screen, I can always stand in front of a broken TV."

"I, um, ran ahead already," Jean said quickly, and tapped her head. "It's kind of like watching a videotape on fast-forward. There was, um, nothing else to see." Her fingers began nervously picking at the polyester threads of the comforter and she focused her gaze on the work, unable to look Carol in the eye.

"What do you mean by 'nothing else'?" Carol asked, folding her arms across her chest.

"Just what I mean," Jean said, still looking at her busy hands. She turned her head slightly—just enough so that her fiery mane fell forward to hide her face. "The information I was looking for wasn't there. Maybe I was wrong about this whole thing—it wouldn't be the first time it happened." She stopped picking and smoothed out the comforter. "I think we'd better get back to the others before they start to worry."

"They're not the *only* ones . . ." Carol said, an edge in her voice.

And with that, both women faded away, leaving the waterbed construct to float away into the troubling darkness.

Jean and Carol snapped back to reality, gasping for air as metabolisms slowed by their shared trance suddenly kicked back into high gear.

Cyclops placed his hands on Phoenix's shoulders as she stumbled back a step. "You all right, hon?"

"I'm fine, Scott," she replied, steadying her breathing. *It's Carol we should be worried about,* she added through their psychic link. Cyclops stared at her, and she quickly shook her head. *Later.*

Carol moaned. "I thought you said that wasn't gonna hurt," she said, massaging her temples with her fingers. "I've had sinus headaches that felt better."

"Sorry," Jean said, still avoiding eye contact. "An unexpected side-effect of the link. I ran through your memories a little too fast for your brain to keep up."

Carol grunted. "Seems like a whole lot of trouble just to find nothing." She winced in obvious pain and rubbed her head with the palms of her hands. "I've gotta sit down for a little bit. Then we better start making plans for getting as far the hell away from here as possible—I wouldn't be surprised to find out that somebody in town had already called for the Guardsmen once the shooting started." Waving off any help, she wandered away to join the other freed prisoners, who were in the process of binding their former captors.

Once their friend had gone, Phoenix quickly filled in her team-mates on what her psychic scans had revealed about the absence of Carol's powers, and her missing memories.

"That don't explain why Ace don't remember *me*," Wolverine commented. "I knew her *before* she got mixed up in this whole spandex lifestyle."

"I think it does, Logan," Jean replied. "Carol's had more contact with you during your time with the X-Men than while you were both working military intelligence; in some way, she associates you more with super hero activity. Therefore, when her memories of having been involved in that 'lifestyle,' as you put it, were removed, her memories of *you* were likewise deleted."

Wolverine grunted. "When did *you* become a psychologist, Jeannie?"

"You go bouncing around inside people's heads as long as I have, friend, and you don't need a shingle hanging on the wall." Jean smiled and wagged a disapproving finger at him. "And that's *Dr.* Jean Grey to *you.*"

Cyclops frowned, and rubbed his jaw with a gloved hand. "All right, so Carol's powers aren't available to us, and Jean's probably right about the rest of the world being unaware of our existence. But, that doesn't mean we just throw in the towel, go back to the citadel, and let the world go hang. If there *are* superpowered individuals who are opposed to Doom, it's vital that we find them and convince them to join us."

"An' where we gon' find us some o' dese 'individuals'?" Gambit asked.

Cyclops tilted his head to one side and stared at Gambit for a moment like he was some kind of circus oddity. "Where anyone *else* would go when they're looking for super heroes, Remy," he replied slowly.

"New York City."

It was the kind of day that made you glad to be alive.

Outside, the sun shone brightly, a cool breeze from the east drifted across lower Manhattan, and, on the balcony, birds could be heard chirping happily as they ate a breakfast of seeds and bread crumbs from a Roadrunner-shaped feeder.

Lying in bed in the apartment she shared with Warren Worthington III, Betsy Braddock grinned broadly as she listened to the sounds of the city as it geared up to meet the new day.

*Her* day. The day she took her first big step toward immortality—starting with that night's performance at the Starlight Room. Warren had made all the necessary arrangements to convince the Minister of Entertainment that he should check out Betsy's act—give her some serious consideration for a possible spot in the Emperor's anniversary celebration.

The rest was going to be up to her.

She stretched, arms extended above her head, back arched, then turned to gaze at the man beside her. Warren was sleeping soundly, arms folded against his chest, head tucked under one of his magnificent white wings, in a manner reminiscent of the way in which birds doze. Betsy propped her head up with one hand and silently watched him for a while, wishing that this moment could last forever. Tenderly, she reached out to stroke one of the primary feathers of the wing that lay closest to her. Warren shifted slightly, his wing flapping gently in reaction to her touch; he mumbled something incoherent in his sleep.

It sounded like "Love you." She was more than happy to settle for the rough translation.

Trying not to disturb him, Betsy quietly stepped from the bed and slipped on a black satin robe. Then, running her hands through her hair to clear her vision of the dishevled lavender locks that had cascaded over her face—how she hated "bed hair"!—she stepped lightly toward the drawn curtains. She pulled them aside to reveal a spectacular view of New York Harbor. The sky was a brilliant blue canvas, stretched out to the horizon without a trace of clouds. To the east, the Brooklyn shipyards were already bustling with activity, as tugboats led massive tankers to and from the docks; to the west, New Jersey was also off to an early start, its highways already beginning to clog with traffic bound for the Holland and Lincoln Tunnels, and, through them, into Manhattan.

And out on the water, sunlight glinted off the polished metal of the Statue of von Doom. The four-hundred-foot-tall armored figure stood proudly at the entrance to the harbor, like a modern-day Colossus of Rhodes, its right hand holding a fifty-foot-long Latverian broadsword as though challenging God Himself to a fight. It was an impressive sight, especially when seen from the ocean, and it had been designed at the Emperor's request by a gifted, world-renowned sculptor named Piotr Nikolievitch to replace the far less imposing French-created statue that had stood there for over one hundred years. Betsy had had the pleasure of meeting the handsome, though somewhat shy, Russian artist at one of Warren's bashes a year ago.

"Is this heaven?" Warren mumbled from under his wing.

"Close enough," Betsy said, turning to face him. "Why?"

"Well, I think you tried your very best to kill me last night," he replied, "so I was expecting to wake up and find myself standing in front of the Pearly Gates."

"Well, you've already got the wings," Betsy said, "but that *wasn't* any sort of murder I was attempting." Her smile widened. "That was what we British call 'unbridled passion.' Perhaps you Yanks have heard of it?"

Warren stuck his head out from under the feathered appendage; his blond hair looked as though it had been subjected to the full power of a wind tunnel. "Oh, is *that* what that is?" He shook his head. "And here I'd always heard about how *restrained* you English ladies are supposed to be."

Reaching behind her, Betsy told hold of the curtains and drew them closed, plunging the room once more into darkness.

"Darling boy," she purred seductively, "who *ever* said I was restrained . . . *or* a lady . . . ?"

It was well after ten o'clock before Mr. Worthington made himself available to his business associates.

Sitting alone on a plush leather couch in the living room, Betsy sipped at a mug of Earl Grey tea while she sorted through a small pile of sheet music that she had spread across the teak wood coffee table before her; from the stereo speakers around her, the soft music of a jazz radio station filled the apartment with the sounds of Miles Davis's trumpet rendition of the Michael Jackson song "Human Nature." Clad in one of Warren's dress shirts, hair tied back in a ponytail, Betsy focused on the matter at hand: looking for just the right pieces to perform that night—ones guaranteed to convince the Minister that she should be included in his roster of acts.

*Nothing too up-tempo,* she thought, *but nothing too melancholy, either. Something Cole Porter-ish, maybe, or Stephen Sondheim.* She picked up one arrangement: "Someone to Watch Over Me." An appropriate number, perhaps, considering that's pretty much what the Emperor did—watch over the entire world—but it was a tad too clichéd; leave that one to Audra McDonnell or Bernadette Peters.

She nervously chewed on her bottom lip. So many choices, so many sets to consider, so many songs that could express to the Minister exactly how she felt about her world, her life, her love for Warren.

So many opportunities to screw up and bore him if she picked the wrong ones.

Betsy shook her head. "That's no way to be thinking, you cow," she muttered. "You'll be fine. In fact, you'll be better than fine—you'll be *tremendous.*"

She nodded, pleased with that incredibly positive assessment of her talents. This was no time to be dwelling on negative thoughts anyway, she reminded herself. Warren had presented her with the opportunity of a lifetime, and she wasn't about to just let it slip away by conceding the battle before she had even fought it.

*Forget any ideas about screwing up,* she told herself. *You're a Braddock, remember—and a Brit. We don't do "screwing up." You will pick the right songs, you will be great, you will impress the hell out of the Minister.*

*And you will get your name on that talent list.*

Betsy smiled broadly. By the time she was finished with her set, she'd have the Minister practically *begging* her to be part of the gala.

All she needed was a chance.

# 8

**B**EFORE SHE knew it, that chance was upon her.

Night descended over Manhattan, and with its arrival a different New York City began to come to life. Office workers and bike messengers and street vendors and sales clerks streamed out of the city at the stroke of five o'clock, to be replaced by leather-and-lace-clad Goths and trendy club hoppers and hunters and huntresses on the prowl for companionship, and even the occasional transvestite dressed to the nines like Tallulah Bankhead or Bette Davis.

It was also the time when The Beautiful People—the rich, the powerful, the noses-eternally-stuck-high-in-the-air elite—came out to play. And to be entertained.

Located just off Times Square, high atop the fifty-four story Osborn Enterprises office tower on Sixth Avenue and Forty-fourth Street, the Starlight Room was one of the city's hot spots where The Beautiful People gathered—a place where one went to spend an evening if one wanted to be considered among those "in the know." On any given night of the week, and especially so on a busy weekend, the spacious restaurant/theater was often jammed to the rafters with celebrities: powerbrokers like Donald Trump and Tony Stark often dropped by with their fashion model dates of the month, as did politicians and actors, musicians and playwrights, poets and authors; even the Emperor and Empress von Doom had visited while celebrating their seventh wedding anniversary.

It was also the spot where, for the past two years, three nights a week, critically-acclaimed songstress Elisabeth Braddock had been "knockin' 'em dead," to use an old Broadway phrase. Show tunes, torch songs, ballads—if there was a song written in the English language in the past fifty years, odds were more than just good that Betsy knew it by heart, and could find a way to perform it as no one else had ever done before. It had often been mentioned in the sterling reviews the New York critics had lavished upon her that her show wasn't simply entertainment—it was an emotional experience.

And tonight, she needed to focus those emotions and yank hard on the heart-strings of one very special audience member.

Standing in the center of her private dressing room—not as small as a closet, but a far cry from the almost Grand Canyon-esque dimensions of Warren's apartment—Betsy was in the midst of her warm-ups, fine-tuning her voice before the show, working her way up and down the musical scale as she watched herself in the large makeup mirror over her dressing table. That afternoon's rehearsals had gone surprisingly well, considering she had sprung a few numbers on the band that they'd never performed, and, even better, her dry cleaner had delivered her "good luck" dress—a red satin, floor-length, off-the-shoulder gown with a thigh-high slit along the right leg. The plunging neckline was provocative without being tasteless, and, in a room that was intentionally dimly lit to create "atmosphere," the fire engine-hued material tended to draw the eye far more than the curve of bosom it revealed. What made it special was that she had first worn it last year, when Warren suggested they move in together. And though the style might be a bit slightly behind this year's fashions, it still seemed to bring her a measure of good luck whenever she wore it in her performances.

And considering the odds at stake tonight, she needed all the help she could get.

A knock on the door caught her attention.

*"Coooommmme iiiinnnn,"* she sang, maintaining her concentration.

The door opened, and Paul Miller poked his head into the room. In his late thirties, his shoulder-length brown hair neatly tied back in a ponytail, Paul was the bespectacled band leader of, and pianist for, The Starlight Orchestra—which, truth be told, was not really an orchestra, since it only consisted of ten members. On the other hand, their original name, the Paul Miller Jazz Group, never really had the *zing* Paul had wanted when they'd been made the house band five years ago, so he had settled on something more upscale and more in line with the elegant setting in which they played.

Paul's eyes widened as he caught sight of Betsy. In the mirror, she could tell by his gaze that he definitely liked the way the gown hugged her like a second skin.

"Hey, kid," he said, nodding appreciatively, "you look *fantastic!*"

*"Thaaannkk yoooouu,"* Betsy replied.

Paul stared at her for a moment more, then shook his head, apparently to focus on other matters. "Oh. Just wanted to stop by and let you know the house is *packed* tonight. Word is the Minister of Entertainment himself's supposed to be putting in an appearance." He smiled. "Try not to embarrass me, okay?"

Betsy stopped singing, and smiled at Paul's reflection in the mirror. "Oh, get out," she said playfully.

Paul laughed. "I'll see you inside. Break a leg, kid!" And with a small wave of his hand, he closed the door.

The Starlight Room was even busier than usual, since word of the Minister's visit had quickly spread through the ranks of the glitteratti—everyone wanted to meet him, to touch the hem of his garment, to suck up to him in the worst way possible.

It had taken an appearance by the Minister's personal—and well-armed—guard to dissuade them of *that* idea.

Now, sitting in a corner of the room—one drenched in shadow so that people would stop staring at them—Warren glanced across the table at his guest, who had moved as far back as possible from the small lamp that shone between them. The Minister of Entertainment was not a tall man, but he carried himself with the arrogance of someone the size of a mountain—self-importance always *has* tended to bring out the worst traits in insecure people. He was high enough in the government to be considered a mover-and-shaker, yet far enough removed from the Emperor to be recognized for the embarrassment that he was.

"Your girlfriend *better* be as good as you say she is, Worthington," the Minister warned. "I'm not about to hire some karaoke singer to stand in front of a jukebox and warble 'My Heart Will Go On' to the Emperor on such a special occasion as his anniversary." He chuckled without mirth. "Although I wouldn't mind doing that to Vic for his next birthday . . ."

"Don't worry," Warren said. "Betsy's everything I've promised, and more. Besides, she was good enough for the Royal Couple when they visited here a few years ago."

The Minister grunted. "That's not exactly a ringing endorsement, friend. Vic's musical tastes tend to swing somewhere between 'The Ride of the Valkyries' and the high-pitched keening of people being ground under his boot heel. And as for Ororo . . ." He shook his head in disbelief. "If I've said it once, I've said it a thousand times: The Partridge Family does *not* make for good, get-down-on-the-ground-like-a-hound party music at an Imperial function." He shrugged. "Hey, but what do *I* know? *I'm* just the freakin' Minister of *Entertainment!*"

Moving out of the light so his face was concealed by shadow, Warren rolled his eyes and groaned softly. This could turn out to be an *extremely* long night . . .

The noisy buzz of chatter in the room died down as Martin

Perkins, the restaurant's manager and emcee, stepped onto the stage. He was greeted with polite applause. In his mid-fifties, his short, dark hair peppered with gray, he cut a dashing figure in a tuxedo as he smiled at the audience, then lightly tapped on the microphone at the front of the stage; thankfully, there was no feedback from the speaker system.

"Ladies and gentlemen," he said, "the staff and management of the Starlight Room are proud to present, now in her second year of exclusive engagements, that stylish chanteuse, that critically-acclaimed British songstress: Miss Elisabeth BRADDOCK!"

A spotlight shone on Betsy as she stepped out from backstage, to be greeted by a hearty round of applause. Smiling brightly, she walked over to Perkins, shook his hand, then moved to the microphone.

"Thank you," she said to those gathered. "I'd like to start tonight with a new number, called 'Spring Rain'. It's an early twentieth century poem by Sara Teasdale that—" she gestured toward Paul, who sat at the piano "—Mr. Paul Miller was gifted enough to set to music." A smile played at her lips. "It's a very special song for a very special man in my life."

There was a smattering of applause, and even a few shouts of approval directed toward Warren. Betsy chuckled as he stood up, politely bowed to the room, then sat down.

When the applause and laughter had died down, Betsy glanced over her shoulder and nodded to Paul. His fingers danced over the keys as he began the musical introduction.

Betsy took a deep breath. Then, eyes closed, fingertips lightly resting on the microphone, she began to sing:

> I thought I had forgotten
> But it all came back again
> To-night with the first spring thunder
> In a rush of rain

Slowly, she opened her eyes, and, a glowing smile lighting her face, could almost picture the scene she was describing, Warren in her arms:

> I remember a darkened doorway
> Where we stood while the storm swept by,
> Thunder gripping the earth
> And lightning scorched the sky

Betsy inclined her head slightly, just enough so she could gaze at Warren, who smiled back; his chiseled, azure features were fairly glowing with pride. She felt her pulse race with exhilaration, and she turned to sing directly to him:

> With the wild spring rain and thunder
> My heart was wild and gay;
> Your eyes said more to me that night
> Than your lips could ever say ...

Three minutes later, the applause that greeted the end of the song was more than appreciated, but it was Warren's warm, beatific smile that meant the world to her.

"Thank you," Betsy said softly to her audience. "Thank you so much."

She glanced toward Warren, and saw him huddled forward across the table, speaking in hushed tones with the Minister. Warren was smiling and nodding her head. Betsy gasped softly, feeling as though her heart was about to explode. Then, drawing a deep breath, she slowly released it as she stepped back from the microphone, and turned to Paul. He smiled and winked at her.

"Go get 'em, tiger-lady," he said quietly, so that only she could hear him.

Betsy smiled and nodded, and the band began playing the next number. As she turned back to the audience, she couldn't help but glance toward the shadowy outline of the Minister. A wicked smile played at her lips.

*Let the begging begin . . .*

To the east, the bells of St. Patrick's Cathedral tolled midnight. To the south, the bright lights of the Empire State Building's upper floors snapped off, their work done for the night. And inside the Starlight Room, the Minister of Entertainment and his entourage departed for his rooms at the Waldorf Astoria, while another singer—a young woman named Alison Blaire—took the stage, hoping to win over the same audience that was still abuzz over Betsy's incredible performance.

As for Betsy herself, she was walking on air, both figuratively and literally—such things were possible, of course, when you had just captivated an audience of New York's elite, and your boyfriend had decided to celebrate the occasion by unfurling his wings and carrying you off into the night sky.

At the moment, they were in a world of their own, one hundred feet above Central Park, slow dancing to a tune that only they could hear.

"Warren?" Betsy asked, chin resting comfortably against his chest, arms wrapped around his waist.

"Yes?"

"Thank you."

"For what?" he asked.

"Everything."

"You're more than welcome, Betts," Warren said. He paused. "You know, you haven't asked about what the Minister said to me."

"I didn't have to," she replied.

"Oh?" Warren asked. "What are you, psychic now?"

Betsy chuckled. "You don't have to be able to read minds to tell when you've won someone over." She tilted her head back to gaze into his dark eyes. "I knew I'd won *you* over when we first met."

"True," Warren agreed. "But my mom always used to say she could read me like a book, too."

"Yeess," Betsy replied, "but why is it that whenever *I* do the reading, it turns out to be *Fun With Dick and Jane?*"

"Hey," Warren countered, "some books of just too *good* to read only once."

Betsy giggled softly and grinned. "So," she said, changing subjects, "when does your dear, old friend the Minister want to see me?"

"Noon," Warren said. "At his office in the World Trade Center. And he's *not* my 'dear, old friend.' You have *no* idea of the sacrifices I had to make tonight, Betts."

"Like what?" Betsy asked, suddenly concerned. "Warren, we agreed that it was up to me—"

"And it *was*, honey. It was," Warren said. "But if I *ever* have to sit through another *second* of his whining about how 'Vic' never listens to his suggestions to 'improve' the Empire's image, make it more fun-oriented . . ." He grunted, as though in great pain, and shook his head.

"Poor baby," Betsy said soothingly, reaching up to caress his cheek.

Warren stuck out his bottom lip and pouted. "Yeah. Poor me."

"Well, if he's as bad as he sounds, then I should get my rest," Betsy said. "So I don't show up looking like some worn-out old hag and wind up falling asleep in the middle of his whining."

"You know, *I* was just going to suggest we turn in," Warren said, feigning surprise. "You *really* must be psychic."

Betsy sighed. "If only that didn't mean that my head was filled by the deviant thoughts you're always broadcasting."

She smiled, and pulled him into a kiss that made it clear how very grateful she was that he was in her life.

They soared higher, then, and, laughing like children, chased the stars until the morning sun arrived to send them to bed.

\* \* \*

Unfortunately, not all the world was filled with lovers.

On the other side of the Atlantic Ocean, in the Islamic Republic of Mauritania, the noonday sun was relentlessly beating down on the harbor city of Nouadhibou—a strip of land, really, jutting out into the water like a sand-covered index finger. It was here that deep sea fishing vessels from around the Empire docked after trawling the coastal waters, and it was from here that massive freighters would carry off shipments of iron ore, bound for the Empire's factories. It was not a large city, as major ports-of-call go—the population was only around 60,000 inhabitants—but it certainly drew its fair share of world-weary travelers.

And it was through the streets of Nouadhibou that one traveler in particular walked.

Stopping for a moment beneath the welcomed shade of a shop awning, Erik Lensherr removed a bright-red handkerchief from a pocket of his voluminous white robes and used it to dab at the sweat that was pouring down his face. Not for the first time, he cursed the necessity of wearing his battle helmet in such a stifling climate, and for lacking the foresight to have designed the damned thing with some sort of air-coolant system. Glancing around quickly to make certain that he wasn't being observed too closely by anyone on the busy street, he adjusted his cloth hood to conceal the helmet once more, and then continued his journey to the docks.

The trek from Araouane had been uneventful—most of it spent crossing the desert at night in a jeep "acquired" by Pietro before he had departed to begin making arrangements for his father's suicidal return to America. Packing what few belongings he considered essential, all Lensherr had to do was get to the Spanish city of Barcelona without alerting authorities to his whereabouts; not all that difficult a task, since he had been successfully avoiding the Empire's law enforcers for over twelve months. And once in Barcelona, he would be provided with false identification, plane tickets that would hopscotch him around the globe before bringing him to America (just as a precaution to throw off any potential "shadows"), and the means to trick any security systems that might have a record of his unique biological makeup.

What he needed right now, though, was a ship so he could get there.

A slight breeze was blowing off the water, and its gentle touch sent an exuberant chill up Lensherr's spine; at last, after spending a year in the middle of the Sahara, he had found some relief from the withering temperatures. The cool air seemed to strengthen him, and he pulled himself up to his full height, allowing just a trace of a smile to show his pleasure.

The docks were extremely busy, with workers helping the crews of deep sea fishing vessels to unload a percentage of their catches and load food and fuel; Lensherr recognized the flags of Russia and North Korea—accompanied, as always, by the flag of the Empire—flying from the masts of some of the ships.

Looking around, he spotted what appeared to be the captain of one of the Russian vessels—a bear of a man, standing a few inches over six feet, with a barrel chest and powerful arms folded across it. Dressed in black despite the heat, his unkempt black beard flecked with gray, he was an imposing figure, to be sure. And it was simple enough to tell that he was in a position of authority: he was the one yelling the loudest at his crew.

Lensherr strolled over to the man. "Excuse me, Kaptain," he said in perfect Russian.

The scruffy man-mountain slowly turned to face him, then, frowning, looked his visitor up and down, twice, before finally responding. "Da?"

"I was wondering: when you set sail, are you, by any chance, stopping off in Barcelona before returning to the Motherland?"

The captain raised a quizzical eyebrow. "Why do you ask?"

"I would like to book passage on your ship, if there is room." From beneath the shadows of his hood, Magneto flashed a gentle, disarming smile.

Again, the captain gave him the once-over and frowned; clearly, he didn't think too much of the robed figure standing before him. Reining in his mounting anger over the man's annoyingly condescending behavior, Lensherr forced himself to remain silent and wait for an answer.

"And why should I be so disposing?" the captain rumbled.

"Because I would be more than happy to compensate you for your time," Lensherr said pleasantly, "and, say, a small, *private* cabin in which to stay?"

The captain grinned—a mildly grotesque expression, considering he was missing four front teeth. "You wouldn't be running from something, would you, my friend?" he asked. "Like agents of the Empire?" His eyes narrowed, and the grin quickly faded. "Or perhaps you *are* an agent of the Empire, eh, come to make trouble?"

*Or perhaps I'll risk being detected by von Doom's satellites and use my powers to turn you inside out, if only to spare myself having to put up with any more of your insolence . . . "my friend,"* Magneto thought darkly. But instead of lashing out, he simply said:

"No—to all of the above. I merely wish to visit friends in Spain, and travel by ship is still the easiest way to leave Mauritania." He smiled again, feeling as though his face might split in two if he had to maintain this saccharine-sweet façade for much longer.

The captain ran a meaty hand through his thick, oily beard for a few moments, considering his options. Finally, he said, "All right. But it will be a *costly* trip, my friend. And I will expect *half* the money the moment you set foot on my ship."

Magneto nodded. "Of course. Thank you, Kaptain."

The captain grunted. "We sail at dawn—if you're not here on time, we won't wait for you. My men and I sleep on the ship; you'll have to find your own accommodations in town for the night." He grinned. "You *are* paying for just the *voyage*, after all."

Gritting his teeth, Lensherr forced a smile, muttered his thanks again, and turned back toward the town, not bothering to point out that the captain had not mentioned exactly how one should define "a costly trip" in monetary terms. No matter—whatever the price, the end result of this circuitous route to the United States was worth it.

As the Chinese philosopher Lao-tzu had once said in the sixth century B.C., "A journey of a thousand miles must begin with a single step." For Erik Lensherr—for Magneto, Master of Magnetism—that first step had now been taken.

The first step on the path to revenge.

# 9

"H UH—PLACE don't look all that different. I was half expectin' all the skyscrapers t'be replaced with flamin' castles."

Turning from the spectacular view he had of Manhattan as it appeared just over the treeline, Wolverine adjusted the wide brim of his darkly tanned Stetson and shot a glance at the other X-Men and Carol. They were seated in a Metro North railway car, seven (hopefully) ordinary-looking passengers among a dozen others spread out around the air-conditioned compartment, inconspicuously making their way down from Westchester County to the center of Manhattan. After spending the night in a Bedford Hills motor lodge, to heal their injuries and get a much-needed rest, they had arose this morning to find an assortment of clothing, a wide variety of breakfast foods, and a small pile of cash, all gathered by the industrious Gambit while they'd slept. He explained that some of the shops and Automated Teller Machines in town had been more than happy to make "donations" to their cause, even though such "contributions" had been received between the hours of one and five A.M. Cyclops had thought of chastising his thievish teammate, but opted instead to let the matter slide since they *were* in need of everything Gambit had provided. The X-Men quickly sat down to feast on sweet rolls, sticky buns, pancakes and sausages, toast and marmalade, and hot coffee and tea. (Never let it be said that, despite their great powers, mutant super heroes are immune to the lure of copious amounts of sugar and caffeine.)

When they were finished gorging themselves and had changed into their "civvies," the team at last settled down to discuss the first order of business: getting into Manhattan. Carol had shot down any ideas of commandeering a transport truck from the camp since large, black vehicles on public roads had a tendency to draw unwanted attention to their occupants; she suggested they make the trip to The City by rail.

Boarding the train at the Bedford Hills station, they had been able to see the aftermath of their night raid when they passed through Salem Center: it appeared that some concerned citizens had alerted the authorities about the rather large explosions that had scorched the night sky and rudely tossed them from their beds—the town, and Graymalkin Drive, were aswarm with hordes of armored soldiers, crisply-uniformed guards, members of the New York State Police, and construction crews apparently dispatched to rebuild the torn and pitted facility. Logan had had to be psychically rendered unconscious by Jean when he realized that, despite his demands to the commandant, the camp had not been leveled; he'd almost managed to leap from the moving train before she was able to send a psi-bolt shooting into his brain to shut him down. When Wolverine finally regained consciousness and calmed down enough to hold a civil conversation, Cyclops reminded him that it was far more important that they get to Doom—if they could reverse what he'd done, then the camps, the tortured prisoners, and the tyrant's position as master of the world would all fade away like the last remnants of a bad dream. Scott's argument had been a sound one, and even Logan had to agree with it. That didn't mean he had to like it, though; he'd sat, brooding, for the last fifteen minutes before at last uttering his remark about the New York skyline.

Now, as the train stopped at the Mt. Vernon station and its

doors slid open, Rogue stood up to stretch her legs, taking care not to disturb Remy, who snoozed peacefully beside her. It was clear to see that Rogue was acting more like her old, outgoing self, now that her bare skin was again protected from any casual contact with passersby—somehow, in his nocturnal foraging, Remy had managed to locate a new leather jacket and a bodysuit to replace her tattered outfit; this one, though, was colored red and black instead of yellow and green, and lacked the distinctive "X" emblem. Upon first seeing it, Nightcrawler had quipped that, with the darker clothing, she was perfectly attired for operating in "stealth mode" when she flew at night.

Unfortunately, unlike the rest of his teammates, Kurt himself was a major problem when it came to the matter of avoiding detection. With his blue skin tone and unusually-shaped hands and feet, he more often than not stood out like the proverbial sore thumb in a crowd, so finding something for him to wear in increasingly warm June temperatures had been a challenge for Gambit, but one the Cajun had been willing to meet. His solution: dark clothing all around—slacks, shirt, a knee-length raincoat worn open, large military-style boots—and a pair of circular sunglasses to hide Kurt's yellow eyes. "If anyone asks 'bout why you got blue skin, or why you wearin' all dis in de summer, *mon brave*," Gambit had said, "you jus' tell 'em you one'a dem Anne Rice fans."

As it had turned out, Gambit had done an admirable job of assembling a wardrobe for the team. Sneakers, jeans, and a crimson blouse for Carol. A light, flower-print summer dress and open-toed sandals for Jean—Scott had decided not to pursue the question, for now, of how the wily ladies' man could know his wife's exact sizes—and tan shorts, green Polo shirt, and low-topped canvas sneakers for Scott; Jean carried their costumes in a large canvas beach bag. Shopping for Wolverine was even easier: work boots, jeans, plaid work shirt, and a cowboy hat. Gambit had settled for sneakers, bicycle shorts, a white muscle T-shirt, and his ever-present duster; like Kurt, his eyes were covered by sunglasses.

The public address system speakers crackled loudly as, somewhere on the train, the conductor made his latest announcement: "Next stop, 125th Street. 125th Street, Harlem. Following 125th Street, this train will be making its last stop at 42nd Street, Grand Central Station. 125th Street, next stop."

A bell chimed pleasantly, and the doors slid closed. With a slight lurch, the train pulled out of the Mt. Vernon station.

"Won't be long now," Rogue said, leaning down toward Jean and Scott. "I just hope somebody's home when we come a-knockin'."

Scott nodded grimly. "That makes two of us . . ."

Warren had already left for his office by the time Betsy awoke.

Unfortunately, he had forgotten to rouse her from her coma-like slumber before he departed. When she finally got around to rubbing sleep-encrusted eyes and rolling over in bed to glance at the alarm-clock on the side table, it was already 10:30.

*"Oh, bollocks!"* she screamed, now fully awake, and clawed her way out of sheets that seemed to have purposely wrapped themselves around her like a mummy's shroud to impede her attempts to get out of bed. She eventually won the battle, though, and was soon racing for the shower.

Moving with a speed she'd never known she possessed—a curiously welcome effect born of equal parts adrenalin and sheer panic—she danced quickly through the shower, blow-dried her hair (noting that she would have to pick up a new bottle of lavender dye, since the color was starting to fade), and began a nerve-racking juggling act that involved running from bathroom to closet and back again, trying to divide her time between applying the proper makeup while searching for the right kind of outfit one should wear when meeting the Minister of Entertainment for the first time.

She was ready to go by 11:45.

Made-up perfectly, perfumed so just, hair done up in a stylish twist, and clad in a dark blazer and matching miniskirt, Betsy stopped to admire the stunning image she presented in the hallway mirror. She arched a delicate eyebrow and, haughtily looking down her nose, cast a withering gaze at her reflection.

"Beg for me, little man," she purred in an overly dramatic Russian accent. "Beg for me, and perhaps I shall perform in your charming, little show." She giggled wildly.

Then, with a joyful laugh, she bolted from the apartment as another adrenalin rush kicked in.

Fortunately, it was a short distance from Battery Park City to the World Trade Center; so short, in fact, that Betsy could have walked there . . . if she had the time. Luck was with her, though—another tenant was just stepping from a taxi cab as she arrived in the lobby. In less than a minute, she was on her way to meet her destiny.

The New York office of the Minister of Entertainment was located on the seventy-fifth floor of the south tower of the World Trade Center. It was not open all year round, since the Minister rarely visited the city, preferring to stay at his Washington, D.C. estate. When he did visit, though, a cleaning crew moved in with all the precision of a military strike team several days before his arrival and scrubbed the place down until it literally gleamed.

Today, of course, was one of those rare occasions when he opened the doors of his office and made himself available to the few people in town he was interested in seeing. Those he was trying to avoid were escorted back to the elevators that led down to the lobby—with or without all their teeth.

The Minister didn't mind fawning sycophants. He just hated it when they did their fawning during business hours.

Betsy stepped onto the main hallway of the seventy-fifth floor, pausing a moment to recover from the pressure on her ear drums created by a higher altitude and an elevator that rose at a speed of 1600 feet per minute. Pinching her nose closed with her thumb and forefinger, she blew hard, then opened her mouth, and was rewarded with the sensation of having her full hearing restored.

And that was when the butterflies in her stomach began flitting about.

"Oh, give it a rest," she muttered to herself. Taking a deep breath, she held it for a moment, then released it, and pulled herself up to her full, spike-heel-assisted height. "Right," she said. "Let's *do* this."

Confidently, she strode down the tiled hallway toward a set of oak-paneled doors; gold-leaf lettering was set into the wood:

MINISTER OF ENTERTAINMENT

OPEN:
WHENEVER

BUSINESS HOURS:
DON'T HOLD YOUR BREATH WAITING

Betsy's eyes were drawn to another line, inscribed above the door frame:

ABANDON ALL HOPE, YE WHO ENTER

"Wonderful . . ." Betsy murmured. Screwing up her courage, she grasped the doorknob, turned it, and walked into the office.

It was like stepping into a child's version of how an office should be designed. Instead of the typical furniture one would expect to find, the reception area was a mass of candy-colored tables and chairs with intentionally twisted legs and seat-backs. Above the receptionist's desk hung ceiling-mounted monitors, on which were being broadcast cartoons and situation comedies and the classic movie *Willy Wonka and the Chocolate Factory.* Betsy smiled, feeling a pleasant chill run up her spine as she watched actor Gene Wilder as Wonka bend down to whisper to the child actress playing the obnoxious Veruca Salt. *"We* are the makers of music, and *we* are the dreamers of dreams," Wilder said softly. Betsy mouthed the words along with him.

On the other side of the room were a collection of pinball machines and old-style video arcade games, their bells and whistles and electronic music battling for attention and combining to create a white noise that rumbled across the black-and-white checkered carpeting to send a tingling sensation through Betsy's toes. And at the far end of the reception area was a wall constructed with a false perspective, so that it appeared the office continued on for another hundred yards. Betsy raised a quizzical eyebrow. Despite what Warren had told her about the man in advance, it seemed that the Minister was an odder egg than even her beau had known.

Her eye was drawn to hung an immense, framed poster hanging on a wall near the front door; it was a promotional item for the hugely-popular animated television show *Obnoxio the Clown*. Sitting curbside on a cobblestoned street, holding a fishing pole that dangled above an open manhole, the star of the show, repugnant in his grotesque green-and-white makeup and costume, glared out at the viewer, as though angered that he was being observed; either that, or he was annoyed by the fact that a dog standing behind him appeared to be urinating on the back of his costume. A word balloon hung above the clown, its tail leading to yellowed teeth sunk into the end of a smoldering cigar: "There ain't no free lunch!" Obnoxio was saying—an infamous, and incredibly overused, catchphrase that he often muttered on the show.

Betsy slowly shook her head. She'd never understood what was supposed to be so humorous about the violent, often vulgar, program, though Warren seemed to think it was outrageously funny. He'd once commented that her reaction was a prime example of the differences between men and women. He called it "Three Stooges Syndrome": a condition in which men thought Moe, Larry, and Curly were the be-all and end-all of slapstick comedy, and women thought it was all incredibly stupid. She just thought it was a lack of ingenuity—though it was to be expected in a country that had never possessed the sophistication to create a *Blackadder* or a *Monty Python's Flying Circus*.

*Americans* . . . Betsy thought, and shrugged.

"Can I help you?" asked a strong, feminine voice from behind her.

Betsy turned toward the source of the question, and found herself facing an attractive Japanese woman; clad in a bright red dress that seemed two sizes too small, she was in her mid-twenties, dark hair cut in a shoulder-length pageboy style. Light green eyes coolly studied her from beneath inky bangs.

Betsy smiled. "Good afternoon. I have a twelve o'clock appointment with the Minister."

The woman looked her up and down for a few moments. "Braddock," she finally said. A sneer creased her perfect, pale-white skin. "Worthington's little songbird."

Betsy started. "I beg your pardon?" she asked, surprised by the venom in the woman's tone. "And just who the hell are *you?*"

The woman's eyes narrowed, and she leaned forward, locking eyes with Betsy. "I am Miss Locke, the Minister's personal assistant," she said, almost growling, "and I am not impressed by pathetic little nobodies who must rely on their boyfriends to suck up to government officials to give them work."

"Oh. Slept *your* way to the top, then, did you?" Betsy asked tersely. The butterflies in her stomach were quickly forgotten, replaced by a roiling surge of anger-laced bile that made her throat burn. She folded her arms across her chest and planted her feet squarely on the carpeted floor, almost daring this uppity secretary to try and throw her out of the office.

The intercom on Locke's desk suddenly buzzed, breaking the tension. Clearly angry that she was forced to break eye contact with Betsy, Locke hurried to answer the summons.

"Yes, Minister?" she asked.

"Miss Locke," said a voice that sounded to Betsy like a cross between singer Paul Williams and a young Mickey Rooney, "do I hear the beginnings of a cat fight out there?"

Locke glared at Betsy; the heat between them was almost palpable.

"I'm sorry, Minister," Locke finally said.

"Oh, don't apologize," the Minister replied. "I *love* a good cat fight—gets the blood racing. Unfortunately, I need to speak with Miss Braddock while she still has a throat to sing with. Could you send her in?"

"At once, Minister," Locke said, still staring at Betsy. The lavender-tressed "songbird" grinned broadly like a Cheshire Cat. Locke sneered and gestured toward the wall behind her desk. "This way."

Betsy followed her around the separation, down a short corridor that ran behind the reception area, and to another set of double-doors. Locke rapped softly on the dark wood.

"Come on in! Don't be a stranger!" shouted the Minister.

Locke opened the doors and, with one last heated look at Betsy, stepped aside to usher her into the office. Once Betsy had crossed the threshold, Locke closed the doors—*just* managing to avoid clipping Betsy on the funny bone.

Now rid of her surly escort, Betsy took a moment to look around. The office was much like the reception area, decorated in the same Wonka-esque style; Betsy half expected an Oompa-Loompa to come sauntering out of a hidden panel in the walls. On the far side of the room stood the only piece of "adult" furniture: a long, wide, oaken desk, on which sat telephones, a personal computer, toy figures—"action figures," she believed they were called—an assortment of papers, and issues of *Daily Variety*. Beyond the desk was a large, black leather chair, its straight back turned toward her; past the chair was a spectacular view of upper Manhattan and the New Jersey Palisades standing proudly across the Hudson River, all on display through windows that stretched from floor to ceiling.

Betsy smiled whimsically as she gazed at her bizarre surroundings. She had heard of the "Peter Pan Syndrome"—a psychological term for men who refused to grow up—but until today she had never seen evidence of anyone who actually suffered from it.

"Quite a view, innit?" asked the Minister. With a start, Betsy realized he was sitting in the leather chair, with his back to her.

"Yes, it is," she replied. She softly cleared her throat and approached the desk. "I'd like to thank you for coming to see my act, Minister—I know we didn't get a chance to speak at the theater, what with your busy schedule and all—and for taking the time to see me today."

"Think nothing of it, Miss Braddock," her host said cheerfully. "Any friend of ol' bird-boy Warren is a friend'a mine, right? Besides, if you didn't have the kinda pipes I heard last night—and the kinda looks I got a gander at—we wouldn't even be having this conversation." He swiveled the chair around to face her.

When she laid eyes on him, it was all Betsy could do to keep from laughing.

The Minister wasn't very tall, and his suit was as brilliant a white as his unruly mop of hair was red; Betsy was reminded of a dish of vanilla ice cream topped with a maraschino cherry. His lack of sartorial tastes went even further beyond belief, as evidenced by an off-putting pistachio-green shirt and an oversized, clownish bowtie with red polka-dots. All in all, he looked less like a high-ranking government official and more like a circus ringmaster—or a used car salesman.

And yet, there was something familiar about the man, though Betsy couldn't quite put her mental finger on it—something that made her wonder if they had met before . . .

Eyes sparkling with dark mischief, he practically leapt from his chair to greet her.

"And please—don't call me 'Minister,' " he said. "The name is *Arcade*, sweets." He smiled broadly and extended his hand in greeting.

"All right, if you call me 'Betsy,' " she replied. Betsy reached out and clasped his hand in hers—

And stiffened as something akin to a powerful electrical current suddenly surged through her body, pinning her to the spot.

She screamed in agony—a short, brief note—just before darkness overwhelmed her.

*"BETSY!"*

Standing on the corner of Forty-second Street and Fifth Avenue, Jean Grey came to a sudden halt, eyes widened in shock. Beside her, the other X-Men and Carol Danvers gathered around as Jean stared off into the distance, her fingertips touching her temples. They did their best to ignore the lunchtime crowds who jostled and bumped into them, though Nightcrawler clearly felt uncomfortable by the open-mouthed stares directed his way.

Scott moved closer to his wife. "What is it, Jean?"

"It's Betsy," she replied. "For just a second, I detected her thoughts—but they were jumbled, confused." Jean turned to gaze at her husband, her bright green eyes filled with concern. "She was in pain, Scott—terrible pain. And . . . *Arcade* was with her." She paused, and turned her gaze downward. "And then she . . . stopped sending."

The X-Men silently looked at one another, their expressions grim.

"And what does that mean?" Carol asked.

"It means," Kurt explained through tightened lips, "that Betsy is either unconscious, or . . ." His voice trailed off.

Carol didn't need a further explanation.

There's an old chestnut that claims that, just before you die, you see your entire life flashing before you, from childhood all the way to your last moment on Earth.

If such were the case, Betsy Braddock could not understand why, then, she was seeing the life of the Minister of Entertainment being played out before her.

It wasn't his complete life story, thankfully; more like a highlights reel of his career. But what made the situation even more peculiar was that she was seeing events that could not possibly have happened—at least, not the sort of events one would associate with a member of Emperor von Doom's cabinet. Scenes of costumed men and women, like those in the "comic book" movies, running through mazes and avoiding movie serial-like death traps and being bounced about in giant pinball machines.

And all of the devices were being controlled by Arcade himself.

*I don't remember ever hearing about the Minister playing at being a cinema villain,* Betsy thought. *Although with that suit of his he could almost have stepped straight out of one of Roger Moore's James Bond movies . . .*

But now other images—not images, but *memories*, she realized with a start—began to form: of herself a few years ago, in a different—and decidedly non-Asian—body, shopping in London (she could tell it was supposed to be her—the lavender hair was a dead giveaway); of a handkerchief being pressed over her face, and the smell of a powerful anesthetic; of that snooty cow Miss Locke carrying her from a van into something called "Murderworld"; of her brother, Brian, dressed in a bright red costume with a yellow, lion-shaped silhouette emblazoned across the chest—like an outfit worn by one of those outlandish super heroes—calling himself "Captain Britain," and coming to her rescue.

And above it all, like a giant, grotesque sculpture of a demonic head displayed at the entrance to an amusement park funhouse ride, hung the sinister, leering face of the Minister of Entertainment.

*What's all this about?* Betsy wondered. *How could any of these be my memories, especially when—thank God—I've never even met the Minister's "personal assistant" before today? And that nonsense about looking Caucasian—when did my imagination get so bloody colorful?*

*But, more importantly, if I've died, then why is it that my head hurts so . . . ?*

"Hey, you okay there, Betsy?" It was Arcade's voice, but it sounded as though it was being broadcast through a bad transmitter, like the muffled sound made by someone speaking into a telephone with a handkerchief over the mouthpiece.

Slowly, Betsy opened her eyes. She was lying on a sofa shaped like a pink-colored carp, her head resting on a pillow that looked like a giant lobster from some children's cartoon; a dampened handkerchief sat coolly on her brow.

"I-I'm not dead ..." she whispered, partly in disbelief.

"Not by a long shot, sweets," Arcade said, "though you had us going there for a minute."

Looking up, Betsy saw him standing beside her, bent forward, hands resting on his knees. Behind Arcade, Miss Locke sneered at her—

*"Try not to cause us too much trouble, little girl," she said, reaching forward to tie a paisley-colored handkerchief over Betsy's mouth; the cloth smelled faintly of lilacs. "Arcade prefers that all participants play the game in their own way, without outside assistance."*

*She checked to make certain that the gag was knotted securely, then stepped back to look at her employer. Arcade, leaning on a thin, bamboo cane, a straw skimmer sitting at a rakish angle on his head, flashed a wicked smile.*

*"Now, the fun begins ..." he said.*

"Back again?" Arcade asked cheerfully. "You know, Warren didn't tell me you were a narcoleptic."

Betsy blinked twice and stared blankly at Arcade, who was now sitting on a chair beside the couch. Obviously, some time had passed since their last brief exchange.

With a start, she realized that she had blacked out again.

But why had it happened? What had caused it?

She was certain it had everything to do with that surge of electricity she had felt when she touched Arcade's hand—but was it something he had done intentionally? If so, for what reason?

And what were these visions she was having during her bouts of unconsciousness—these melodramatic scenes of facing dire peril at the hands of the Minister and his assistant? She *had* had the odd feeling that they'd met once before, but surely it must have been at a party, or at the ballet, or a movie premier she had attended with Warren—not as a helpless kidnap victim being used as a prize in a bizarre game intended to trap her brother. Maybe it was just her fear of failing Warren—of failing herself, really—at play here, and her subconscious mind was causing her to see the Minister and Miss Locke as a threat to her desire to finally make a name for herself.

Couldn't *that* be it?

And yet, there was something about the visions—something that her mind was insisting was real; that they were not fanciful manifestations created by an overactive imagination, but actual suppressed memories of an actual terrifying event in her life.

But why, then, couldn't she remember experiencing it?

What in God's name was going on with her?

A soft grunting noise drew her attention back to reality and over to Arcade's assistant. Clearly disgusted at the sight of a woman who appeared to have had a fainting spell brought on by all the excitement of meeting the honest-to-God Minister of Entertainment himself, Miss Locke turned on her heel and left the office.

"W-what is happening to me . . . ?" Betsy asked.

"I haven't the slightest idea, sweets," Arcade said. "Soon as we shook hands, you went stiffer than Tony Stark on a three-day bender and keeled right over. And then, just as I was about to explain all that to you after you woke up, you plopped down again and took another catnap."

Betsy paused to replay the initial event in her mind. She nodded slowly as it all came back to her. "But, didn't you feel the shock when we touched? The electrical shock?"

Arcade stared at her, obviously confused. "Shock?" He chuckled. "Well, I left my joy buzzer in my other pants, so that couldn't have been the cause of it. But I might've accidentally rubbed my feet on the carpet before we touched . . . although that's not the kind of thing that can knock you out, you know?"

"No, I suppose not . . ." Betsy said slowly. Pushing off from the lobster-pillow, she sat up and removed the cold compress from her forehead. "I'm sorry for all the melodrama, Minister. That's never happened to me before." She shook her head. "God, I feel like such an a—"

"Hey, it's all right," Arcade said, waving his hands in a dismissive gesture. "No harm, no foul. Besides, you've just provided proof positive of what I've always suspected: I've got a real *electric* personality." He reached out a hand to her and smiled, and—

*"I hope your brother gets here soon, ducks," the leering gamesmaster said to her. Betsy tried to lash out at him, to claw at that insipid, arrogant face, or kick him in the groin to wipe away that infuriating smile, but bound as she was, hand and foot, to a gleaming white wooden stallion on a merry-go-round, such actions were impossible.*

*"I'd hate to see such an exquisitely beautiful woman—such as yourself—wind up splattered across ten square meters of Derbyshire," he continued, "because their super heroic sibling was off rescuing cats from trees when he should have been watching out for his loved ones." He reached out to stroke Betsy's cheek with a gloved hand, and—*

"—your boyfriend can attest to *that* fact," the Minister was saying.

Betsy started. "W-what . . . ?" She looked up to find herself sitting in front of Arcade's desk on one of the candy-apple red chairs scattered about the office. The Minister was back in his big leather seat, white-booted feet resting comfortably on the desk's ink blotter.

Betsy shook her head to clear her thoughts; her cheeks reddened. "I-I'm sorry, Minister. My mind must have . . ."

"Taken a little stroll?" Arcade asked. Betsy bobbed her head once without looking at him. Arcade shrugged. "Happens to me all the time." He eyed her suspiciously. "Are you *sure* you're okay?"

Betsy nodded vigorously. "Oh, *yes*, I am. I'm *fine.*" She saw Arcade's eyes narrow as he studied her face. *"Really,"* she insisted.

"All right. Just checking," Arcade said. "Anyway, I was just saying that Warren can back me up when I say that I thought your stuff was outstanding last night. You put a lot of heart in your performance, and it really showed."

Betsy blushed. "Thank you."

"And that little number you threw Warren's way. That poem?"

" 'Spring Rain,' by Sara Teasdale?" Betsy offered.

Arcade thumped a fist on the desk. "*That's* the one! *Fantastic* number! I saw how the audience was just eating it up with a spoon—wasn't a dry eye in the house by the time you were done yanking on their heart-strings. A regular Celine Dion ballad." He shrugged. "Not exactly Wayne Newton, but hey—it's a helluva lot better than 'I Think I Love You,' and it'd have the Empress crying all over her party dress, and *that's* what's important." He paused. "You have permission from this . . . this . . ."

"Teasdale."

"Right. Her. You have her permission to use that song?"

Betsy suddenly found it difficult to catch her breath. Was this conversation going where she *thought* it was heading . . . ?

"Well?" Arcade asked. *"Is* this Teasdale going to cause any trouble?"

"Uh, no," Betsy replied. "She passed away quite a long time ago."

"Perfect!" Arcade exclaimed. "I *love* quick and easy solutions to potential problems—they make my life *so* much simpler."

"Umm . . . excuse me, Minister . . ." Betsy began.

*"Arcade,"* the Minister happily insisted.

"All right . . . Arcade." Betsy paused, part of her brain screaming at her to ask the question, the other part warning her not to back him into a corner and force him to make a decision too soon. She *had* to know, though. "I don't mean to be too forward," she said slowly, "but are we talking about me actually *participating* in the anniversary gala?"

"Well, for *now*, we are," Arcade admitted. "But I can't set anything in stone until I hear back from some of the other acts I've been talking to. Believe you me, the last thing I'm about to do is tell The Wayouts that I've gotta bump 'em from the schedule so some unknown chanteuse from a midtown Manhattan lounge can take their spot and serenade the Royal Couple instead." He shivered. "Those guys would rip off my legs and beat me to death with 'em before I could choke out an 'I'm sorry, and I'll make it up to you.' "

"But you *are* saying I have a chance?" Betsy asked. Her heart was pounding so loudly in her ears, she wasn't even certain she had put forth the question.

"Sure—*everybody's* got a chance, sweets, but I really won't know for sure about the line-up for another day or so." Arcade shrugged. "You'll just have to bear with me until you hear back one way or the other. Fair enough?"

Her mind suddenly a blank, Betsy found it difficult to do anything more than simply nod.


"Any luck?" Scott asked.

Jean shook her head. "I can't detect any other activity from Betsy. It's like her 'signal' was cut off in mid-transmission. And without knowing the direction it came from, I can't get a fix on her location."

Depressed, she glanced at her husband, who smiled encouragingly. After receiving Betsy's psychic SOS, the X-Men had elected to move to the opposite side of Fifth Avenue in order to get away from the constant flow of pedestrian traffic that crowded the busy intersection; for the past fifteen minutes, they had been sitting quietly on the stone steps of the New York Public Library, waiting for Jean to track down their missing colleague. Off to one side, Carol and Nightcrawler sat at a small table, conversing quietly as they sipped at cans of soda; his unusual skin coloration was concealed, for the time being, by the shade of the open umbrella that jutted up from the center of the table. Rogue and Gambit were also sitting together, snuggled close, heads almost touching as they talked in hushed whispers. They looked like any other couple gathered on the steps: two people—not mutants, not super heroes—deeply in love and enjoying their own company.

As for Scott, Jean, and Logan, they were still focused on the matter at hand: trying to reach Betsy. Scott was sitting back, elbows resting on the step behind him, watching the nonstop hustle and bustle that was New York at lunchtime; it seemed that not even the machinations of Victor von Doom could do much to disrupt the faster-than-life speed of the Big Apple. Beside him, Jean looked thoroughly annoyed, chin resting in the palms of her hand as her elbows balanced on her knees; she stared into space, brow furrowed. Slouched on the steps on Jean's other side, Logan was doing his best not to look like a third wheel as he sat beside the happy couple.

Groaning softly, Jean leaned forward to grasp her sandaled feet and hang her head in frustration between her legs, allowing her hair to flow down and conceal her features. Scott reached out a hand to gently rub her back.

"I don't understand it," Jean muttered from beneath her mountain of crimson locks. "Even if Betsy were unconscious, I should *still* be able to pick up *some* trace of her subconscious—a random thought, a brief replay of the last few seconds before she blacked out . . . *Something.*"

"You *sure* she's in the immediate area, Red?" Logan asked, his cowboy hat set low over his dark eyes. "If her mental hollerin' was as loud as you say it was, maybe she's someplace *else* in the five boroughs. Hell, she coulda been sendin' that message from *Hoboken* fer all ya know."

Jean's head snapped back up and she stared at Logan for a moment. Then, wincing as though in pain, she growled softly, and sharply rapped the sides of her head with her knuckles. "Dumb, dumb dumb," she muttered. "The image of Arcade that she broadcast was so clear, the sensation of his threat so evident, I just assumed Betsy was somewhere in our vicinity." She looked at Wolverine. "Thanks, Logan."

"No charge fer the service, darlin'," he replied with a half smile.

"Any news?" Carol asked as she and Nightcrawler walked over to join them. She glanced at a large clock suspended above the entrance of a cigar shop of the corner of Forty-second Street—it was 1:30 P.M. "Time's a-wastin' if you folks want to try and track down some of your long-john brethren."

"That can wait for the moment," Scott said. "Right now, we've got a friend who appears to be threatened by one of our most dangerous enemies. She might be in need of our help and, Doom-controlled world or not, the X-Men always take care of their own."

"Pretty words, Summers, but ultimately useless," Carol said, with the tone of someone who no longer believed such sentiments. "Try saying them again with the same conviction if you ever wind up in one of von Doom's camps like I did. I promise you: one week of beatings and starvation and fighting for crumbs of food, and that 'all for one, and one for all' Musketeer crap will become just a faint memory as you focus on more important things—like battling each day just to keep *yourself* alive."

"Well, Carol," Scott replied slowly, clearly avoiding being drawn into an argument, "if we succeed in our mission and set everything back to the way it all should be, it'll be this version of the world that becomes the faint memory. And locating another X-Man is just as important as contacting the Avengers for help now—it's one more ally lending her powers to our cause." Not bothering to wait for Carol to respond, he turned to Phoenix. "Jean, I want you to run a telepathic scan as far out from this spot as you're able to go. Start with the island, then sweep the other boroughs. If that fails—" he glanced at Wolverine, and smiled wryly "—follow Logan's suggestion and try Hoboken."

"All right, Scott," Jean said. "It might take a while, though."

"You take all de time you need, Jeannie," Gambit piped in. "We not goin' nowhere till you finished with what needs doin'." Jean turned in his direction and saw that Remy was lying on one of the steps, head resting comfortably in Rogue's lap; he grinned broadly as his Southern Belle ran slender, gloved fingers through his dark, unruly hair.

Jean smiled. "Thank you, Remy. I appreciate your patience."

"My pleasure," Gambit said.

Jean's grin broadened. *Dat Gambit, he a suave one, no?* she thought.

Drawing her legs up, Jean assumed a meditative lotus position and closed her eyes. Slowly, she willed herself to tune out the ear-throbbing urban sounds around her, then slowed her breathing and cleared her mind.

*Betsy, are you there?* she broadcast. *Betsy? It's Jean. If you can "hear" me, please respond. Betsy . . . ?*

Down at the World Trade Center, Betsy had just stepped into the elevator that would take her back down to the lobby when the screaming started in her head.

*BETSY! PLEASE ANSWER ME! IT'S JEAN! BETSY, YOU'VE GOT TO RESPOND!*

It was sudden and demanding and so completely over-whelming—like an icepick being driven through her eye and into her brain—that the pain temporarily blinded her. She stumbled forward into the car and slammed against the far wall, clutching the sides of her head. Thankfully, the elevator was empty, so she didn't need to try and mutter some lame excuse for her behavior to a fellow passenger; not that she could have said anything at this point—the throbbing in her brain was so intense she could barely form a coherent thought.

"S-stop i-it. P-please st-stop i-it . . ." she mumbled pitifully, tears streaming down her cheeks. But the pain didn't let up, and her legs were suddenly unable to support her weight any longer; she slid down along the wall to lie in a heap on the cool, tiled floor.

And now a torrent of images pounded at her mind: a con-cerned, redheaded woman; a man with claws like an animal, but the heart of a warrior; a black-costumed man with a goatee, raking razor-sharp fingers across her eyes; an obese, yellow-skinned *thing* with eyelids held open by metallic pincers that sunk deeply into its flesh, and a smile like that of Satan himself; the English-woman version of herself, trapped in a room filling with water as the Minister of Entertainment/but not the Minister of Entertainment watched, her cries for help cut off by a colorful strip of cloth; the correct, Japanese version of herself, but dressed in a dark blue swimsuit and leggings of some kind, a swash of red color—like paint, or a tattoo—running from just above her left eye down to her left cheekbone; a blue-skinned demon with a pointed tail, leaping at her; a peaceful world that looked nothing like Earth, watched over by a kindly, dark-haired woman in white who lived in a floating citadel; a baldheaded man in a wheelchair.

What did it mean? What did *any* of it mean? And why wouldn't the flood of indecipherable visions stop? Why wouldn't they get out of her head before she was driven to the brink of madness, for surely that wasn't long in coming?

But *still* the images formed and dissolved, moving faster and faster, and *still* the voice echoed through her mind, growing louder in volume, demanding that she respond. . . .

A few blocks away, in a building on Pearl Street, an alarm began sounding.

The offices of the Imperial Agency for Superhuman Activities, New York Center, were located in a forty-story, Art Deco-designed building that, from the outside, looked no different from any of the hundreds of other glass and steel and stone structures that towered above the thin, winding streets of lower Manhattan.

Unlike the other structures, however, the glass was capable of withstanding a point-blank burst from a laser cannon, the stone was thick enough to shrug off a blow or two from the Hulk, and the beams that supported the building were composed of steel mixed with adamantium and a variety of other super-strong elements. In short, the building could withstand anything short of a nuclear strike on Manhattan, or a gathering of hell-raising Norse gods intent on having a memorable night on the town.

It was almost as strong, some often pointed out, as the woman in charge of its personnel.

In her early thirties, blond-haired and blue-eyed, Dr. Valerie Cooper was that rare kind of person who possesses good looks, an incredible intellect, and an annoyingly superior attitude that, in this case, meant she considered herself God's gift to science (and there where those in the scientific community who would actually agree with that assessment). For the past decade, she had made a career of keeping superhumans in line, coordinating her office's activities with those of Anthony Stark's and Sebastian Shaw's, and, on the rare occasion, even reporting directly to Emperor von Doom himself. Her rule of thumb in dealing with the superpowered men and women who tended to pop up over the years was simple: you either worked for the Emperor and wore your leash and collar like a good little obedient dog, or you were put down before you posed a threat to the civilian population. After all, nobody liked a bad dog.

A *lot* of bad dogs had been put down on her watch.

Nine years ago, it had been the good doctor's people who, at von Doom's command, had eliminated a good portion of the super-villain community so that the Emperor could focus on more important matters of state. And though some people might call her a killer, and some might consider her a saint, the bottom line was that Val Cooper enjoyed her work, was proud of her work, and wasn't the type to allow even the lowest Morlock to escape her scrutiny.

Such dedication to her profession, of course, made being assigned to her division akin to a sneak preview of what it might be like to be consigned to the blackest pit of hell . . .

"Kill that damn noise!" Cooper bellowed as she entered the thirty-first floor monitoring room. She turned to a brown-haired, female technician as the alarm cut off. "What's the situation?"

"TK meters, Ma'am." The tech—whose nametag said BUR-

ROUGHS—pointed to a monitor at her station. "We're picking up an incredible surge of psychic power—it's off the scale!"

Cooper folded her arms across her chest and raised a quizzical eyebrow. "Location?"

"Midtown Manhattan. Forty-second and Fifth." Burrough's eyes widened as she glanced at another screen. "Ma'am, the sender isn't registered in the systems."

Now it was Cooper's turn to register surprise. "An unknown psi-talent? How can that be possible?"

"I've no idea, Ma'am," Burroughs replied. "Your orders?"

Cooper tapped a slender index finger against the tip of her nose as she paused to consider her next move.

"Scramble the Hunters," she finally said. "Fill them in on the situation, and have them load for bear; we don't know *what* we might be up against here. Then notify Psi Division—have them send one of their people over so our team's got someone capable of warding off a mental assault." She pointed a demanding finger in the technician's face. "And make sure they're *all* aware that the target's in the middle of a *densely populated* area. I don't want them tearing up half of Manhattan in some senseless donnybrook if they can convince the target to surrender peacefully." She frowned. *"I* sure as hell don't want to have to explain the cause for massive property damage and incalculable civilian injuries to the Emperor."

Burroughs nodded in understanding, then paused. "And if the target refuses to cooperate, Ma'am?"

Cooper's eyes glittered with unbridled malevolence. "Then the Hunters are to *terminate* the target—with extreme prejudice."

# 10

I F EVER there was one specific person for whom Extra-Strength Tylenol had been created, that person would have to have been Elisabeth Braddock.

Hair and clothing disheveled, feet set squarely on the warm asphalt walkway, she sat on a bench at Battery Park, head down, looking for all the world like someone who had just been trampled by every bull and bear that had ever run rampant through the Wall Street area. Above her, a flock of seagulls made slow circles in the afternoon sky above the harbor; every now and then, one of the birds let loose a piercing cry that rang through Betsy's skull like a fire alarm. A few hundreds yards away, a tour group was lining up to board a boat that would take them to the Statue of von Doom, where they would be given a brief history lesson on the Emperor's rise to power. Betsy had taken the tour once, last year, when Warren had been out of town on business; it had been a pleasant way to spend an afternoon, with the smell of salt water in the air and a cool breeze blowing in from the Atlantic Ocean.

Now, though, just the act of elevating her head slightly to look at the beaming faces of the children as they ran wildly across the boat's twin decks was enough to send daggers into the base of her skull. Dully, she wondered how such a day laden with promise could have gone so terribly wrong. Not expecting a reply, she hung her head down to lessen the pressure building behind her sinuses and fished in her purse for the small bottle of Tylenol she had purchased after staggering out of the elevator back at the World Trade Center.

She'd certainly been a sight to see, then, hadn't she? The impression she must have left on the minds of the Doom Youth Scout troop when the elevator doors had opened to reveal an attractive, purple-haired woman sprawled in a corner, mumbling for someone to "stop"!

Thankfully, the voices and the barrage of images *had* stopped, just before she had resorted to banging her head against the elevator's walls and floor in the desperate hope that unconsciousness would bring a blessed end to the torment. Why they had stopped, she didn't know; nor did she really care.

Fighting the child-proof safety cap, Betsy eventually managed to shake out a couple of tablets from the bottle. With a grimace, she shoved them into her mouth and dry-swallowed. Now, if she could just manage to get back to the apartment without passing out again . . .

*Man, could I get lost in all'a that hair . . .*

Betsy raised her head—a little too quickly, as her throbbing temples pointed out—and looked around for the speaker. Her gaze fell upon a young black man in his early twenties seated on a bench across from her. He was dressed in a tightfitting white T-shirt—emblazoned with the logo of the New York Yankees—and a pair of black spandex shorts. One sneakered foot rested idly on the support bar of a mountain bicycle. A walkie talkie was strapped to his waist, and a large, black portfolio was propped against the edge of the wooden seat, within arm's reach. A messenger of some sort, obviously taking a break from his errands to admire the feminine scenery.

"I beg your pardon?" Betsy asked him.

The messenger looked back at her, clearly caught off-guard by her question. "Huh?" he replied.

"You said something about my hair?"

The messenger started, as though he'd been caught at doing something bad. But instead of apologizing, he vigorously shook his head. "I didn't say nothin.' "

Betsy frowned; she wasn't in the mood for this nonsense. "Of course, you did," she said. "I clearly heard you say you'd like to get lost in all my hair." To emphasize the point, she tugged at a few lavender strands. "Not that I'm not flattered—I am—but I think it's somewhat inappropriate to just go blurting out things like that in public."

The messenger's eyes widened in surprise, and he slowly rose to his feet. "B-but," he stammered, "I didn't *say* it. I was just *thinkin'* it."

Now it was Betsy's turn for shocked expressions. "But, that can't be," she insisted. "I heard you plain as day."

*Holy—she's some kinda freaky* mutant *or something. or maybe one of those Imperial probe types I heard about—Readin' my mind an' stuff. I gotta get outta here!*

Betsy froze. She had heard that, too. But this time she had been facing the man—*and he hadn't spoken those words aloud.*

*Oh, my God,* she thought, feeling a horde of butterflies being released into her stomach. *It's starting again. But, how am I doing this? What's happening to me . . . ?*

"Look, lady," the messenger said, as he straddled the seat of his bicycle, "I'm tellin' you the truth. I didn't say *nothin'* out loud, and I didn't say nothin' to *you*. All I was doin' was checkin' you out, an' thinkin' about what fine hair you got. But I *never* said *anything* out loud. An' if that ain't good enough for you, then that's *your* problem. Me—I'm outta here." And with that, he began pedaling away.

"Wait!" Betsy said, waving at him to stop. "I'm sorry! Please, I don't understand why this is . . ."

But the messenger was already riding out of the park, not bothering to look back.

"Please . . ." Betsy whispered, feeling tears well up in the corners of her eyes. Her head was beginning to ache again, and she squeezed her eyes shut to try and stave off the next wave of pain before it broke. She needed to get home, lie down, and—

*Wow. Check out those legs,* another voice said. *Go right up to her neck, don't they? I'd sure like to—*

She wheeled around to find a thirtysomething police officer standing a dozen paces behind her, an admiring smile plastered on his face as he openly gazed at her. With a start, he realized that he was being observed by the very object of his keen interest; cheeks blushing, he quickly averted his gaze.

"You'd like to *what?*" Betsy asked angrily, rising to her feet. She took two wobbly steps toward him, but then—

*Can't believe Doom's raising the price of gas again. You'd think he's already got enough money . . .*

Yet *another* voice? Confused, Betsy turned from the policeman and saw a business-suited man walking by, not looking at her at all; he was too busy reading a newspaper.

Reading. But his lips weren't moving. Yet she could still "hear" him as he continued scanning an article on pending price increases announced by von Doom's cabinet.

But it wasn't like what had happened in the elevator. There were no images this time, no suppressed memories suddenly leaping to the front of her brain—this was nothing less than a deluge of other people's thoughts. It was as though her head had been turned into some kind of enormous receiving dish for every random idea, every dark secret scratching at the corners of someone's mind, every hidden desire being unconsciously broadcast by the people around her.

And it wouldn't stop; in fact, it only got worse with each passing second.

*been meaning to tell Barbara how I feel like to tell old man Ferguson where he can stick it how can I tell Kevin I'm infected gotta be a way to get out of this freakin' lowpaying job why doesn't anybody understand never should've let Jack talk me into that weekend in Atlantic City Mets better get some good pitchin' soon can't let Sandra go and ruin my marriage bet nobody'd care if I stepped in front of a bus wonder if Bill's interested in going to the cabin this weekend can't believe I have to reschedule another dental appointment they'll never find the body NOT WHERE I HID IT why can't I be as thin as those supermodels a shame a looker like her turns out to be such a nutjob GREAT LEGS THOUGH AND MAN JUST LOOK AT ALL THAT HAIR*

"STOP IT! STOP IT!" Betsy screamed, her hands pressed to the sides of her head. "JUST LEAVE ME ALONE!"

Around her, passersby came to an abrupt halt. She could "hear" each of their thoughts—some of them feeling concern for her, some annoyed by the antics of the crazy woman melodramatically clutching her head, some wondering what she might be like in bed when the "voices" weren't talking to her. Most though, spared her only a moment's glance before continuing on their way—a typical New York reaction to an atypical situation: *Not my business*, their thoughts said. *Somebody else's problem. Move on.*

Fighting to regain control of her mind, Betsy realized that she had to get out of the park, back to the apartment. She couldn't remain here any longer—at any moment, the police officer who had been admiring her legs might call for

*Dispatch, I need an ambulance at Battery Park. Possible psychiatric patient causing a disturbance. request assistance.*

Frantically, Betsy looked around. The policeman was standing far enough away so that she wouldn't have been able to hear him under normal circumstances, but now . . .

Before the officer could react, she was pushing through the crowd and racing through the park, trying to see through bleary eyes as she looked for an exit. All she needed to do was get to the apartment complex—get to the complex and she'd be safe. But it seemed so very far away . . .

"Warren . . ." she cried softly, tears streaming down her cheeks, head pounding like an incessant drumbeat. "Help me . . ."

* * *

With a heavy sigh, Jean Grey shook her head and turned to her husband.

"I'm sorry, Scott," she said. "It's no use. She's just not sending."

With a slight nod of his head, Scott Summers reached out to rub Jean's arm consolingly. "It's all right, hon. You did your best." He smiled encouragingly at her, but Jean's expression made it clear she was disappointed in herself for failing to locate Betsy.

"We movin' out?" Logan asked from beneath his hat.

"No other choice," Scott replied, a frown creasing his handsome features. "We can't afford to wait any longer." He ran a hand through his dark-brown hair and kicked at a loose piece of concrete near his feet in frustration. "Damn it."

Now it was Jean who offered the comforting gesture, sliding her right arm around his waist and pulling him close. "I know how you feel, hon," she said quietly. "None of us want to leave a team member behind, especially in the middle of a crisis. But we don't have a lot of options open to us, and reversing Doom's handiwork *has* to remain our top priority."

"I know," Scott said. "But still . . ."

Jean moved her arm from his waist and reached up to gently tousle his hair. "I'm sure Betsy will be fine, Scott," she assured him. "She's an X-Man, after all, and it'll be a sorry day for us all when one of our people can't handle a third-rate loser like Arcade." She smiled, and reached up to stroke his cheek with her left hand. "We have to keep telling ourselves that, have to maintain a positive outlook, or we won't be able to complete this mission." Her smile broadened as she leaned close to whisper in his ear. "As a wise man once said: 'The needs of the many outweigh the needs of the few.' "

" 'Or the one,' " Scott said, completing the quote. He turned to look at Jean, a half smile playing at his lips. "Since when did AMC start running *The Wrath of Khan*?"

"They didn't," Jean replied. "*Star Trek* movie marathon on the Sci-Fi Channel. I caught it just before we left to help Roma."

Scott shook his head in mild disbelief and leaned forward to kiss her; Jean met him halfway.

*Love you, Red.*

*Love you too, "Slim."*

Beside them, Logan suddenly sat bolt upright, batting his Stetson away with one hand. He jumped to his feet and cocked his head to one side, obviously straining to hear something above the noise and traffic on Fifth Avenue.

"Logan?" Scott asked. He and Jean rose to their feet.

"We got company," Logan said. "I'm pickin' up some weird kinda turbine sound, comin' from—" he turned around and pointed to the sky above the public library "—there."

Its hull gleaming brightly in the midday sun, the armored transport sliced through the air, moving swiftly from the west toward Fifth Avenue. As it drew closer, the sound created by the powerful turbines that kept it aloft drowned out every other noise in the area and rattled windows for blocks around. And then, as quickly as it had flown, it came to an abrupt stop just above the library and remained there, hovering.

As one, the other X-Men and Carol moved to stand beside Logan, Scott, and Jean, assuming combat-ready positions.

"How you wanna play this, Cyclops?" Rogue asked.

"Let them make the first move," Scott replied. "And when it comes, try not to let them draw any of you away from the rest of the team."

"I'll try keepin' that in mind when the explosions start goin' off," Rogue said. She glanced at Gambit. "Can't be a proper fight *without* somethin' explodin'—right, sugah?"

Gambit flashed an easy smile. "Couldn't've said it better myself, *chere.*"

With a hiss of pressurized air being released, a hatch opened on the bottom of the craft.

"All right," Scott said grimly. "Here it comes."

Slowly, a large metal platform descended from the transport, occupied by a half-dozen costumed men and women. As it moved closer, they were able to get a better view of the group: a dark-haired woman in a tight leather outfit, a gun strapped to her right thigh; a blond-haired man in a red leather jacket, green buccaneer-style boots, and a black costume trimmed in green—the upper half of his face was concealed beneath a mask that was green on the left side and black on the right; a blond-haired woman in an identical costume to his, though the display of colors on her mask were reversed, and her thigh-high boots were golden; behind them stood a cloven-hoofed cyborg of some sort, another dark-haired woman in a red-and-gold costume, and what appeared to be a sentient oil slick, on top of which floated an inky-black approximation of a human face.

"Looks like somebody left the door open at the Legion of Losers Hall," Wolverine said.

"You *know* these people?" Carol asked.

"Some of 'em," Wolverine muttered, his eyes narrowing in anger. "Don't recognize the three in the back, though." He pointed to the leather-clad woman. *"That* one calls herself 'Mastermind.' The Cajun an' me ran into her a couple years ago. She's a telepath, like her old man—tried messin' with our heads, makin' us think I was some kinda serial killer." His lips pulled back in a feral snarl. "An' she was workin' with Arcade then."

"All roads seem to lead back to that little sociopath, do they not?" Nightcrawler commented.

"Just a small cog in a giant machine, Kurt," Jean replied. "Besides, our kind of business *thrives* on coincidence."

"The brother/sister act in the matching costumes," Scott explained to Carol, "call themselves 'Fenris,' after the wolf in Norse mythology. They're mutants, with an ability to generate concussive blasts."

Behind him, Rogue looked over to Gambit and smiled.

"See? I told you," she whispered. "Explosions."

*"Big* time, *chere,"* the Cajun agreed. He slipped a hand into the pocket of his duster to pull out one of the six new decks of playing

cards he had purchased after getting off the train at Grand Central Station.

"All right, people, I'll only say this once," Mastermind stated, her voice amplified by a hidden speaker on the platform. She pointed a commanding finger at the X-Men. "By order of his royal majesty, Emperor Victor von Doom I, and under the authority vested in me by the Imperial Agency for Superhuman Activities, Psionics Division, you are to surrender the telepath and then submit to arrest without incident. Failure to comply with these orders is punishable by death."

"Well, at least now we know how they became aware of our presence," Carol said. She glanced frostily at Jean. "Between poking around in my so-called 'memories' and this, you've got a helluva track record going, sister."

"Knock it off," Scott snapped. "You have a grievance to air out, do it *after* we've gotten out of this situation."

"What's your answer, boys and girls?" Mastermind demanded. "I don't have all day to stand around while you pick at your navels."

"The answer is *no*," Scott replied. He raised a hand as though to scratch his chin; he was actually placing it close enough to his visor to flip open the ruby quartz lens when needed.

Mastermind smiled; at another time, in another situation, it would have almost seemed pleasant. "No big surprise there, huh, handsome? Well, Cooper's going to have my head on a platter for this, but . . ." She shrugged, and glanced over her shoulder to her team. "Do it."

The brother and sister team of Fenris shared the same crazed expression, lips pull backed in a half smile/half snarl; to Jean, they looked like wild beasts scenting blood and wanting their fair share of it. They clasped hands, and immediately their bodies began to glow as a powerful charge of energy took shape between them. Mastermind stepped to one side, allowing them the pleasure of the first strike.

As the platform touched down on the plaza outside the library, Wolverine triggered his claws.

"Bring it on, chumps," he said with a growl. "I still got some frustrations to work out from this mornin' . . . an' I'm *more'n* willin' t'work 'em out on *you* . . ."

At last, she was safe.

Huddled in a corner of the living room, Betsy finally allowed herself to relax, to uncoil from the fetal position she had assumed in an effort to silence the voices running rampant in her head. Her head didn't ache quite as much as before, but every muscle in her body felt like a limp noodle after being held in so tight a position for so long. If only she could get the droning voices out of her thoughts, she could—

With a start, she realized they were gone.

The voices—the endless torrent of other people's thoughts that had driven her to the brink of madness during her blind race from Battery Park—had stopped their continuous chatter; in their place was nothing but sweet, blessed silence.

No, she thought, not silence—just a return to the types of *normal* sounds she was used to hearing: the hum of the central air conditioning system; the tick of the clock above the mantelpiece; the beat of her own heart. No strange visions of another life she couldn't remember living, no incessant buzz enveloping her mind about what to buy for dinner or who to get to mind the kids tonight or how expensive dating was getting or the racket created by those blasted kids upstairs with their 'N Sync CDs or how much someone hated her for being so beautiful and so damned skinny— only the sounds of her little corner of the world, assuring her that all was right and good, and that she could be at peace here.

But, how long *would* this peace last? How long before the thoughts of her neighbors in the complex began invading her mind?

"Don't dwell on it," she told herself. "Just take advantage of it."

Slowly, pressing her hands against the walls, she raised herself to her feet and smoothed out her miniskirt; looking across the room, she realized that, at some point, she had kicked off her shoes, but couldn't remember doing so. Using a wall to support her, she used a cuff of her jacket to wipe away the tears and snot that had crusted on her face.

*Some sight* I *must be, eh?* she thought. *Thank God there are no* mirrors *handy.*

Gathering her strength, she pushed off from the wall and, moving at a snail's pace, shuffled toward the bedroom.

Betsy had just enough energy left to shrug out of her jacket and skirt before flopping across the bed. As she gratefully drifted off to sleep, she prayed that she would awaken free of any further pain.


"You think *this* is pain, darlin'? Just *wait* till I get my hands on you—*then* you're gonna know what *real* pain is."

For a man with half a clip of .45-caliber bullets in him, Wolverine was doing surprisingly well, considering he should have died after the first three tightly-spaced rounds penetrated his chest. However, not only was he *not* dead, but he had advanced on Mastermind to put her within striking distance of his claws.

Such were the wonders of a mutant healing factor.

"This wasn't how it was supposed to work," the dark-haired woman muttered. "*You* were supposed to go after the big guns while *I* twisted your gal pal's psyche inside out like a corkscrew."

"Stop it," Wolverine replied. "Yer gonna make me cry. Anyways, you an' me got some old scores t'settle."

"I haven't the slightest idea what you're talking about, you little psycho," Mastermind said, stepping back and reaching for another clip of bullets. "Not that that matters to you in the least, I'm sure."

Sunlight glinted on adamantium as his claws slashed out, cutting the barrel of Mastermind's gun in half. "Hope ya weren't too attached t'that thing," he said, and took another step toward her.

But instead of turning and running from the pint-sized engine of destruction, Mastermind stood her ground . . . and smiled. "Hope you're not too attached to your *brain* . . . Shorty." Her brown eyes flashed.

The claws that tore into Logan's head were not real—he knew that for fact. They were actually psychic probes transmitted from the young woman before him, peeling back the layers of his mind, exposing his deepest secrets, his darkest fears, his most unsettling jealousies.

The claws hurt like hell, but they weren't real, he kept reminding himself.

That knowledge, though, didn't stop him from screaming.


"Wolverine!" Phoenix cried.

Standing beside Cyclops, she was in the midst of helping him battle Fenris—using her mental powers to hurl at them everything from garbage cans to a Starbucks coffee kiosk to the paving stones that formed the floor of the library plaza—when she heard Logan howl in excruciating pain. In her mind's eye, she caught glimpses of the agonies he was being forced to endure under Mastermind's psychic assault: images of sinister-looking laboratories and flesh-searing explosions and the sociopathic villain Sabretooth gouging out huge chunks of his body with the assassin's own sets of claws and Magneto using his incredible powers to literally strip the adamantium coating from Wolverine's bones *through the pores of his skin* and then enduring even greater levels of searing pain as the indestructible metal was once more bonded to him a year later.

And, most surprising of all, of the moment when she and Scott had stood on the altar at their wedding and first kissed as husband and wife. That image seemed to be stuck on playback, moving forward and then rewinding, to start the process over again without any end in sight. Of all the memories being used against him in Mastermind's vicious attack, *this* was the one causing him the greatest pain.

*Oh, Logan* . . . Jean turned to her husband. "Scott, I've—"

*"Go,"* he said. "I can handle this."

"I'll be right back," she promised.

"And I'll be counting the moments till then, love," Cyclops replied. He triggered his visor once more, and the ground beneath Fenris shattered in a blast of crimson energies, tossing the siblings high into the air.

Bright green eyes flashed, and Jean took to the air, rushing forward to aid her fallen comrade.

Carol Danvers was completely out of her element.

For a moment, when these costumed stormtroopers of von Doom's had stepped from the levitating platform, she felt certain that she could provide some help to the X-Men—try and draw one of the combatants after her to cut down the odds.

That opinion had changed once the brother/sister team of Fenris loosed the devastating energy that they had formed by simply holding hands. The blast had scattered the X-Men like tenpins and shattered one of the stone lions that stood guard at the entrance to the library plaza. Carol had been tossed a good twelve or fifteen feet into the air, and it was only through sheer luck that she had landed in the row of hedges that lined the perimeter of the library grounds; luckier still to have survived the short flight with no broken bones.

Now, as she watched the battle being waged in the center of Manhattan from the relative safety of a hot dog cart that had been abandoned by its owner at the first sign of trouble, Carol began to wonder why she just hadn't run for the hills after the camp was liberated. True, she was grateful to these strangers for helping her escape from a living hell, but whatever had possessed her to *join* them on their quixotic campaign, instead of melting into the shadows and trying to create a new life for herself? Was it really because she shared their desire to oust von Doom from his throne? Or was it because they had treated her as one of their own?

Watching the X-Men working in unison—covering one another's backs, gently chiding one another in the heat of battle—

she began to understand that these people functioned not just as a team, but as a *family*. And, despite the fact she didn't know them from Adam (though they insisted otherwise), despite the hostility she had felt toward Jean Grey for obviously withholding information from her after their trip through her mind, despite the fact she had thought them insane for wanting to confront Victor von Doom on his home turf, they had welcomed her into their hearts and made her feel a part of that family.

An old saying sprang to Carol's mind: Friends may come and go, but family is forever. In the middle of a crisis like this, could she really just run off and abandon her new family?

Near the main set of steps leading to the library's main entrance, Phoenix made a perfect two-point landing, positioning herself between Mastermind and Wolverine. Carol was suddenly struck by the absurdity of the scene: a leather-clad *femme fatale* facing off against a redheaded fury in a pretty, yellow summer dress, while a short, hairy man with foot-long pitchfork tines sticking out of his hands writhed on the ground, clasping his head in agony. For a moment, she wondered where the movie cameras might be hidden.

That ridiculous question was quickly tossed aside as she spotted the red-and-gold-dressed woman from the platform—Carol had heard Mastermind refer to her as "Shakti"—cast a spell that caused a gale-force wind to send Rogue flying across Fifth Avenue and into the sixth floor windows of an office building. Bystanders who had stopped to watch the fight now scrambled for cover as glass, masonry, and office supplies rained down on them. Momentarily free from attack, the dark-haired sorceress turned her attention to Phoenix, who appeared to be in the midst of some mental catfight with Mastermind. To Carol, it looked like the two combatants were quietly standing their ground, eyes locked, though Lord only knew on what kind of psychic battlefield they were waging their private war.

What Shakti seemed to see, on the other hand, was an invitation to strike down an unwitting enemy.

*Well,* two *can play at* that *game,* Carol thought. *But first, I need a weapon . . .*

She spotted a heavy, gray paving stone lying nearby. Without hesitation, she leapt from her hiding place, grabbed the object, and charged straight at Shakti's unprotected back.

She didn't even realize she had stepped in an oily patch on the ground until it sprang to life, slithering up her legs and over her body before she could cry out in surprise.

*"NO!"* Carol tried to scream, but the oily film covered her face, flowing into her nostrils and tear ducts, pouring into her open mouth like a living river of ink. Her body convulsed from the panicked sensation that she was drowning, a half mile from any body of water. In horror, she felt the entity taking control of every nerve, every muscle in her body, forcing it to ignore her mental commands.

And there was nothing she could do about it.

Nor could she stop the entity from changing the direction of her attack, then raising the paving stone above her head, to bring it crashing down on the back of Phoenix's skull. Jean stiffened for a moment; then, with a whisper of a sigh, she collapsed in a heap on the warm gravel.

Mastermind smiled at her. "Thanks for the assist, Divinity. Not that I couldn't have handled the witch by myself."

"Too much time, your method takes," Carol heard herself say in a voice that was not her own. "Time should not be wasted so."

The entity called Divinity kept talking to Mastermind, asking what the telepath planned to do with Wolverine before he regained consciousness, but Carol was no longer listening. There was another odd sensation beginning to flow through her body, one that had started in her toes and was slowly creeping up her legs, her torso, into her very thoughts. It was an icy chill, of all things— something she never would have expected to feel in the middle of June, with the sun shining so brightly and not a cloud in the sky. But even as it reached up to caress her mind with the gentleness of a lover, she recognized it for what it was—a terrible thing she had held at bay for years, denying its touch; something she thought she had managed to finally elude when she saw the sun rise on a day filled with such promise.

It was Death.

And she had come to take Carol home.

Cyclops staggered back a step as he felt his wife being struck down from behind—a disadvantage, to be sure, of sharing a psychic link with a loved one in the midst of a battle.

"J-Jean . . . ?" he muttered, one hand rising to massage his pulsing forehead. In horror, he looked over to where she lay on the ground. Standing over her was Carol Danvers, a heavy, blood-smeared stone in her hands; she was covered from head to toe in an oily substance, eyes widened in shock, her mouth opened in a silent scream. Next to Carol was Mastermind, who prodded Jean's unmoving body with the pointed toe of a leather boot.

"JEAN!" Cyclops screamed.

A flash of ruby quartz in sunlight, and Mastermind was propelled up the library steps and into the antique wooden framework above the main entrance. She collapsed in a heap on the landing.

Despite the dangers presented by turning his back on an enemy—even though both members of Fenris were lying, dazed, on the ground—Scott couldn't stop himself from doing so; Jean was lying so still, so lifeless. He had to know if she was merely unconscious, or . . .

He took one step toward Jean—

And was blown across the length of the plaza as Fenris—groggy, but still functional—unleashed another burst of destructive energy.

Amid the splintering of every bone in his right arm as he crashed into a used book kiosk, Cyclops heard one other sound: Carol Danvers' death rattle as the oily creature that had enveloped her flowed off her body, leaving behind a desiccated, lifeless husk that crumpled to the ground.

And then darkness claimed him.

"Now, y'all went an' got me *mad!*" Rogue shouted as she soared above Fifth Avenue.

It had taken her a while to dig her way out of the five offices through which she had crashed after being hurled away from the battlezone by Shakti's miniature cyclone—five offices and count-less walls that had crumbled like papier-mâché before she had finally come to rest in the break area of the law offices of Stern, Mantlo, Moench & McGregor. To say the partners, their employees, and the few clients seated in the waiting room had not been pleased by her unexpected—and highly destructive—visit would be an understatement; suffice to say, there had been enough derisive expletives and angry promises of lawsuits aimed her way to make certain that Rogue would avoid entering even the airspace above a courthouse for years to come.

Mad as hell, her hair drenched in half-and-half cream and smelling of used coffee grounds, Rogue had done her best to ignore the threats and insults and quickly exited back the way she had come, eager to dole out a little payback to the villainess who had caused her all this trouble in the first place.

But as she returned to the plaza, she was greeting by the sight of Fenris striking down Cyclops—and Divinity draining the life-force from Carol Danvers.

"Oh, God . . ." Rogue whispered. "Carol . . ."

Any further concerns for her erstwhile teammate were smashed from her mind as a devastating bolt of energy blew her out of the sky.

Tumbling head over heels, Rogue dimly realized that seeing Carol being murdered had distracted her long enough for Fenris for launch their attack. Unable to regain her equilibrium, she could only brace for the impact just before she crashed into the sidewalk, hard enough to create an eight-foot-wide crater.

Rogue slowly struggled to her feet, unable to clear her addled thoughts. Something warm dripped into her eyes, and she recognized it as blood, seeping from a deep cut in her forehead—possibly the result of a hairline skull fracture. The shock of seeing herself bleeding began pumping adrenaline through her system, and her mind slowly cleared. Her head was spinning, her eyes couldn't focus, and her legs felt as though they were made of gelatin, but she knew that if she didn't stand up, didn't strike back, she was more than likely going to join Carol on her trip to the afterlife.

But she wasn't prepared to die—not yet.

Unfortunately, she never saw the remaining stone lion at the entrance to the plaza come to life under Shakti's direction, never saw it rise on its haunches and eye her hungrily—at least, not until it had sprung at her. But by then, it was too late.

Before she could leap out of its path, the lion was upon her, driving the air from her lungs and smashing her head against the pavement with the full weight of its body.

As the world dimmed around her, Rogue wondered if Carol had felt any pain in her last moments of life.

She also wondered if she was about to be able to ask Carol that question directly.

"Things are not going well, *mein freund*," Nightcrawler commented as he and Gambit clashed with the cloven-hoofed, technology-based lifeform that had identified itself as Technarx. Despite a rapid series of well-placed kicks and blows delivered by quickly teleporting around his foe, Kurt had been unable to find a weakness in its armor.

"You can say *dat* again, 'Crawler," Gambit replied. He spared a glance over his shoulder to see Rogue being dragged over to Shakti by the animated stone lion; it held one of the unconscious mutant's arms in its granite jaws.

*Don' you go lettin' yo' feelin's for dat girl get you* killed, *Remy,* he sternly warned himself. *Dat Rogue, she a tough one—she'll be fine. 'Sides, you got problems of your own t'deal wit'.*

As if in response to his thoughts, Technarx swung in his direction, its right arm shooting forward. Gambit leapt to one side, striking the metal-and-circuit-sheathed limb with a charged playing card. The resulting explosion made the techno-organic mutant screech loudly and reel back in pain.

"Maybe you oughtta *BAMF!* on outta here while I cover you," Gambit said to his teammate while they had a momentary breather. "Give you some time to go contact de FF, or de 'Vengers, an' get us some back-up."

"And leave you in such dire straits?" Nightcrawler asked. "I think not, Remy. Besides, in case you have not noticed, if our little tête-à-tête with Doom's flunkies has not drawn the attention of such well-respected heroic groups, what makes you think they would be willing to come to our aid *now?*" A slight movement seen from the corner of his eye caught Kurt's attention. He glanced past Gambit, who turned to look in the same direction.

Fenris was staring back at them.

"Now, we shall wash the last of this *scum* from our streets," said Andrea Strucker, the female half of the team.

"Indeed. The Emperor will be *most* pleased with our work, dear sister," replied her brother, Andreas.

Smiling malevolently, the siblings joined hands.

"Perhaps, friend Gambit," Nightcrawler mused aloud, "discretion *is* the better part of valor. But if I am to fight another day, I shall not do so *alone.*" He reached out to grab his friend, preparing to teleport them both away from the battlezone—

—only to be roughly pushed aside by his teammate. The reason why became immediately clear: Technarx had recovered, firing a stream of techno-organic circuitry at the blue-skinned X-Man in an attempt to snare him. Remy had not hesitated in shoving Kurt out of the way.

Much to his own misfortune.

As Nightcrawler watched, circuits and wires and metal plates began to take form, spreading over Gambit like an infection gone wild, transforming him into a creature that was only partly a man. Remy's one remaining eye swiveled toward Nightcrawler, the sorrow in it unmistakable.

*"Kurt . . ."* he/it rasped, in a voice that sounded like two pieces of metal being rubbed together.

And then the Gambit-thing collapsed.

"Oh . . . oh, my God . . ." Nightcrawler said huskily. He jumped forward, all thoughts of escape pushed aside by his blinding desire to do something—anything—to help his friend.

He hardly felt the impact of the Fenris-created energy blast that sent him hurtling into unconsciousness.

# 11

**W**HEN BETSY finally awoke, it was to Warren's gentle kiss on the nape of her neck. She uttered a soft, appreciative moan. "What time is it?" she asked groggily.

"A little after eight," he replied. "I just got home a few minutes ago. I called around five-thirty, to tell you when I'd get in, but you didn't pick up." He paused. "You feeling all right?"

Betsy rolled onto her back and gazed deeply into his loving, concerned eyes, not knowing what to say. Should she tell him about her strange episode in Arcade's office, or her collapse in the elevator, or the multitude of voices that had been running non-stop through her head until she thought it would burst from the pain? As her sleep-addled brain began to function again, she suddenly realized that the voices still hadn't returned—maybe, God willing, she was free of the madness.

She doubted that, though.

But, what would he say if she *did* tell him about everything that had happened? How would he respond?

She knew *exactly* how he'd respond: the same way he always had in the past when she had a troubling experience—with compassion, and understanding, and that boyish smile that used to make her feel that all was truly right with the world again.

Unfortunately, the kind of trauma she'd undergone this afternoon could not be made better with just a warm smile and a peck
on the cheek. Something had happened to her today—something
had been awakened inside her mind, and now that the beast had
been freed, there was no putting it back in its cage.

And with that realization, Betsy also knew, though she wished
it weren't so, that *nothing* would ever be truly right from this day
forward . . .

"I'm fine," she lied.

Warren stared into her eyes for a few moments, as though
searching for some kind of evidence to refute her claim; he found
nothing. Slowly, he smiled.

"Okay," he said, and brushed away a few loose strands of
lavender hair from her eyes. "You hungry?"

Betsy's stomach gurgled in response, and she giggled as she
placed a hand over her mouth. "I'm absolutely famished." She
rolled off the bed and onto her feet. "What did you have in mind?"

"I don't know," Warren replied. "What do you feel like?"

Betsy rolled her eyes. This was the same conversation they always had whenever they decided to stay home for an evening, and
she knew how it would end: with her foraging through the kitchen
for whatever food could be turned into a quick and easy meal.
One of these days, Warren was going to have to learn how to
cook . . .

"You know," Betsy said, wrapping an arm around his waist to
lead him from the bedroom, "dining would be much simpler for
us both if you'd kept the servants around."

"Oh, so *now* you think I should've kept the staff here," Warren
shot back, slipping an arm around her in kind. "What happened
to all that talk about wanting to avoid living the oh-so-clichéd
pampered existence of the rich and famous?"

Betsy sighed. "Well, that was before I realized you were forcing
me to live a life that revolved around an almost steady diet of
Ramen noodles and grilled cheese sandwiches."

Warren's face slackened, and his eyes glazed over as he stared into the distance. "Mmmm ... grilled cheese sandwiches," he moaned, in a fair approximation of Homer Simpson.

Betsy laughed, and they exited the bedroom, bound for the kitchen. As they passed through the living room, she spotted the MESSAGE light blinking on their answering machine.

"That your call from before?" she asked.

"One of them is," Warren replied. He changed the course of their direction to bring them over to the machine, then pushed the REPLAY button.

"You have ... TWO ... messages," the answering machine stated in its flat, mechanical voice. "Message One: 'Hey, Betts, it's Warren. I'm running a little—'" Warren pressed the ERASE key.

"Message Two," continued the machine. "Betsy, sweets, it's your old pal, Arcade. You there? Pick up, please." Pause. "Betsy? Hello? Pick up pick up pick up!" Pause. "Okay, so you're not there. I won't hold that against you. Probably whooping it up with Studley over there, right? Anyway, here's the reason I'm calling, and you ain't gonna believe it: Purely by the greatest coincidence, it turns out ol' Vic von D wasn't exactly thrilled by the thought of the Wayouts trashing the stage at the Arts Center during their act—at least, that's what his Press Secretary was telling me. So, here I am, stuck with a gap in my events schedule and nobody to fill it." Pause. "Or am I wrong ... ? Gimme a call, babe, and let's make some magic! Later!"

For some odd reason, Betsy found it incredibly difficult to catch her breath. The reason for her condition, though, became readily apparent—she'd been holding it throughout the playback of Arcade's message.

Smiling, Warren leaned close to her ear. "Betts," he whispered, "it's okay to exhale."

The air came flowing out of her in a rush, and her knees quivered. She latched onto Warren before she wound up doing a header into the carpet.

"Did ... did he ..." she said breathlessly. "Did he just ... just say ..."

"Say what?" Warren asked. From his expression, it was clear he was taking some sort of sadistic pleasure in watching her reaction.

Betsy inhaled deeply, summoning all her strength. *"Did he just say I'm in the show?"* she blurted out.

"Sounded something like that," Warren replied with a shrug. He reached for the REPLAY button. "Want to hear it again?"

"No!" Betsy cried, slapping his hand away. "Not just yet." She placed a hand over her heart; it was galloping like a racehorse. "I don't think I could take the strain." She stepped away from Warren as a warm feeling—a sense of tranquillity—slowly spread through her body. Tears welled up in her eyes, and she placed a tremulous hand over equally trembling lips to try and calm herself before she collapsed in a nervous heap.

*It had finally happened.*

After all the years of struggling with her career and trying to make a name for herself and swallowing insults about her relationship with Warren, she had finally gotten a chance to prove her worth—to make her mark on history. And she had gotten that chance by using her strengths, her determination, and her talents.

*Her talents.*

Betsy began to grin, and the smile was so wide, so full of joy, she was almost afraid it would cause her face to split.

And then, with a scream of sheer delight, she ran through the apartment, turning cartwheels and bouncing off the furniture like a giddy child on the first day of summer vacation.

"I think," Warren commented, "this calls for *more* than a grilled cheese sandwich . . ."

The Emperor was not in the mood for dining.

Slouched in a high-backed leather seat behind his desk in the Oval Office of the White House, Victor von Doom sat alone in the dark, brooding.

Spread across the executive desk were over two dozen color photographs, and a set of reports compiled by S.H.I.E.L.D., the

Psionics Division, and the Imperial Agency for Superhuman Activities—all of them documenting the attack on the Salem Center prisoner center from the night before, and the battle that had erupted in midtown Manhattan that very afternoon between Imperial Hunters and a group of unregistered, superpowered men and women. It had been during a cursory examination of the pictures—when, to his great surprise, he had recognized the faces of the I.A.S.A. prisoners—that the Emperor had lost his appetite.

"The X-Men . . ." von Doom muttered to the darkness. "To think that—for all the preparations made, all the minor details attended to, all the potential . . . problems that were eliminated at the very start—a group of self-righteous cockroaches like Ororo's former teammates could have escaped my notice is unconscionable, for Doom is not a man given to mistakes." He frowned, staring off into space. "How, then, could they have avoided being affected by the improvements that I have brought to the world?" He mulled this question over for a while, chin resting in the crook of one hand between thumb and forefinger. Then his eyebrows began to rise as a theory slowly took shape in his mind. "Unless they were not *on* this world when the transformation occurred . . ."

A soft knock on the door roused him from his reverie. He turned toward the portal, teeth bared in anger.

"Who *dares* disturb the thoughts of Doom?" he barked loudly.

"His loving wife," came the reply from the other side of the door.

"Ah." Slowly, von Doom relaxed, and a pleasant smile came to his face. He rose to his feet, adjusting his red silk tie and smoothing out a wrinkle in his dress shirt as he did so, and pressed a button on the desk that activated the room's lights. The Oval Office was bathed in a soft, white glow.

"Enter," he said, with a gentleness that would have shocked even those who knew—and feared—him well.

The door opened, and Lancer stepped aside to allow Ororo entry to the room. The Empress looked resplendent in a black gown that complemented her figure as well as her snow-white hair. A tiny smile bowed her lips as she met the imperious gaze of her husband.

"My liege," Ororo said, with a slight bow of her head.

Looking past his wife, von Doom nodded to Lancer, who quietly shut the door. Now alone with Ororo, the Emperor smiled broadly and stepped around the desk to properly greet her, embracing her and pulling her into a deep, loving kiss.

When they at last parted, Ororo paused a moment to regain her composure.

"I was not away from you all that long, Victor," she said breathlessly. "A mere two days while I visited the children at their school in Switzerland."

Taking her hands in his, von Doom lightly kissed her fingertips. "Each moment without your shining presence, my beloved, is an eternity spent in Hades."

Ororo placed a hand to her cheek as the blush of embarrassment colored her face, then smiled broadly. "If that is true," she replied, "then I shall have to see how receptive the great Victor von Doom is to his Empress if he is left to his own devices for an entire *week.*"

The Emperor laughed heartily. "The Earth itself would tremble from the strength of my longing." Tilting his head downward, he kissed her on the top of her head.

"Then, if only for the sake of the world," Ororo said solemnly, "I shall do everything in my power to never leave your side for any lengthy period of time."

"A *wise* choice," the Emperor replied. He smiled. "But enough about the safety of the world—surely it can run properly without the need of Doom's guiding hand for *one* evening. Would you care for a drink? I have recently received an excellent Latverian Merlot from my mother; we can speak of the children as we share a glass."

"All right," Ororo replied.

With a slight bow, von Doom strode across the Oval Office to a small cabinet set into an oak-paneled wall. Opening its door, he reached in to extract the crimson-hued libation and two crystal goblets.

"What are these, Victor?"

Von Doom froze at the sound of papers being shuffled, his hand still resting on the bottle of wine. Slowly, he turned to find Ororo standing at his desk, a look of mild interest on her comely features as she inspected the photographs.

"Simple affairs of state, my dear," he replied quickly, walking back to join her. "A band of misguided souls who had foolishly allowed themselves to be swayed by the inflammatory propaganda of that murderous scum, Magneto. My agents have already taken them into custody."

"Then, they are mutants?" Ororo asked. "Like myself?"

Von Doom waved a dismissive hand. "They are *nothing* like you, My Lady. Mutants they may be, but Magneto's rebellious curs are no more your equal than a lump of coal is to a diamond. Mark my words, though: One day soon, they—*and* their cretinous master—shall learn the price for opposing the rule of Doom."

"Still," Ororo said slowly, gazing down at the pictures, "there *is* something about these people that I find . . . hauntingly familiar." She picked up a close-up photograph of Phoenix—her head bandaged, her normally pale skin looking deathly-white from the loss of blood caused by her head injury—as she was being loaded into an ambulance. "This woman in particular—I *know* her from somewhere . . ."

As he watched his wife struggle with a memory she could not quite bring to the surface of her mind, von Doom's lips curled back in a fearsome snarl. This sort of behavior on her part would not do at all . . .

"Ororo," he said firmly, *"look at me."*

The Empress glanced up from the pictures to discover, much to her surprise, that her husband's eyes were *glowing.* "Victor, what is—" she began.

*"Silence,"* von Doom commanded. Immediately, Ororo became quiet, standing stock-still as though rooted to the spot. A glaze settled over her eyes as she found herself unable to look away from those troubling orbs that blazed hotly from beneath knitted brows.

"I *know* what is happening to you, my queen," he growled.

"Now that you have been confronted by reminders of the rabble which whom you once associated, your mind is struggling against my control, attempting to make you aware that, in days past, we were *not* the closest of lovers, but the bitterest of *enemies*. Warning you that all you have experienced of late, all that you have come to know as fact in this world of my making, is but a *sham.*"

Von Doom frowned. "You are a strong-willed woman, Ororo; in time, you *would* be able to free yourself from my influence. But, having at last made his dream a reality, Doom will not allow anyone—not even his lovely bride—to awaken." His dark eyes flared even brighter. "You will forget having seen these photographs, forget we have discussed anything but the welfare of Kristoff and Qadira." He pointed a commanding finger at her. "But always remember this: Your will belongs to Doom. Your mind, body, soul—all these belong to Doom." He gestured toward the bay windows of the office, balling his hands into fists. "This entire *world* is Doom's, to do with as he sees fit. And there is nothing you—or any of your former meddlesome associates—can ever do to change that." He leaned forward, eyes narrowing. *"Do you understand?"*

"Yes," Ororo replied softly, eyes wide but unseeing. A slight tremble ran through her body.

The Emperor smiled malevolently. "Excellent, my love . . ."

By the time Ororo's mind cleared, the photographs and reports had been locked inside a bottom drawer of the executive desk; the Emperor possessed the only key.

"And Qadira?" von Doom asked pleasantly. "She is doing well, also?"

Ororo opened her mouth to answer, then stopped. She looked around, to find herself seated on an leather couch, Victor sitting beside her. Two glasses of wine stood on the table before them.

"Is there something wrong?" the Emperor asked.

"I-I am not certain," Ororo said hesitantly. She was obviously confused; it was also obvious that she couldn't quite figure out just what exactly was troubling her. "What were we talking about . . . ?"

"You were telling me of our children's exploits in school," von Doom prompted. "I was pleased to hear of Kristoff's excellent grades and high intelligence quota—the future of the Empire rests squarely on the boy's shoulders. You were about to tell me of our daughter."

Ororo nodded slowly. "Oh . . . yes." Her knitted brow relaxed as she turned to focus on their conversation. "Qadira is quite well, though she seems to have something of a rebellious streak in her, according to the headmaster."

"Like her mother," von Doom commented, with a hint of a smile.

Ororo laughed softly. "And her father."

The Emperor nodded solemnly, and opened his mouth to reply— only to be interrupted by the unkingly rumbling of his stomach.

"Victor, have you dined yet?" Ororo asked. Her tone was somewhat akin to that of a mother worried about her child's eating habits.

Von Doom shook his head. "No. But, now that you are here—" he smiled, a wicked sparkle in his eyes "—I find myself absolutely famished . . ."

"You call this slop *food?* I've had roasted *camel* that tasted better!"

With an angry growl, Erik Lensherr sent the gold-trimmed serving plate flying across the dining room. It shattered against a pale blue-colored wall on the far side, just missing the fiery-tressed head of his hostess—a blue-skinned woman named Raven Darkholme—as she stepped from the kitchen. Bits of tuna fish and pasta curls stuck to the wall as canned peas and smashed pieces of pottery rained down on the stark-white carpeting. Raven stared at the mess, then turned to her guest.

"I am *not* cleaning that up," she said coldly.

As one of the mutant overlord's field agents, Darkholme was more often referred to by her codename: Mystique—an appropriate name for a woman whose past was as mysterious as the unique powers she possessed. Clad in white leather boots, white gloves, and just enough white, gauze-like material to provide a modicum of attire for when she stepped out in public, she was every bit the modern-day equivalent of Mata Hari—beautiful, strong-willed, deceptive, and not above using her sexuality as a lure to get what she wanted. She was an expert in her field, able to create explosives from simple household items, crack any government computer system, slip undetected into some of the most secure military facilities in the world, eliminate any target from as close as five feet away and still manage to escape some of the Empire's most highly-skilled Hunters, and wire every inch of her home to keep prying "mentos" from eavesdropping on her thoughts.

Unfortunately, her years of hard work as a secret agent meant that she had never had the time to master certain skills—like the basics of Home Economics.

"How can one of my finest operatives *live* like this?" Lensherr muttered over the rim of his wine glass.

"What do you *expect* from me, Magneto?" Mystique snapped, pointing to the mess hanging on the wall. "I'm a *spy,* not a gourmet chef—I'm rarely here in South Beach most of the time. If you want a five-star meal, go down to Ocean Drive—I'm sure one of the restaurants there would have a board of fare suitable for your delicate palette." She paused, and a shark-like grin slowly crept over her features. "Oh, but you can't *do* that, can you?" She nodded, in complete agreement with herself. "That's right—you're a wanted man. The 'Butcher of Paris,' I believe the Ministry of Information has tagged you. Were you to set a single foot outside this modest home, it would only be a matter of seconds before one of my less-than-trustworthy-but-always-nosy neighbors notified von Doom's stormtroopers that you were back in the States." She tapped a slender index finger against her chin and gazed at the ceiling, deep in thought. "Mmmm ... I wonder what they're serving as a last meal at The Vault—" her eyes lowered to fix on Lensherr "—if you were to *make* it that far without 'accidentally' being killed while trying to escape."

Lensherr said nothing, opting instead to meet Mystique's haughty gaze with one of cool indifference. Idly, he wondered how quickly he could smash that look from her face were he to cause the iron in her blood to form a clot in her brain—and then have it burst.

"I, on the other hand," Mystique continued, "have no such fears of being discovered." Instantly, her face, her body, even her clothing, began to blur and twist and assume a new form; within seconds, she had become the spitting image of Victor von Doom, right down to the Mandarin power rings worn on each finger. "When one is a shapeshifter," she said, her voice a perfect imitation of the Emperor's, "who can say *what* one's true face really is?"

Lensherr applauded without any trace of enthusiasm; obviously, his roundabout trip to Florida from Mauritania hadn't done anything to improve his mood. "Bravo, Mystique, bravo," he said sarcastically. "I'm certain such useless displays of your abilities make you extremely popular in the circles in which you travel; as for myself, I refuse to be goaded into childish brooding by false images of a man who will soon be slain by my own hand."

The faux von Doom wagged a disapproving finger at "his" guest. "You *really* should work on your sense of humor, Erik. All this talk of dead men and retribution—it makes you incredibly soporific at times."

"Is that so?" Lensherr replied, raising an eyebrow. "My plans for overthrowing von Doom make you drowsy, Raven?" Now, it was his turn to smile menacingly. "Well, if you feel fatigued by my company, then perhaps you should retire for the evening. I shall be more than delighted to tuck you in—permanently."

A knock on the front door put a swift end to any further verbal jousting. In the time it took Lensherr to glance from the portal back to Mystique, she had undergone another transformation—a wrinkled, hunched-over, white-haired woman in her eighties was now standing before him. Arthritic fingers smoothed out the dark-blue dress and white apron that had replaced von Doom's pressed business suit. Slowly, the octogenarian moved toward the front of the house, pausing to reach into a closet and pull out a formidable-looking handgun; Lensherr recognized it as an Israeli-made Desert Eagle .45.

"Who is it?" Mystique called out in a quavery, high-pitched voice.

"Pizza delivery," replied a male voice from the other side of the door.

Still moving forward, the old woman slowly, quietly, pulled back the slide on the top of the gun to chamber a round. Lensherr followed her out into the hallway, grabbing his helmet from the top of a coat rack, prepared to go into battle. By the time Mystique reached the door, the Eagle's hammer was cocked, and the gun was hidden behind her back. She unlocked the deadbolt, released the security chain, and slowly opened the door.

"Oh," Lensherr heard the old woman say in Mystique's normally silky voice. "It's you clowns." She stepped back, and a pair of men entered the front hall. Both of them carried pizza boxes; the air in the hallway filled with the aroma of tomato sauce and melted cheese. One man was tall and thin, with sharp, hawklike features and a Julius Caesar hairstyle that had gone out of vogue with the demise of gladiator movies in the late 1950s. His name was Forge, and he was both a Cheyenne Indian shaman *and* a mutant gifted with an ability to create incredible—and frequently deadly—mechanical devices from the smallest piles of spare parts and wiring.

What Forge possessed in sheer brain power, the other man more than matched in sheer physicality. Powerfully built, with movie star looks and shoulder-length red hair tied back in a ponytail, Fabian Cortez, like his associates, was a mutant. *Un*like his fellow conspirators, though, Cortez's unique ability was that he was able to amplify *other* mutants' powers, often beyond their control; thus, if a member of *Homo sapiens superior* could fire energy blasts from his or her hands, that person, under Cortez's influence, would be able to level mountains—with the unfortunate side effect that the recoil would more than likely help provide enough velocity to put them in orbit around the Earth.

A mixed blessing, to be sure.

Mystique closed the door and shifted back to her natural, midnight-blue form, then cautiously uncocked the hammer of the Desert Eagle and placed it on a small table nearby. "What've you got in the boxes, boys?"

Forge lifted the top of the one he held; inside, a vegetable-laden pizza quietly bubbled, fresh from the oven. "Having already sampled your culinary skills, Raven, we decided to bring our own food." He sniffed the air, and his features twisted in disgust. "Tuna casserole again, huh?" He shook his head. "How can one of our finest operatives *live* like this?"

Mystique grunted in reply and strode back to the dining room, ignoring Lensherr's amused expression. The three men followed her.

"So," Lensherr began as they convened at the table, "has my son told you of my plans?"

"A small portion, lord," Cortez replied. "Merely that you wish to put a swift end to the rule of that annoying flatscan, von Doom."

"Flatscan." A term coined by Cortez ages ago to define humans—"those genetic dead ends unblessed with our mutant abilities," as he had put it. Lensherr allowed a trace of a smile to crease his face. What *better* way to describe the bottom-most rung on man's evolutionary ladder?

Lensherr nodded. "I understand that the tenth anniversary of that braggart's rise to power is to be celebrated shortly, and that his aides fear I will take that opportunity to try and strike him down." He smiled maliciously. "I do not wish to shatter their expectations."

Mystique glared at him. "And why am *I* just hearing this for the first time? You've been here two days, Magnus, and you never once hinted that you were planning something so incredibly . . . *foolish.*"

"I keep my own council, Raven," Lensherr replied curtly. *"Your* function is to provide me with information and support my actions—not voice your opposition. I have made my decision—" his eyes narrowed "—and the matter is not open to debate."

"Well," Forge said around a mouthful of pizza, "the timing couldn't be better to start making our preparations. From what I've heard through the grapevine, some major dust-up in New York that happened today has got von Doom's nose out of joint." He paused. "That reminds me . . ." He stood, bowed to Lensherr. "Excuse me for a moment—I need to check on something." Lensherr waved a dismissive hand, and Forge headed for the living room.

"As I was saying, Cortez," the mutant overlord continued, "the concept of destroying that armor-plated scum before an audience of billions has great appeal for me. I'm certain my . . . performance will be the talk of the entire planet the next day—the *first* day of the Age of *Homo superior.*"

Cortez nodded eagerly, eyes shining brightly with undisguised passion, as one would expect from an acolyte devoted so completely to a cause—and a charismatic leader.

"Uh, folks?" Forge called from the living room. "I think you all better take a look at this."

Stepping from the kitchen, the trio were greeted by the machinesmith, who waved them toward the couch.

"What—" Lensherr began.

"Just watch," Forge replied. He pointed to the television, on which could be seen an image of a dark-suited, blond-haired woman in her mid-twenties, holding a microphone. She was standing before the cordoned-off battlezone that had once been the New York Public Library plaza; police officers and Guardsmen kept curious passersby from getting too close to the crime scene. Forge pressed the volume control on the remote.

"—high-ranking official at the Ministry of Information reported that the unprovoked attack on a group of Hunters that took place here in midtown Manhattan this afternoon was initiated by sympathizers of the notorious Magneto, the so-called 'Butcher of Paris,' " the woman stated.

"You see, Magnus?" Mystique said, glancing at Lensherr. "The media just *loves* you."

"*Silence,*" Lensherr snapped.

"Despite severe injuries to some members of the team," the reporter continued, "the Hunters were able to apprehend the superpowered terrorists before they could carry out their plans to detonate a small nuclear device that they had smuggled into the city. It is now expected that, with the assistance of anti-terrorist experts from the government organization S.H.I.E.L.D., information will soon be acquired from the prisoners that will ultimately lead to the capture of their infamous leader.

"Joy Mercado, CNN."

Forge lowered the television's volume as the broadcast cut to a commercial for the upcoming release of the *Doom's Patrol* motion picture. He turned to Lensherr. "Pietro didn't mention anything about you sending in an advance team to stir things up."

"Because I did not order one to do so," Lensherr replied. "Whoever these 'terrorists' are, whatever their motives may be, they acted without my knowledge. Do you really think I'd be so foolish as to have any use for a bunch of sycophantic bomb-carriers idiotic enough to openly confront a group of highly-skilled Hunters?" He pressed his lips together in a firm, straight line and sat back on the couch to think. "Yet, such actions—whether they be true, or mere fabrications created by von Doom's propaganda machine—demonstrate that there *are* still those who share our opposition to that Latverian windbag; perhaps we even share the same dream of making our race the supreme form of life on Earth." He nodded slowly, settled his chin between the thumb and forefinger of his right hand, and stared into space. "And if these individuals are powerful enough to have injured a pack of von Doom's bloodhounds . . ." His voice trailed off, and he sat silently.

After a few moments, Forge politely cleared his throat. "Uh, Erik? You want to clue us in as to what you're thinking?"

Slowly, Lensherr's glazed-over eyes cleared. He leaned forward, then turned to Cortez. "Contact my son. Have him speak with his associate in Washington. I want to know where the prisoners were taken, and how much time remains before they are to be executed."

"It will be done, dread lord," Cortez said immediately.

"Just a moment. What sort of scheme is running through that devious mind of yours, Magnus?" Mystique asked, arms folded across her chest.

"An inspired bit of deviltry," Lensherr replied, a mischievous smile curling his lips. "If these alleged 'followers' of mine are as opposed to von Doom as we, perhaps an alliance is in order."

"And how, pray tell, do we go about signing up these new recruits to the cause?" Mystique shot back.

Lensherr's smile broadened. "It's quite simple, child. All we need do is get to them before they're killed during their interrogations . . ."

# 12

"**Y**OU HAVE a lovely frontal lobe," an unknown male voice commented.

"W-what . . . ?" Phoenix asked. Her head was pounding like a drum beat, making it extremely difficult to focus her thoughts. She licked dry lips and opened her eyes, then quickly shut them as a blinding light momentarily seared her retinas. Wincing in pain, she tried to raise a hand to shade her eyes, only to find she was unable to move her arms.

"I wouldn't bother moving around too much," her unseen companion said. "You're still on the mend from that concussion you received, and the restraints on your chair are locked in place."

Slowly, cautiously, Phoenix half opened her eyes; just enough to provide some vision and give her an idea of her surroundings. She tried to move her head, but it was held in place by some sort of device she couldn't see; a coarse leather strap bit into the flesh of her throat when she made the slightest movement. She was in the center of a room with metal walls and large glass observation windows, the lighting low except for the halogen lamps shining directly on her. By turning her gaze downward, she could see that she was sitting in a high-tech chair of some sort, her arms and legs held fast by massive clamps.

And that she was wearing her costume.

Now, her eyes opened fully, all traces of her headache vanishing in an instant; her lips pulled back in a snarl. Looking around, her gaze fastened on a bear of a man, standing just off to one side. He was close to seven feet tall, with a build that rivaled the Hulk's; like the green-skinned behemoth, the man's closely-cropped hair was a bright emerald hue, but his skin tone was a normal pink coloration. Dressed in dark slacks and shoes, a starched white dress shirt, and an even whiter laboratory coat, the man studied the redheaded mutant with an even stare.

"Who are you?" Phoenix demanded.

"My name is Dr. Leonard Samson," the man replied. "I'm one of the assistant directors here."

"And where is 'here'?"

"Psi Division Headquarters. In Langley, Virginia."

"And are *you* the one who dressed me in my costume?" she demanded. To her surprise, Samson actually blushed.

"Uh . . . no," he replied. "The nurses did that some time after you were brought in."

She frowned. "Any particular reason for that, Doctor?"

"Well, you and your friends have made us all curious . . . uh . . ."

"Phoenix," Jean replied. "Like the bird."

Samson nodded. "I understand the mythological reference. As I was saying, Phoenix, your group—and you in particular—have piqued our interests. It's not often we come across unregistered telepaths who also possess telekinetic abilities. Or who can single-handedly mind-sweep an area the size of Manhattan."

"I'm glad you're impressed," Phoenix replied sarcastically.

"By dressing all of you in those colorful uniforms of yours," Samson explained, "we were hoping that the Imperial Identification Network might be able to recognize you in your costumed identities, since there seem to be no records of your civilian lives." He shook his head. "No luck there."

Having quickly grown tired of the conversation, Phoenix closed her eyes and focused her thoughts at him. *All right, Doctor, I've had enough idle chatter for one day. I want you to tell me everything about this place, and where my friends are. Then you're going to release me and show me a way out of here.* She paused, waiting for his mind to respond, to provide her with information.

But, for some reason, nothing happened.

Samson gazed at her for a moment, then slowly nodded in understanding. "Ah. You're probably wondering why you can't get inside my head." He smiled, then shrugged when she didn't respond. "Sorry—professional humor. There's a neural inhibitor attached to the base of your spine; basically, it shuts down the synapses of your brain that allow you to activate your powers. Your friends have also been tagged with them." He flashed a boyish grin. "We can't exactly have you people running around the facility fully-powered, possibly damaging billions of dollars of delicate equipment, can we? The taxpayers would kill us—not to mention the Emperor."

Phoenix paused to mull this over. No powers, trapped in a building full of telepaths, telekinetics, and armed guards, and no immediate means of escape...

*All right—stay calm,* Jean told herself. *You've gotten out of tougher scrapes—against Magneto, the Brood, Apocalypse . . . Hell, you've even come back from the dead once or thrice. All you need is some* time *to figure a way out of this.* She frowned. *But I don't have* time—*none of us do. Not with Roma getting ready to destroy this plane of reality, and Saturnyne probably still egging her on to do it . . .*

"Where *are* my friends?" she asked.

"Elsewhere in the facility," Samson replied. "Being questioned by other members of the staff." He paused. "Except for the one who died, of course."

Jean's eyes widened in shock. *Scott . . . ?* she thought.

"Who—who was it?" she asked hesitantly.

"A woman," Samson answered. He picked up a clipboard from a nearby control console, studied the sheets of paper attached to it. "Carol Danvers, according to the fingerprint match."

Jean allowed herself to breathe again, grateful to learn her husband still lived, but now a feeling of guilt swept over her. What right did *she* have to feel contentment, knowing that one of her friends had been lost, knowing that she had withheld information from her—information gathered from her own mind?

*Oh, Carol, I am so, so sorry . . .*

"Says here she was a guest at the Westchester detainee camp," Samson continued. He glanced up from the clipboard. "I imagine, then, it was your group that was responsible for the camp's destruction two days ago."

"Just what are you planning to do with me?" Jean asked, ignoring his leading comment. She rolled her eyes upward, to indicate the device into which her head was strapped. "I doubt you intend to experiment with hairstyles; if you are, though, I like mine just the way it is."

"*I* am not planning anything, Phoenix," the green-haired assistant director replied. "But there are some people from S.H.I.E.L.D. on their way here to ask you questions."

A nervous shiver ran through Jean's body, and she forced herself to remain calm. Back when the world was normal, she and the X-Men had had more than a few run-ins with the members of the super-secret intelligence organization. They weren't exactly the most likable people in the universe—or the most trustworthy, given the fact that the Psi Division of this reality was based on a much smaller version that operated from the depths of the S.H.I.E.L.D. helicarrier.

"The Cerebrum Scanner," Samson continued, pointing to the machinery above Jean's head, "serves two functions: The first is to break down any psychic barriers you may have erected around your mind—that's done through a combination of electroshock treatments and telepathic contact with a number of our agents. The second is to extract memories that you may have been trained to suppress. I understand Magneto has taught his followers well in ways to resist psi-probes. Rest assured, though: it won't take the machine very long to break through that kind of conditioning."

"This is a *mind ripper?*" Phoenix said angrily. "You're just going to *tear out* my memories and paw through them, rather than ask me questions that, I assure you, I don't have any answers for?"

Samson shook his head. "Not me—the S.H.I.E.L.D. people will be running the interrogation. And I certainly *hope* it won't come down to them forcibly extracting the information they're seeking from your brain." He shrugged. "But that, as the saying goes, is entirely up to you." He glanced at his wristwatch. "Look, I hate to chat and run, Phoenix, but I have a Board of Directors meeting to attend—your group's presence has started a great deal of buzz around Washington, what with all the renewed talk of Magneto possibly coming out of hiding to attack the Emperor. We've been on alert since you were brought in."

"Well, don't let *me* keep you," Phoenix said sarcastically.

Samson grunted. "I'm sure the S.H.I.E.L.D. people will be along any minute." His lips curled into a half smile. "Try not to go wandering off before they get here, all right?"

Jean stared daggers into the back of his head as he walked away.

Alone with her thoughts, Phoenix nervously chewed her bottom lip, and wondered exactly what kind of techniques were used by *this* version of the espionage organization to extract information from their prisoners ...

It was the closest thing to having a red-hot poker shoved into her eyes.

Strapped to an examination table, her powers deactivated by a neural inhibitor, Rogue screamed in agony as the psychic probe slowly burned through each layer of the complex mental defenses that Professor Xavier had created for all his students, for exactly these kinds of situations.

For Rogue and the other X-Men, as it had been for Carol Danvers, the key to the defense was in finding a "happy place"—the center of calm that existed in the subconscious—and building protective walls around it. In Rogue's case, that sanctuary came in the form of a small brook that ran near her home, though she hadn't been back there in real life for years. Still, it was the perfect setting to which a troubled mind could find some measure of tranquillity—the soothing murmur of the water, the gentle whisper of a soft autumn breeze that prickled the skin, and a glint of golden sunlight that shone brightly from between the mountains in the distance.

And it was on the edge of that imaginary brook that Rogue now huddled, trying her best to ignore the tremors that ran through her mental landscape, to shut out the pain that caused her real body to convulse as each layer of her mind was peeled away. She knew it was a losing battle, though—prior experience with psi-powered opponents had made it quite apparent that if they wanted information, not even barriers created by the world's most powerful telepath would stand in their way for long.

That didn't mean she was willing to just hand over information to spare herself any further torture—the last thing she wanted to divulge was that the X-Men's goal was nothing less than the total destruction of Doctor Doom's worldwide empire. Fortunately—or rather, unfortunately, given the mounting fervor with which they relentlessly battered her mind—the type of information her captors were seeking was related to another, though related, matter: the whereabouts of Magneto. That knowledge wasn't in her possession; she had told them that from the start.

Of course, they hadn't believed her.

Sitting by the brook, Rogue watched with increasing horror as the sunlight began to fade, and the air grew colder.

A storm was brewing, just over the horizon . . .

Standing beside the mutant, her gloved hands savagely pressing against the prone woman's temples, Psi Division Director Emma Frost was quickly losing patience. She had decided to start with the skunk-haired powerhouse because she appeared to be the

weakest link among the prisoners, what with her wealth of inse-
curities lying on the surface of her mind, all just waiting to be
turned against her by a highly-skilled telepath.

Unfortunately, after forcibly creating a psychic link with this
"Rogue" in the first stage of the interrogation, matters had become
far more complicated than Frost could have imagined. Now, an
hour later, the armpits of her white blouse were soaked with perspiration, and her white, shoulder-length hair was a damp, disheveled mass of tangles.

"It doesn't matter how long this is going to take," she snarled
through gritted teeth. "Eventually, I'm going to break through . . .
and then I'll scoop out all your lovely thoughts like the finest
sherbet—and devour them." Taking a deep breath, she focused her
incredible psychic powers on the next "wall" in Rogue's mind and
drilled away at it like a jackhammer cracking through stone.

*TELL ME WHAT I WANT TO KNOW, YOU LITTLE BACK-
WOODS WITCH!* she screamed through the psychic link. *TELL ME
ALL ABOUT MAGNETO—WHERE HE'S HIDING, WHAT HIS
PLANS ARE—OR I'LL BURN OUT EVERY SYNAPSE IN YOUR
BRAIN, AND LEAVE YOU A DROOLING VEGETABLE!*

Tears streaming from her eyes, Rogue whimpered as the attack
continued, and tried to focus on a bubbling brook that she could
only see with her mind's eye.

*Jean, where are you . . . ?*

Cyclops's entire body was a mass of bruises and broken bones.
His head was pounding from a hairline fracture, his torso ached
from a half-dozen purplish welts scattered across his chest and
abdomen—a dull, throbbing pain, made worse by the leather straps
that bound him to the metal chair in which he was sitting—and
the bones of his right arm were just about held together by a
thread. The shattered limb had been fitted with a cast on the trip
down to Langley, but it wouldn't be of any use to him for at least
six to eight weeks—not counting the additional weeks of rehabil-
itative treatments . . . should the universe live that long.

Yet, despite his massive injuries, his concerns were centered on his wife. He remembered how the attack at the library had started because Doom's thugs had come for Jean. And after that terrible blow to the head she had taken, was there a chance she might be—

Scott shook his head. No. He refused to believe she was gone. Their psychic link had been broken, but that only meant they were unable to communicate for the moment. Jean *was* in this place—somewhere—and if he ever got the chance to find her, hold her, smell the sweet fragrance of her hair once more, then no one—not Doom, not Magneto, *no one*—would ever be able to keep them apart again.

*Just hold on, Jean. Hold on . . .*

"This is the leader?" a male voice asked from behind him.

Cyclops started. He recognized that voice.

"Shaw!" he shouted. "Sebastian Shaw! Where are you?"

With surprising quickness, Shaw stepped around to place himself within Cyclops's range of vision, then yanked the visor from the younger mutant's head. Instinctively, Cyclops shut his eyes, prepared to hold back the torrent of destructive energies that were sure to follow, but the burning, rushing sensation that always accompanied a surge of optical power never came about—the neural inhibitor at work, he surmised. Slowly, he opened his eyes.

Shaw was standing in front of him, his attention focused on the visor, turning it every which way in his hands; clearly, he was trying to figure out how it worked.

"Where are the others?" Cyclops demanded.

"I'd be more concerned for my own well-being, were I in your position, young man," Shaw replied. He placed the visor over his eyes. "Ruby quartz, eh? I imagine that allows you to see the world through the proverbial rose-colored glasses." He chuckled at his little joke. "Don't worry about your friends—they're receiving the same sort of hospitality any traitor to the Empire would get after they've been brought in for questioning."

An image of Jean—lying face down on the plaza, being kicked

by Mastermind—formed in Scott's mind's eye, but he fought down the urge to uselessly struggle against his bonds and snarl impotent threats at his captors. Better he remain calm and play for time.

"And when does Doom plan to show up?" he asked. "It wouldn't be like him to miss an opportunity to gloat over a fallen enemy—especially when they're old friends of his wife."

*That* got Shaw's attention. He lowered the visor and raised a quizzical eyebrow. "Friends of the Empress, are you?" He slowly shook his head and made a "tutting" sound. "I never would have imagined Ororo could be so desperate for companionship that she would resort to trawling amongst the rabble." He shrugged. "Ah, well—such are the eccentricities of the rich and powerful. As for the Emperor, he couldn't be here—he has far more important matters to address than what to do with a poorly-organized group of mutants who've lost their way and forgotten their stations in life." Shaw smiled maliciously. *"That* particular topic, I'm pleased to say, has been entirely left up to *me* to resolve."

Handing the visor over to a young man wearing a lab coat, Shaw removed his jacket and began rolling up his shirt sleeves.

"You're probably wondering what I'm doing," he said. "Well, I know the Psi-Division enjoys poking around in people's mind, flipping through their memories like magazines on a newsstand, but I've always prided myself on being a bit more hands-on with my questioning—especially when it comes to matters involving Magneto."

Scott was nonplused. "You're going to *beat* the answers out of me?" he asked. "While I'm tied to a chair with a broken arm?"

"Not at all, my boy," Shaw replied. A fire burned in his dark eyes. "I'm going to thrash you to within an inch of your life, and *then* I'm going to ask my questions. It spares us both that whole annoying process of raising the level of punishment each time you refuse to answer, and dispenses with the time-consuming work involved in stripping away the psychic barriers protecting your mind. This way, by using my power to increase my strength kinetically, each blow I land becomes more powerful than the last, until I am literally grinding your bones to paste. With such ex-cruciating pain coursing through every fiber of your being, the matter of mental barriers becomes a non-issue." Shaw handed his jacket to his assistant and stepped toward Scott. "Shall we begin . . . ?"

The first blow pulverized Scott's already shattered humerus.

After that, his mind burning with pain, he could only pray that Shaw's arms would begin to tire long before the Black King wound up killing him.

He was dying.

Lying on a cot in the darkness of his cell, Remy LeBeau breathed laboriously, each inhalation and exhalation an effort of almost Herculean proportions. The circuitry and machinery that had started growing on his body back in New York had continued to spread until he now looked more like a robot pretending to be a man.

And he felt so very, very cold . . .

He'd awakened shortly after arriving at the facility, to be greeted by the sight of a dozen or so men and women huddled around him, all of them covered head-to-toe in yellow Hazardous Material protective suits. There had been a lot of talk about "techno-organic viruses"—whatever those were—and the dangers of exposure and a lot of other scientific mumbo-jumbo Remy didn't understand. Some Asian woman in green latex, standing in an adjoining observation room, had inquired as to his chances of survival. She'd been told they were nil—he had only hours at the most left to live, a day if he was lucky.

"Then I have no use for him," she'd said angrily, and walked away.

He'd been dumped in the cell soon after that brief exchange, isolated from the rest of the facility while his captors waited for the final stages of the metamorphosis to run their course. They wouldn't have all that long to wait.

Remy shuddered. His heart was beating much slower now, his skin icy to the touch. He didn't even react as the latest strands of monofilaments forced its way through his pores, tearing through his flesh like razor-sharp hairs.

He couldn't really feel much of anything, as a matter of fact.

Death was close now. Her chilly hand was pressing down on his chest, drawing away what little warmth remained in his body. A feeling of loss washed over Remy, and he choked back a sob. It wasn't that he feared death—Lord only knew how often he'd played "tag" with her since his days as a young pickpocket on the streets of New Orleans.

It was because he knew that he was going to die, alone, without ever having given his heart completely to the one woman who had found the soul of a poet deep within the breast of a simple thief.

A tear trickled from his remaining eye; it smelt of machine oil.

"Ah, *chere,*" he mumbled, his voice sounding more like an electronic burbling. "I'm sorry we didn't make dat concert . . ."

*Heavenly Father, grant me the strength to survive this ordeal . . .*

Kurt Wagner had always been a devout Roman Catholic; in his younger days, he'd even considered joining the priesthood. An ironic situation, given his demonic appearance.

Of course, the lure of the seminary had been ultimately replaced by a higher calling of sorts—the chance to aid Professor Charles Xavier in bringing about his dream of humanity and mutantkind one day walking, hand in hand, down the path to everlasting peace. It had been the right choice to make, Kurt had always been certain of that, and up till now he had never been proven wrong. Thus, secure in mind and spirit, he had devoted his life to The Dream, rarely feeling the need to bother the Almighty with pleas for assistance.

But if ever there was a time he truly needed the Lord's help, that time was right now. He couldn't teleport, couldn't melt into the shadows—there were none, the room being filled with blinding light—and the drugs he'd been given were wearing down his resistance to the psychic probing of the two people sitting across from him.

The woman was Wilhelmina—tall and willowy, with the face of a supermodel and the kind of condescending attitude one could only find in a follower of a despot like Doctor Doom. The man was William—broad-shouldered, powerfully built, with a head that seemed attached to his body without the benefit of a neck. Both wore dark blue uniforms with high starched collars.

"Talk, Wagner!" the woman demanded. "That bucketheaded leader of yours can't be worth all this pain and suffering! Do you *like* working for a mass-murderer? Was the bombing of Paris just another 'acceptable loss' for the realization of his precious 'dream'?" She pointed a commanding finger at him. "You *will* tell us everything, you blasted freak, or I'll reach into that feeble little mind of yours and rip out every memory you've got!"

"Please, Kurt," urged William. "Just tell us what you know, and we'll end the interrogation right now—" he glanced at his partner "—before it gets out of control."

Kurt's mouth slid into a lopsided grin. "This must be . . . the 'good cop/bad cop' scenario . . . I've seen so often . . . on American television . . ." He rolled his head around on his shoulders to look at the woman. "You are far too . . . attractive . . . to play the . . . 'bad cop,' *fraulein* . . ."

William slapped his hands down on the table and jumped to his feet. "This is ridiculous!" he barked. "I'm *tired* of playing around with this freak!" He leaned forward and punched Kurt in the face with a meaty fist, almost pitching him from his chair. The wiry X-Man chuckled softly as a thin line of blood—a bright red streak against a midnight-blue field—trickled from the corner of his mouth.

"*Now* . . . who's the . . . 'bad cop' . . . ?" he said.

Wilhelmina rose to her feet and walked around the table. She grabbed Kurt's chin and forced him to look into her eyes. "You like movies, don't you, Kurt?" She smiled as his eyes widened in surprise. "Didn't think I'd gotten in there, did you? But I *did.*" The telepath chuckled. "It seems Miss Frost was wrong about which one of you was the weakest link—and won't *she* be angry when she finds out." Kurt tried to pull his head away, but she held on fast. "I'm not all the way in, of course—that will take some time. But I *have* been able to sift through the thoughts lying on the surface of your mind—quite an eclectic bunch of images, I must say: movies you've seen recently . . . your friends . . . religious icons. Are you a religious man, Mr. Wagner?"

"Why should *you* care?" Kurt growled.

"Actually, I *don't,*" Wilhelmina replied. "But reading your personal messages to the Almighty for help gives me such . . . wonderful ideas. William?"

The big man's eyes flashed, and Kurt was suddenly airborne, tossed across the room by the sheer force of William's telekinetic powers. He slammed hard against the far wall, the breath crushed from his lungs, and hung there, arms spread wide, two feet above the floor.

Wilhelmina reached into one of her boots and pulled out a pair of throwing knives—a gift from her grandfather when she had turned sixteen. Fluorescent light played along cold, thin steel as she gazed at Kurt's prostrate form.

"Such wonderful ideas . . ." she purred.

*Like the man said, "I can't be dead—I'm achin' too much all over."*

Logan opened his eyes. He certainly couldn't be dead—not unless St. Peter now operated his *This is Your Life on Earth* review of prospective heavenly candidates in a sterile examining room. And not unless St. Peter had been replaced by a group of gibbering scientists, dark-uniformed psi-agents, and heavily-armed guards. Their backs were turned to him; obviously, they thought he was still unconscious.

As they yammered away about who he might be, and how poorly the other interrogations were going—at least, that was the talk around the facility—he heard one of the scientists mention the neural inhibitors that had been implanted in the prisoners, and how well *they* were still functioning. What his captors hadn't realized, though, was that, in Logan's case, the inhibitor had shut down his heightened senses, and his mutant healing factor—but, hopefully, not his claws.

*An' that's the big mistake that's really gonna cost ya, boys an' girls,* he thought, eyeing his captors. *The kinda mistake that can kill.*

Of course, such dark thoughts could not go unnoticed in a facility crawling with telepaths and telekinetics.

"The prisoner!" one of the male telepaths cried. "He's awake!"

Logan couldn't wait any longer. Knowing what would happen if he *did* release his deadly bio-weapons without an active healing factor—he'd gone through *that* painful experience a few times too many during his missions with the X-Men—Logan nevertheless prepared himself for the ordeal. He gritted his teeth, tensed the muscles in his forearms, screwed his eyes tightly shut.

And then triggered his claws.

The inhuman howl that filled the examination room sent a chill up the spine of everyone standing around him—and those passing in the outside hallway. Before the scientists or telepaths could recover from the shock, Logan had torn through his restraints and leapt at them, lashing out with deadly precision.

He crashed through the door and out into the hallway, ignoring the burning sensation in his arms, and the blood pouring from the open wounds created by the claws when they broke through the skin on the backs of his hands. Normally, his healing factor would have handled the damage already, stanching the bloodflow and repairing the torn skin, but the inhibitor was still functioning, still denying him

*If I don't make this jailbreak count for somethin' an' find a way outta here 'fore my injuries get t'me,* Logan thought, *I'm gonna feel pretty damn stupid passin' out from loss o' blood.* He staggered around a corner—

And was struck by a volley of tranquilizer darts.

They pierced his arms, his legs, his throat—close to two dozen feather-tipped missiles, each filled with enough sedatives to bring down an elephant. Yet the man known as Wolverine remained standing.

"That the *best* you losers can do?" Logan snarled.

A rush of adrenaline surged through his body and, roaring like a maddened lion, he rushed toward the guards, fully intending to dispose of as many of them as possible before his brain was disconnected from the control of his muscles. He got within striking distance of his first target—

And then the sedatives finally kicked in. So powerful was the dosage that Logan didn't even feel his nose break as his face violently struck the linoleum flooring.

"Well," one of the guards remarked, "that oughtta keep the midget from makin' any more trouble for a while..."

Two hours.

They'd left her alone for the better part of two hours.

Phoenix closed her eyes and tried for the tenth time to slip into a meditative trance. Unfortunately, as before, she wasn't able to attain a higher level of consciousness due to some physical matters beyond her control: her stomach rumbled with hunger; there was a maddening itch between her shoulder blades that couldn't be soothed even by rubbing against the back of the chair; her left calf muscles twitched slightly—the first signs of an oncoming cramp from having remained in one position for too long. And her butt had fallen asleep.

The door opened, and Phoenix opened her eyes to see a woman clad in skintight green latex stride into the room. She was accompanied by a tall, wiry man in his fifties with short, graying hair and a pencil-thin mustache; he was dressed in the black leather uniform of an agent of S.H.I.E.L.D. Though she didn't know who the man was, it only took Jean a moment to recognize the woman.

"Viper?" she said.

The woman smiled, without warmth. "You know of me," she

replied, clearly satisfied with that knowledge. "Good." She gestured toward her associate. "This is Agent Maynard Tyboldt—he's going to assist me while we indulge in a little girl talk. I'm sure you know what I mean: You tell me how a group of Magneto's super-powered bootlickers can move about the Empire freely for who knows how many years, without being detected by either the Psi Division or S.H.I.E.L.D.; where your cowardly leader has been hiding himself for the past year; and what his plans are now that the White House has started releasing details about the Emperor's anniversary celebration. Maybe then I'll be able to get von Doom off my back." She snorted. "Tell *me* I don't know how to do my job . . ."

"Look," Phoenix said. "I don't *know* where Magneto is; I haven't had any contact with the man for quite a while. And even if I *did* know, what makes you think I'd be willing to assist you in killing him? Besides, there are far more important things at stake than providing a salve for your wounded pride."

"Ah. Insulting your captors to start things off, eh? That's *really* not a smart move, love." The Director sighed. "And here Samson was convinced you were the most intelligent among the prisoners—I'm beginning to think his opinion was influenced by nothing more than a pretty face. So much for the cool detachment of scientists." She pursed her lips. "Of course, you're not the only plaything available to me. I wonder what that hunk with the eyebeams could tell me—given the proper stimulus . . ."

Though she knew better than to allow herself to be baited so easily, Jean couldn't stop her lips from pulling back in a snarl.

Viper raised an intrigued eyebrow. "Well, *that* certainly produced my first response of the day." She leaned forward, her voice dropping to a conspiratorial whisper. "Tell me, dear, are you two more than friends? Lovers, perhaps?"

"*Please*, Viper, you've got to release me—you've got to release my friends," Jean urged. "The world is in terrible danger."

Viper slowly shook her head in mock sadness and stepped back.

"You know, I was hoping that, after a year in hiding, Magneto would have provided his followers with a better script, but you're still spouting the same old rhetoric: the Emperor is bad, the Emperor is evil, the Emperor will destroy us all in the end. I will admit, though—you're much more passionate in your beliefs than most of the other traitors I've . . . talked to." She shrugged. "But we'll have plenty of time to discuss ideologies—after we've ripped yours from your mind." She turned toward Tyboldt. "You may begin the extraction process, Doctor."

Tyboldt nodded and walked out of Jean's view; she heard him moving around behind her, flicking switches and pressing buttons. The chair began to hum, increasing in volume until the vibrations made the fillings in Jean's teeth rattle.

"Viper, pl—" she began, only to be silenced as the beautiful S.H.I.E.L.D. director gently placed a latex-encased finger against her lips.

"Sshhh," Viper said gently, and smiled—like a mother reassuring her daughter that the only monster she needed to fear . . . was the one right in front of her. "The time for civil conversations has passed." She gently stroked Jean's cheek. "Now I don't want to hear another word from you, young lady. You should save your strength—" the smile became a shark-toothed grin "—you'll need it for screaming."

"No!" Jean cried. "You've got to listen to—"

Any further protestations were cut short as Viper jammed a rubber ball-like device between Jean's teeth and secured it to the straps holding her head in place.

"Can't have you biting your tongue off, love," the S.H.I.E.L.D. director explained. "We wouldn't be able to talk later—and we *are* going to have oh-so-much to talk *about*, correct?" She looked past Jean, to Tyboldt. "Level One."

The first electrical shock surged through the chair, causing Jean to jerk spasmodically against her restraints for three or four seconds. When the power was shut down, she slumped back against the chair, feeling dizzy and nauseous, unable to think clearly. Instantly, she felt the touch of a dozen minds—prodding, probing, trying to worm their way past her psi-screens.

She wouldn't let them.

"Level One no good," Tyboldt said. "She's resisting."

Viper glanced at Jean; a tear was running from the redheaded mutant's right eye. "Putting up a fight? Good—I despise weak people." She gestured to Tyboldt. "Level Two."

Now it felt as though every inch of her body was on fire; she could smell strands of her hair burning. The shock lasted a few seconds longer this time, making it difficult for her to focus her eyes, making the pounding in her head start up again as the momentarily forgotten effects of her concussion washed over her consciousness, threatening to drag her into darkness.

And again the probing bored away at her mind, stronger this time—or was she beginning to weaken . . . ?

Whatever was happening, she refused to give Viper her satisfaction. She wouldn't scream.

"Still unable to break through," Tyboldt reported, glancing at his monitors. He shook his head in wonderment. "Amazing. Even with the inhibitor running, even with a head injury and two doses of electroshock, she's still able to hold off a dozen of our best agents." He looked up from his instruments. "Director, if these readings are correct, I'm beginning to think this young woman might be the most *powerful* telepath on the planet." There was an almost reverent tone to his voice. "If we could somehow convince her to work for the Empire . . ."

The head of S.H.I.E.L.D. wasn't as impressed. "I'm a spy, Tyboldt, not a recruitment officer—in my line of work, this redheaded bimbo is one of two things: a source of information, or a threat to the Empire that needs to be eliminated. Telling me she's the most powerful *anything* on the planet just guarantees a quick trip to the morgue for her. If you're so completely awestruck by the workings of the mutant brain, feel free to take her apart at the autopsy when we're done here. I'd *also* love to see what makes her tick ... but only *after* I've gotten what I want."

Tyboldt said nothing, wisely choosing instead to return his attention to the monitors before him.

Viper leaned close to Jean; snot and a few spots of blood had crusted along the edge of Phoenix's nose, and she was breathing heavily. "Just thought you'd like to know," the Director said quietly. "There are thirteen levels of extraction. I understand no one has ever made it past the fifth level ... without becoming a catatonic vegetable in the process. I wonder how high *you* can go ..." With a smile, she stepped back from the chair.

*"Level Four."*

The lights in the room dimmed as blue-tinged electricity crackled across Phoenix's body, violently snapping her head back. A thin line of blood trickled out from beneath the straps securing her chin.

And then, despite her gag, despite her every effort to deny her captors gaining any pleasure from her torture, Jean Grey howled like one of the damned.

Viper sighed dramatically. " 'Listen to them—the children of the night. What music they make ...' "

# 13

I F I may be so bold as to ask, Supreme Guardian, exactly how long do you plan to allow this nonsense to continue?" Saturnyne asked.

Sitting with perfect posture on a straight-backed chair in the throneroom of the Starlight Citadel, the Omniversal Majestrix turned to gaze at her superior. Roma stood beside the scrying glass, her eyes narrowed as though she were trying to peer into its pitch black depths. Despite the fact that she had been able to place the X-Men on their home planet, she was still denied viewing the events on that world. With a sigh, the Supreme Guardian stepped back from the large glass globe and turned to speak with her highest-ranking multidimensional agent.

"One week was given to the X-Men to set matters aright, and one week they shall have," Roma said. "I gave them my word, Saturnyne—I cannot go back on it now."

"I understand, m'lady—your word has ever been your bond. But three days have already elapsed on Earth 616, and no changes have occurred," Her Whyness pointed out, rising to her feet. "In fact, the Chaos Wave is now beginning to spread *beyond* the planet's boundaries!"

"The 'Chaos Wave,' Saturnyne?" Roma asked, one eyebrow raised quizzically.

"I thought perhaps the effect might need an official title, Supreme Guardian," the white-haired Majestrix replied. "It certainly sounds better than 'that reality-threatening thing that could destroy us all.' "

"Quite so." A small smile played at the corners of Roma's mouth. "Once more your categorical gifts have served me well, Saturnyne."

Her Whyness gave a small nod. "Thank you, m'lady."

The soft hum of an antigravity device echoed in the vast chamber, and the two women turned to face the main entrance. Seated in his hoverchair, Charles Xavier glided into the throneroom, telekinetically bringing the device to a halt at the crossing. He nodded respectfully to them both.

"Am I interrupting, Your Majesty?" he asked.

Roma gestured for him to approach. "Nothing of importance, Professor. Saturnyne and I were just discussing the use of . . . labels."

Xavier looked confused by Roma's peculiar response, but clearly was too polite to ask for an explanation.

"Have you received any word from my students?" he inquired. "I've tried on a number of occasions to make telepathic contact with Phoenix, but it appears that the same forces which prevent you from viewing my Earth through your scrying glass are also blocking my mental probes."

Roma sadly shook her head. "I am sorry, Professor, but there has been no contact with them since I sent them through the carrier portal. And the more time your students take in locating the source of the disturbance, the more advanced

"Which is exactly why we cannot wait for them any longer, Supreme Guardian," Saturnyne said. "I know how much your word means to you, but I urge you to think of the omniverse—the safety of innumerable dimensions far outweighs the lives of a—" she waved a hand in a dismissive gesture "—mere handful of mortals."

"You say that as though my students and I were nothing more than disposable items to be used and discarded at your whim, Majestrix," Xavier countered, eyes narrowing in anger. "Cannon fodder in your eternal quest to maintain order in the cosmos. Yet we 'mortals' were the ones you turned to when neither your Tech-net nor your Captain Britain Corps were able to end the destructive tendencies of your—dare I say—'evil twin,' Opul Lun-Sat-yr-nin."

Saturnyne's lips formed a thin line as she scowled at the Professor. The Omniversal Majestrix did not like being reminded of her failures by lesser beings.

Xavier chose to ignore her heated gaze and turned to Roma. "Your Majesty, I am well aware of the risks you are taking by allowing my X-Men this chance to repair the damage that has been done to our home dimension. But they did not go blindly into this mission—they, too, knew what was at stake, and were more than willing to risk their lives in this attempt to set matters aright, rather than stand idle and watch our world die." He maneuvered his hoverchair closer, placing himself between Roma and Saturnyne. "I beg of you," he said to the Supreme Guardian, "do not let that effort be for naught. Think—as my students did—of the countless billions of innocent life forms across the universe who would be sacrificed without ever knowing why they had to die."

"Sometimes, Professor," Saturnyne said coldly, "it is better to *not* think of such things."

Xavier stared at her for a moment. Although he would never consider scanning Saturnyne's thoughts, there was something about her attitude in this entire matter that he could not under-stand—it was as though she were holding back vital information.

"If I may be so bold as to ask a question of *you*, Majestrix," he said, "I would like to know why someone so dedicated to the pres-ervation of order and the elimination of chaos is so adamant about depriving my students of their chance to save our home dimension. I should think you'd be on *our* side, supporting our efforts to the bitter end."

For a moment, the stern, icy features of the Omniversal Majestrix softened; a blush of embarrassment bloomed on the perfect, pale-white skin.

"You *would* think so . . ." Saturnyne murmured. She turned her gaze from Xavier, to focus it instead on the scrying glass, took a deep breath, then slowly released it. Xavier waited patiently for her to continue.

"Several years ago," she finally said, "I faced a situation not unlike the problem we have today. I was heading the Dimensional Development Court, an offshoot of the Supreme Omniversal Tribune. It was my duty to travel to certain variants of Earth—the ones whose slow development was holding back the progress of all other Earths throughout reality—and orchestrate the 'push' that would set them on the proper track." She frowned. "One of the transformations didn't go as planned—there was an unexpected outside influence that twisted The Push. It drove the inhabitants mad, eventually caused the entire planet to collapse in upon itself—it was unlike anything we had ever seen. But it didn't stop there; it continued to spread beyond Earth, to the stars. Entire planetary systems were warped by the effect—billions upon billions of life forms screaming in horror as they watched their universe die."

Saturnyne paused, nervously chewed on her bottom lip for a moment. "There was no natural way to stop it, you see—this retardation of reality that became known as 'The Jaspers Warp.' In the end, the Tribune was left with no other choice but to wipe that dimension from existence, before its sickness could spread to other levels of the omniverse." Arms clasped across her chest, the Majestrix hugged herself, as though a chill had suddenly run up her spine.

"Then, you've seen this happen before," Xavier said. "If that's true, Saturnyne, then *you* of all people should be eager to see my students succeed. Given enough time, I am certain they will find a way to—"

"You don't *get* it, do you, Xavier?" snapped Saturnyne, turning back to confront him; she was once more the ice queen. "Having lived through this sort of nightmare, I already *know* how it will all turn out: *badly.* They won't slow the infection, they won't stop the infection, and it will continue to spread unchecked throughout the universe until Roma is ultimately forced to destroy that entire plane." She paused, her cool façade slipping once more.

"Don't you see, Professor? Your X-Men were doomed to fail right from the start," she said quietly. "No matter how mightily they may struggle, no matter how noble their efforts, they are going to *fail.* And *that* is why I am so adamant that Roma end this charade—for why should others have to live with the knowledge that their actions were directly responsible for billions upon billions of deaths . . ."

Xavier gazed silently at the Majestrix, and his heart went out to this woman, this agent of order who would always be haunted by the memory of the one time she had lost to the forces of chaos. "Saturnyne . . ." he began.

Rather than let him continue, Her Whyness drew herself up to her full height, head held high, and turned away from him. Disheartened, Xavier looked to Roma, who had quietly watched this exchange with great interest.

"Your Majesty," Xavier said, "I implore you: do not give up on my X-Men now. I understand the Majestrix's motivations, but the next four days could be critical to their efforts. To destroy an entire dimension without giving it every opportunity to go on living . . ."

The Supreme Guardian clasped her hands behind her back and walked toward the scrying glass. "My father, Merlyn, has always thought the people of your world hold great promise, Charles Xavier—that, one day, they will rise above their petty differences and live in harmony." She paused. "He has never mentioned if he feels that way about any of the countless other Earths in the omniverse." Roma reached out to stroke the surface of the glass. The darkness within swirled for a moment, then grew still once more. "I have come to understand that you and Merlin are of like minds in this matter, Professor."

"Universal peace has always been my dream, Your Majesty," Xavier replied. "My goal—and that of my students."

Roma nodded. "Dreams are such fragile things, my friend—so quickly forgotten with the rising of the morning sun, so easily dispersed by the harsh light of day." She turned to face the Professor. "But *you*, Charles Xavier, have ever held fast to your dreams, to your hopes, despite the hatred and mistrust directed at your kind, despite the long years of struggle to create a lasting peace between human and mutant." A gentle smile came to her lips. "With so powerful, so compelling a dream as that . . . who, then, am I to rouse the dreamer from his slumbers?"

"Supreme Guardian . . ." Saturnyne began. Roma quickly raised a hand to quiet her before she could continue her protest.

"To honor that dream, Professor, I shall not change my decision," Roma said. "Your X-Men shall have all the time remaining to them—but not a moment longer. Not even *I* am willing to further jeopardize the structure of all reality for such noble beings as your students. Four days—and then I shall have to, as you mortals say, 'take matters into my own hands.'" She glanced at Saturnyne. "There shall be no further entreaties for reconsideration of my judgment until then."

Her Whyness choked down whatever she had been about to say, nodded once in curt acknowledgment, and remained silent.

"Thank you, Your Majesty," Xavier said gratefully. "You will not regret this decision."

"I pray that you are right, Charles Xavier," Roma said solemnly. "For if I have chosen wrongly, yours is not the *only* dimension that will suffer from my poor judgment . . ."

It was a dream come true.

Standing on the roof of the Von Doom Center for the Performing Arts—a building formerly dedicated to the memory of the late U.S. president John F. Kennedy, long before the rise of the Empire—Betsy Braddock pinched herself to make sure she wasn't still napping onboard Warren's private Lear jet; the sharp, brief pain on the flesh of her forearm proved that she was wide awake. She really *was* in Washington, she really *was* gazing out on the spectacle that was the world's capitol at night, she really *was* a scheduled performer for the anniversary gala in honor of the Emperor.

*But if this really* is *a dream, and pinching myself is just part of that dream,* she thought happily, *then I don't* ever *want to be awakened* . . .

Around her, a party was being held in honor of the performers—champagne flowed, caviar was consumed, and the air was filled with the strains of a string quartet performing classical music; Betsy had recognized one piece as a Max Bruch composition for violin. But there was more to the celebration than just good food and good music. With Warren at her side, Betsy had even had the opportunity to meet some of her idols in the entertainment industry; as to be expected, some were gracious, some were pompous, and some were surprisingly uncomfortable with their celebrity. Everyone, though, seemed determined to make an impression with their carefully-chosen attire—the women wearing expensive gowns, the men in tuxedos—and Betsy was no exception, wearing sparkling gold jewelry and a black, full-length silk dress. Her lavender hair billowing in the slight breeze coming off the Potomac River behind her, she gazed at the lights of Washington, D.C. and smiled like a little girl on Christmas Day, eager to open all the wonderful presents laid out beneath the tree.

"Some view, huh?" Warren asked, wrapping his arms around her waist, and resting his chin on her shoulder. Betsy turned around to face him.

"I like *this* one better," she said, gazing into his eyes.

Warren chuckled. "You sure know how to stroke a guy's ego, you know that?" Betsy smiled. "So, how did rehearsals go?"

"A little awkward," she admitted. "I'm not used to the acoustics of a place as big as the Concert Hall—that thing is huge!" She paused. "It's a little daunting, too. I mean, I *know* I'm in the show, but still . . . to step out on that stage and realize that this is all really happening . . . that I'm actually going to sing for the Emperor . . ."

"And how about the headaches?" Warren asked, clearly concerned. "Still having those?"

Betsy nodded hesitantly. "But they're not as bad now," she lied. "It's probably just nerves—once the show actually starts, I'll be fine. It's just *getting* there that's driving me half-mad."

Warren eyed her suspiciously, but didn't press the matter.

Unable to make eye contact with him any longer, Betsy turned around and rested her head against his chest, then clasped her arms around his. For all the clichd, stiff-upper-lip British exterior she was maintaining around her one true love, she began to wonder just how long she could keep her secret from Warren. Although the remainder of the night when Arcade had left his congratulatory phone message had passed quietly—meaning she had been spared any more attacks by thoughts not her own, and did not suffer from further visions of the Minister of Entertainment acting like some melodramatic movie villain—the "voices" had returned the next day, when she had stepped from the apartment complex to buy some groceries. By concentrating almost to the point of causing a migraine headache, she had been able to block a majority of the thoughts of her fellow shoppers, but she had still returned to the apartment as quickly as possible, fearful that she might lose control at any moment. Since then, Betsy had continued to work on suppressing her mind-reading abilities, often times relying on her musical talents, repeating song lyrics in her head to "shout down" the voices; it had, surprisingly enough, worked wonders to quiet the intrusive thoughts, but if she had to listen to one more rendition of Englebert Humperdinck's "After the Loving" . . .

This party was a test of sorts for her: if she could block out as much of the psychic chatter being generated by the hundred-odd people around her—including the thoughts she was starting to pick up from Warren—then there was some hope that she'd be able to get through her performance, when the Concert Hall below her would be filled with close to a thousand of the Emperor's most famous (and most fawning) subjects and ever-watchful security personnel.

"Some view," she finally said, gazing out at the Washington skyline. Wordlessly, Warren tilted his head downward, to eye her plunging neckline.

"I like *this* one better," he commented.

Betsy laughed. She didn't need to read *his* mind to know what he was thinking....

"You *can't* be serious about this," Mystique said.

"Oh, but I am, Raven," Magneto replied. "Quite serious."

Shaking her head in disbelief, Mystique looked around the hotel room in which had gathered the mutants who had answered the call of their master—men and women who shared the dream of destroying Victor von Doom and placing their lord in the seat of power. A lofty goal, and one Mystique shared, but she wasn't all that certain that these were the people who could bring that dream to reality ...

Lounging on a loveseat was Scanner—a blond-haired woman in her early twenties, bright-eyed and eager to show her leader that her bioelectrical powers would make quick work of his enemies in a fight. Seated beside her, Unuscione, on the other hand, was dark of hair and mood, forever angry at the world; her talent was in the creation of psychokinetic forcefields that operated on both defensive and offensive levels—an appropriate power, for someone used to keeping people at arm's length. Vindaloo, munching on a stick of beef jerky as he leaned against a table, was a lanky, dark-skinned Indian, his waist-length black hair tied in a loose ponytail; his was the power to emit a gel-like liquid from his hands that he could turn into napalm-like blasts. Mellencamp was a broad-shouldered, lizard-like mutant, his scaly hide gleaming as though polished, his snake-like tongue drilling through the apple he was noisily chewing at the moment. Sitting next to him on a couch, trying to ignore her comrade's grotesque eating habits, was Amanda Voght, a quiet, dark-haired woman with the ability to turn herself into mist—a useful talent, when one required a fogscreen to move about undetected. Rounding out the group were Magneto's son, Pietro; the sycophantic Cortez; and Forge, who was fiddling around with the innards of the lone television in the room, making who-knew-what out of its wires and circuits.

And seated in the center of the room, looking incredibly regal in his crimson-and-purple costume, his battle helmet polished until it gleamed, was Magneto, Master of Magnetism. Their leader. Their god.

An eclectic gathering of mutants, to be sure, but one that could give even the deadliest Hunters of the Empire a good drubbing.

Still . . .

"Let me see if I have this straight," Mystique said. "You want us to break into Psi Division Headquarters, of all places, and rescue a bunch of melonheads *stupid* enough to have gotten themselves caught and interrogated by Doom's psychic stormtroopers."

Magneto nodded. "That *is* the plan."

"That's not a plan—that's *suicide!*" Mystique objected. "Absolute suicide! Who's to say they'll be of *any* use to us after a day of having every thought in their heads ripped out and put under a microscope?" She shook her head. "I know you want to rub your superiority in Doom's face, Magnus, but I thought the idea was to do that at the celebration, in front of a live audience. We shouldn't be doing anything that would tip our hand this early, like blundering through a spur-of-the-moment rescue of people you don't even know! Doom doesn't even know you're in the country—we should use that to our advantage. Our best bet is to keep a low profile, make all the necessary preparations, and then catch him unaware. The party is in two days. We don't have all that much time to get ready, you know."

"You did not seem so reluctant to carry out the mission when my father first presented it," Pietro said.

"That was before your friend in D.C. told us *where* they were being held!" Mystique replied. She looked around at her fellow conspirators. "None of you have the *slightest* idea of what I'm talking about, do you?"

The blank stares she received more than answered her question.

"Look, this isn't like Valhalla Mountain," she explained, "where hopping into the trunk of someone's car automatically gets you past their defense grid. And it's not The Vault." She snorted. "I've walked in and out of that place a *dozen* times without being detected. But *Psi Division?*" She shook her head. "That's just insane. Its security measures *alone* make the White House look like it's being protected by two sharp sticks and a rubber band. And do you know why it's insane to attack it? *Because the damned mentos can tell when somebody's going to strike, even before the first stages of a plan have been implemented.*" She looked around at the group. "Do you know how *dangerous* it is for us to even be *this* close to the compound? If it wasn't for the psi-screens Forge and I set up in this room, we would've had Hunters and Guardsmen banging down the doors already!"

The acolytes glanced at one another, then gazed toward their leader for guidance.

Mystique grunted in frustration; she wasn't getting anywhere by playing to the audience. She turned to Magneto. "Please don't do this, Erik. Remember Paris, when you tried to devise a similar attack against Doom, and tipped your hand too soon? Remember the lives it cost you—Drake, Dane, Neophyte, Kath, Callis—"

"Are you *done*, Raven?" Magneto asked. His eyes shone with unbridled anger from within the shadows of his helmet.

Mystique's golden eyes narrowed, and her lips pulled back in a snarl; clearly, her arguments had fallen on deaf ears. *"Yes,"* she replied through gritted teeth.

"Good," Magneto said curtly. "Then please be seated."

Mystique stomped over to the couch and sat down hard at one end, forcing Voght and Mellencamp to move side; then, she folded her arms across her chest and glowered silently at their leader.

"Thank you," Magneto said. He rose to his feet and looked around the room, making brief eye contact with each of his acolytes. "My friends, for all her histrionics, Raven *is* correct: this *is* a dangerous mission—though far from being as suicidal as she makes it sound."

"That's *your* opinion," Mystique muttered under her breath.

Magneto chose to ignore her. "However, it is my firm belief that these people who were captured by the Psi Division—people who appear to be mutants like you and I—may hold the key to victory for our cause. It is apparent that they share our opposition of von Doom and, based on the information provided to us by Pietro's contact, we now know that one member of that group—a young woman called 'Phoenix'—could be the most powerful psi-talent in the world, which makes her feared even by von Doom's scurrilous Thought Police. Adding her talents alone to our ranks would make us impregnable to anything the Empire might throw at us; adding her fellow members' abilities would make us unstoppable." He paused. "I know I am asking much of you. Failure on our part could result in losing our chance to strike at von Doom—" he glanced at Mystique "—or, yes, even death. If any of you wish to back out, do so now—there will be no feelings of enmity toward you, by either myself, or any member of our group.

"But know this: What I plan to do this night is something I would not hesitate to do for any of you—for *any* of our kind.

"It is a risk I am willing to take . . . for The Dream."

The mutant overlord stood silently as each of the acolytes looked at one another, each searching the other's eyes for a sign that would indicate a lack of faith in their savior. Yet, not even Mystique seemed ready to back out now.

It was Scanner who finally spoke for them all.

"Dread lord," she said without hesitation, "how may we serve you?"

# 14

H E HADN'T told them anything, much to his captors' dismay. In the darkness of his cell, Nightcrawler lay curled in a fetal position on a broken-down cot, trying his best to ignore the painful throbbing in his palms. The bleeding had stopped some time ago, but the burning sensation hadn't lessened at all—he could still feel the superheated metal of Wilhelmina's knives piercing his flesh, still remember the way in which she had used her telepathic powers to increase the level of pain he felt by a factor of ten, and still prevent him from passing out.

It had been the longest four hours of his life.

Despite the damage to his hands, Kurt believed he could still consider himself lucky—the blades hadn't sliced through any nerves. "Lucky," of course, was a relative term in this hellhole: lucky to still have the use of his hands; lucky that he hadn't bled out as he was dragged through the halls to this cell after his interrogation; lucky to still be alive.

It was a momentary respite; he knew that. The Psi Division was waiting for the pain to wear away at his resolve, waiting for it to slowly bore through the psychic defenses that had withstood even the worst physical and mental punishment he had ever endured. When they felt he had been sufficiently weakened, he would be dragged back to the interrogation room, and the process would begin again.

He wasn't sure if he could survive a second round of questioning.

Staring into the darkness, Kurt wondered how his friends were holding up to the torture. During the trip to his cell, he thought he had seen Rogue being dragged from another room, eyes wide with horror, yet seeing nothing. Then, one of the guards had told him to mind his own business, and a metal club came crashing down onto the back of his head; he awoke on the cot.

And what of the others? Where were they in this madhouse? Were they even still alive?

Kurt angrily shook his head. Giving into despair would do him no good. He *had* to believe there was a way to endure; had to believe that an opportunity for escape would present itself soon, before time ran out for everyone in this dimension. Right now, faith in such intangibles was the only thing keeping him sane.

*What is it that Paul the Apostle says in the Bible?* he thought, then nodded in remembrance. *"Faith is the substance of things hoped for, the evidence of things not seen."*

Ignoring the pain, Kurt clasped his hands together and began hoping for a sign.

The soft rapping on his chamber door came five minutes later.

She was alive—that was the only thing of which she was certain.

Slowly, Jean Grey opened her eyes. She was still strapped into the torturous Cerebrum Scanner, still gagged—but still strong enough mentally to have held off the psychic probing of the facility's best agents, right up to the moment before the tenth level of electroshock treatments had smashed her down into darkness.

Much to her surprise, she discovered that she was alone. Viper and Tyboldt were gone; more than likely, they had departed after failing to revive her. That didn't mean they wouldn't come back, though, eager for another chance to break her.

The door suddenly opened, and Jean had to fight the urge to

cry out in panic. But it wasn't Viper, this time—rather, it was a statuesque African-American woman in her twenties who stepped into the room. She was wearing a lab coat and a simple gray dress, and carrying a small metal tray; on the tray were a small bottle of colorless liquid, and a syringe. Behind the woman walked a guard; the man was in his thirties, sandy-haired and deeply tanned, with a scowl seemingly etched onto his face. He swept the room with the automatic rifle he carried as he entered, then brought its muzzle to bear on the phoenix emblem on Jean's chest.

"That's right—keep an eye on her," the woman said mockingly to him. "She looks like she's about to bust out of that chair any minute now." With a soft snicker, she placed the tray on an arm of Jean's chair.

"Yeah, well, you techies might think it's pretty funny," the guard shot back, "but I heard one of these freaks broke out of his restraints and ripped up a few of your people earlier today. Bet you wouldn't be laughin' if some guy with Ginsu knives comin' outta his hands was comin' after you."

"Ginsu knives, eh?" the technician asked. She picked up the syringe and the bottle. "Does that mean he can cut through an ordinary person, yet his blades are still fine enough to slice a tomato?" She chuckled at her own joke.

Jean's eyes widened as she watched the woman sink the needle into the bottle, pull back the plunger, and start to fill the barrel of the hypodermic.

"What's that stuff?" the guard asked.

"Phenobarbital," the woman replied, tapping the side of the needle with a finger to remove any air bubbles. "It's a sedative."

"And what, exactly, is that gonna do?"

"Well, if it's a *sedative,*" the woman said, with more than a trace of annoyance, "I'd imagine it's going to put her to *sleep.*"

The guard scratched his head in confusion. "But, she was sleeping just a little while ago. Why would you want to put her out again?"

The woman turned to face him, a sneer on her lips. "Look, don't you have something else to do—kick in another prisoner's teeth, maybe slap around somebody *else* who's tied to a chair?"

The guard shook his head. "My orders are to remain with the prisoner until Viper gets back. That includes any time you spend getting Bird-Girl here ready to go sleepy-bye."

The woman gestured with her chin past the guard's shoulder. "Then you can start taking your coffee break, soldier-boy."

Clearly confused, the guard turned around, expecting to see Viper approaching—only to cry out in surprise as the woman clamped a hand over his mouth and plunged the syringe into the base of his skull. Convulsing wildly, he crumpled to the floor for a few moments, then lay still. A thick cloud of mucousy foam billowed from between his lips, and his glassy eyes rolled up in his head. A few more twitches, and he lay still.

"Idiot," the woman muttered. "Oldest trick in the espionage handbook."

As Jean watched, the woman's features blurred, her clothes changed color and style; within the space of a heartbeat, she had turned back into Mystique. Jean almost said her old enemy's name aloud, then remembered the rubber ball in her mouth. Holding her breath, she waited for Raven to make her next move.

To her surprise, it was to remove the gag and unfasten the straps that held her head in place. Jean started to whisper a thanks, only to wince in pain as her jaw muscles cramped from the strain of being held in an open position for countless hours.

"Don't try to talk," Mystique said. "You're going to be in some pain for a while, so just listen: I'm here with friends to get you and your teammates out of this torture chamber." She moved to a control panel and pressed a sequence of buttons; with a soft clang of metal, the restraints around Jean's arms and legs retracted. "I still don't know why Magneto thinks you're so important to the cause, but just the fact that you're still alive, as he had believed, makes me start to think I shouldn't question him as much as I do."

Jean started. "M-Magne—" She whimpered as a bolt of pain shot through her jaw.

"I told you to keep your mouth shut," Mystique said scoldingly. "Yes, Magneto. And you have *no* idea how much effort it took on my part to keep him from just barging in here and tearing the place down around our ears." She dragged Jean from the chair, since the fiery-tressed mutant was to weak to stand on her own. "If you have any questions, I'm sure he'll be more than willing to answer them—*after* we've gotten away from here."

Slowly, Jean tested her legs; she was unsteady, like a new-born filly trying to find its feet.

"Just a second," Mystique said. She reached into a pouch attached to her skull-decorated belt and pulled out a metal band like the one she was wearing around her head, and placed it around Jean's. "It's a psi-scan blocker—it should hold up long enough for all of us to get out of here before any of the mentos start picking up our thoughts." She grabbed Jean around the waist. "Let's go."

As they stumbled toward the door, Jean pointed to the guard lying on the floor.

"W-what about t-that m-man?" she asked, though the pain caused by talking made her quickly wish she had remained silent.

"Oh—him." Mystique shrugged. "He's dead."

Jean stared at her in shock. "Thought you s-said 'pheno—' "

"Phenobarbital?" Mystique asked. Jean nodded, and the shape-shifter softly laughed. "Hell, no—that was window cleaner. Why waste a perfectly good sedative on a piece of trash like him?"

Stepping outside the interrogation room, Mystique shifted into a perfect replication of Viper, checked to make sure no one was in the hall, and then guided Jean away from the interrogation room.

Two corridors away, a pair of guards slammed open the door to Rogue's cell. Their names were Morales and Poe. The former was a hulking Latino in his mid-thirties, with short, wavy, black hair and a chilling smile; the latter was a Caucasian in his late twenties, not as muscular as his partner, with dark-brown hair and a severe case of acne-scarring. From the way in which they barged into the cell, it apparently could never be said that they did not enjoy their work.

"Rise and shine, sweetness!" Morales barked, and hauled the exhausted mutant to her feet.

"Wh-what're y'all doin'...?" Rogue asked sleepily. Her legs felt like mush, her head like a punching bag leaking sand.

"Miss Frost wants to have a word with you," Poe said. There was just enough of a hint of malice in his voice to get his prisoner's attention.

Rogue snapped awake, eyes wide with fear. "N-no..." she gasped, and started struggling. Despite her mental anguish, she managed to find the strength to push the men into the hall, kicking and lashing out with her fists in a vain attempt to break free.

"Get the stun gun!" Morales yelled to his partner, just before a hastily-thrown elbow broke his nose. He cried out in pain and stumbled back, blood pouring from his nostrils.

The second guard managed to catch Rogue in the right temple with his fist. As she staggered into a wall, momentarily stunned, he reached down to his utility belt and unclipped a small, black device. He pressed an activation button on its side, and a jagged bolt of electricity rippled between two metal contacts on one end. Poe stepped forward, intending to jam the stun gun against Rogue's waist.

"What are you idiots doing?" demanded a sharp female voice.

Rogue and the guards turned to find Viper standing a few feet away, a disgusted sneer on her emerald lips.

"Umm...Director," Poe said, with just the proper tone of fear. "We were ordered by Miss Frost to bring this prisoner–" he gestured toward Rogue, who was slumping against a wall "–to her office for interrogation."

"Well, you can disregard that order," Viper said. *"I'm* taking charge of the prisoner."

Both guards looked confused. "Ma'am . . . ?" replied Morales, trying his best to look respectful while keeping his head tilted back to staunch the flow of blood from his broken nose. From the corner of his eye, he glanced at his partner.

"No disrespect, Director, but that goes against Psi Division regulations," Poe said. "I shouldn't have to remind *you* that S.H.I.E.L.D. has no claim to our prisoners—not without a direct, written order from the Minister of Defense." His hand was hovering near his utility belt—and the gun holster attached to it; the shiny black handgrip of a .9mm pistol could be plainly seen.

Viper's dark eyes narrowed. "Are you refusing my command, you worm?"

Poe shivered in undeniable fear for a moment, but he stood his ground. "Yes, Ma'am."

Viper sighed. "Very well."

The throwing knives that suddenly appeared in her hands—and then in their throats—silenced both men before either could raise an alarm.

Viper looked over her shoulder. "You can come out now, Red."

Using the wall for support, Jean staggered from the adjoining corridor to join her. "Is all this killing really necessary, Mystique?" she asked; it was becoming a little easier to talk.

The faux S.H.I.E.L.D. director grabbed her around the waist. "You know, if I were in your position, I'd do my best to see every last one of these soulless buzzards burn in hell for what they'd done to me and mine."

"That's the difference between you and I," Jean replied. "*You* see them as 'soulless buzzards.' *I* see them as innocents, twisted by the hate-filled dreams of one man."

"Von Doom." The shapeshifter grunted. "Maybe we *do* share the same goal, after all." She gestured toward Rogue. "Let's collect your friend and see how the others are doing."

They were doing just fine, actually.

Making use of the information provided by Pietro's contact,

Mystique's fellow acolytes had moved quickly through the facility, aided, as it turned out, by some of the contact's highly-paid spies—psi-agents, surprisingly enough. They had allowed the group entry to the complex, and had even provided the locations of the prisoners. It seemed that Pietro's mysterious friend was networked throughout the Empire, making deals and gathering information behind von Doom's back, without any apparent fear of reprisal.

It had also made Mystique wonder if someone other than Magneto was, perhaps, vying for possession of the throne.

Of course, the X-Men themselves weren't much help in carrying out the escape. Wounded, broken, their psyches ravaged and mutant abilities deactivated, they could only rely on the kindness of people who would have otherwise been their bitterest of enemies, solely dedicated to their extermination. For the moment, the concept of the entire world being unaware of their identities was a blessing in disguise for the half dead super heroes.

Now, the acolytes and their charges were assembled in an interrogation room, waiting for the last of their group to join them.

"Somebody give me a hand," Mystique said as she entered with Jean and Rogue. Scanner and Vindaloo stepped forward to remove Rogue's weight from her shoulders, then guided the weary Southern Belle toward a chair.

Jean's worried gaze swept across the faces before her, glancing briefly at Kurt and Logan as they nursed their injuries, looking for one face in particular. It only took her a moment to find it—much to her horror.

"Oh, my God! Scott!" Jean cried.

Scott sat on the floor against a wall, his right arm wrapped in a metal brace, his left hand gripping the ruby-quartz visor—a device useless to him at the moment. His face and bare chest were covered with fist-sized bruises and deep cuts. The swelling around his eyes made it impossible for him to see, and blood had crusted around his nose and mouth.

"Jean . . . ?" Scott tried to rise, but the effort was too much for him. He sank back to the floor.

"God ... oh, God ..." Jean gasped hoarsely. With Mystique's help, she staggered over to join her husband. Gingerly, she touched his swollen face. "Who—who did this to you, honey?"

"It was ... Shaw," Scott gasped. "Sebastian Shaw."

Jean's lips pulled back in a snarl; a low growl issued from her throat. *"Where is he?"* she asked.

"What's *this?*" Mystique asked in mock surprise. "Miss Peace-and-Harmony turning into a lioness protecting her mate? What happened to all that talk of how everyone in this place is an 'innocent'?"

Jean sneered. "That was *before.*"

Mystique smiled. "I'm starting to *like* you, Bird-Girl. Unfortunately, much as I'd like to see you cut loose, *you* don't have any powers, and *we* don't have time for vendettas." She looked to Cortez. "All right, Fabian, we got in—now, how do we get out? We're going to look a little conspicuous trying to walk through the main gate with the Emperor's favorite new guests. And the mentos have probably already spent the entrance fee they were paid, so I doubt they'd be willing to show us the back door for free."

"I've already worked that out." Cortez pointed to Nightcrawler. "This one is a teleporter, normally capable of moving himself and a passenger across short distances. By providing him with additional energy, I should be able to increase that range by a factor of three."

Mystique nodded. "I see. So, if we all join hands, and you boost Blue Boy's jaunting power, he might be able to take all of us along for the ride."

"That is the plan," Kurt said.

Mystique shrugged. "No crazier than any *other* plan I've been hearing these days. Let's get to it."

"Remy!" Rogue suddenly exclaimed. "Where's Remy?"

Mystique looked to Cortez. "We're missing one?"

"Ah ... yes," Cortez replied slowly. "There were ... unusual complications. We can't take him with us."

"Then we're not leaving," Jean said. *"No one* gets left behind."

Jean and Mystique stared hard at one another, neither batting an eyelash. Both were unwilling to back down, so it became a waiting game as to who would give in first.

Jean won.

"All right, Cortez," Mystique finally said. "Why don't you just show us these 'unusual complications' so we can get out of here?"

Cortez nodded and headed for the door. "Follow me."

*I'm gon' miss dat smile*, Remy thought.

Lying on his cot, he gazed into the darkness, his mind's eye forming a picture of Rogue as he waited for the end to come.

*Dat smile . . . De way de corners o' her mouth turn up just so t'make her dimples show, de way her nose crinkles up an' twitches, de way her eyes sparkle like de Mississippi under de full moon. I'd give jus' 'bout anyt'ing t'see dat smile one mo' time . . .*

That wasn't entirely true, though. All he *really* wanted was one last opportunity to *speak* with Rogue, and let her know how he felt about—

"Remy . . . ?"

*It was her.*

Remy smiled. Maybe he *was* about to die, but maybe the man upstairs had decided to throw a little mercy his way before the end, and provide him with that last chance he had so desperately wanted. If so, he wasn't about to screw it up.

Gambit forced his lips to move, to form one word that came out in a gasp of air from metal-coated lungs: *"Chere . . . ?"*

Remy tilted his head upward, just enough to see the door to his cell open, and Rogue start to enter.

"No, you little fool!" shouted a male voice. A powerful hand gripped Rogue's shoulder and pulled her back into the hallway. A brief struggle followed

Remy struggled to a sitting position on the edge of the cot, then to his feet. It was hard to move—most of his flesh was gone, replaced by cold, lifeless metal and plastic circuitry. Vaguely, he wondered if this is how it would have felt to be an old man—the

aching body, the shortness of breath, the strain on a weakening heart to move atrophied limbs.

Not that he would ever have the chance to find out, of course.

"Let me go, Cortez!" Rogue shouted. "I've got to help him!"

Slowly, painfully, Remy dragged himself to the door and opened it all the way. He was greeted by a chorus of stunned gasps and the wide-eyed, fearful stares of his friends and a group of people he recognized as enemies of the X-Men in the "real world."

"*Bonjour, mon braves,*" he gurgled electronically.

"*Mein Gott . . .*" Nightcrawler whispered.

"Look at him!" Cortez said to Rogue, pointing at Remy. "Your friend has been infected with a techno-organic virus—you lay a *finger* on him, and the same thing will start happening to you! *That's* why I had decided to leave him behind."

Rogue seemed to be in a daze. "I . . . I can't touch him?"

Cortez shook his head. "I'm sorry—it's a highly contagious pathogen. And from his condition, I'd have to say he's in the last stages of the infection. He . . . doesn't have much time left."

"Ironic, *non?*" Remy said to Rogue, leaning against the door frame for support. "All dis time we been wantin' t'have de chance t'kiss widout de fear o' your powers absorbin' mine—you always worryin' 'bout what it might do t'me—an' now, when it don' matter none anymore, it's *me* who can't touch *you.*"

"No, Remy!" Rogue said. "We'll get you outta here, find a cure—"

Remy sadly shook his head. "No, *chere*. Ol' Gambit, he done played his last hand—now de time has come t'call it a night, I t'ink."

Desperately, Rogue turned to Cortez. "We can come back for him, right? After Kurt has gotten us out of here, we can come back—we can take Remy with us. Can't we . . . ?"

Somberly, Cortez glanced at Nightcrawler; the blue-skinned teleporter looked as though his soul was being torn from his body.

"Kurt . . . ?" Rogue said softly.

Nightcrawler looked up at her with haunted eyes. "I . . . I . . ." he began, then fell silent.

"I think any more than one jaunt would tear your friend apart," Cortez said gently. "He'll be lucky if the strain doesn't kill him the first time."

Rogue's mouth moved, but no words would come out. Her panicked eyes refocused on Gambit. The Cajun shrugged and flashed a small smile.

"Dat's okay, *petite*," Remy said. "*Somebody* got t'keep dese pigs distracted while you get away. Sound like de perfect job for de Six-Million-Dollar Mutant, *non?*"

The quivering of Rogue's lower lip made it clear she didn't find his comment humorous in the least.

"And what are you going to use for weapons?" Mystique asked. "They confiscated anything you were carrying when you were brought in."

Gambit chuckled softly. "But, I got *one* t'ing dey ain't got," he burbled electronically. He tapped on his stiff metal wrappings with his remaining hand. "I got *me.*"

He looked around at his friends as they began to realize—in horror—just what he was saying. "You jus' make sure you stop dat crazy tinhead Doom, *mon braves*. De whole universe is countin' on you—" he winked his one eye "—an' ol' Gambit, too."

"*No*, Remy—you can't *do* this!" Rogue said. "Remember what Cyclops was sayin' before: If we can find a way t'change everything back, then we can cure you, too—make it like this never happened! All you've gotta do is hang on till then!"

Remy shook his head. "I wish it was dat easy, *chere*, but de plain an' simple truth is I'm dyin', an' no amount o' hangin' on is gonna stop it." He turned to Mystique. "Can we have a minute?"

"*Only* a minute," Mystique replied, but there was no caustic bite to her tone of voice—it actually sounded tinged with sorrow.

Gambit stepped back into his cell, and motioned for Rogue to join him.

"Remy, you've got to—" Rogue began, but soon fell silent as Gambit gestured for her to be quiet.

"Please, *chere*—let me say what I need t'say while I still got de time t'do it. Jus' hear me out, okay?" Rogue nodded, and Remy took a deep breath to steady himself—as much of a breath as the constricting metal would allow—then began:

"Rogue, I always wanted t'tell you how much you meant t'me, how much I cared 'bout you, but ev'rytime I tried, I couldn't find de right words, an' den I'd wind up chasin' you away." Remy paused. "I'm sorry. I'm sorry for puttin' you t'rough all dat heartache. Sorry for all de pain I caused you over de years. Sorry I could never find de courage to say . . . to say, 'I love you.' " A warm, easy smile came to his lips.

"I love you, Rogue," he said gently. "Always have, always will. You de only woman I ever met who could beat a t'ief at his own game; you did dat t'me de first time we met—when you stole away my heart. I jus' wanted you to know dat."

Rogue stared at him for a moment, clearly uncertain of how to reply.

"An' you waited until now to tell me?" she finally said in a quiet voice.

Remy flashed a lopsided grin. "You know me, *petite*—always de master o' timin'." He gestured toward the others, and turned away from her. "You . . . you better get goin'."

Rogue stood there, quietly trembling, unable to say anything, until Jean gently placed her hands on her shoulders and led her back to the group.

"God be with you, *mein freund,*" Kurt said to Gambit.

"I'd 'preciate it if you'd put in a good word or two for me, Kurt." Remy flashed a melancholy smile. "I got me a feelin' I'm gonna need all de help I can get when I meet de Big Man."

"It would be my honor to do so," Kurt replied.

"Take care'a yerself, Cajun," Logan said.

Remy smiled. "I'll see you on de other side some day, *mon ami*— we'll drink a toast t'de wild ol' days."

"Don't be lookin' fer me *too* soon, Remy," Logan replied. "I still got plans."

Gambit chuckled.

"Come *on*, people," Mystique urged. "We've got to go *now*."

Reluctantly, the X-Men turned from their friend to join the acolytes. Placing their hands on Kurt and one another, the group watched as energy crackled around the teleporter and Cortez, then around themselves.

Immediately, alarms began sounding as the build-up of teleportational forces was detected.

The clatter of boot heels on linoleum caught their attention. A platoon of armed guards dressed in riot gear was pounding down the corridor; behind them charged Samson, Viper, Tyboldt, and Miss Frost.

"Well, what d'you know?" Remy said. "De gang's all here." He turned back to his friends. "Go. *Now*."

For the briefest of moments, Rogue and Gambit made eye contact; it was clear her heart was breaking. He almost asked her to stay, then forced himself to say nothing; instead, he smiled encouragingly.

"I love you, Remy," she said softly.

And then, with a massive burst of brimstone and imploding air, the X-Men and the acolytes were gone.

"Good-bye, *chere*," Remy whispered.

"Damn it! They got away!" said Frost.

"You! Put your hands above your head and lie flat on the floor!" Viper yelled at Gambit as the guards assumed firing positions.

Remy chuckled—an eerie, electronic sound that issued from between icy lips. "I only *got* de one hand, *fille*—but I'll do what I can wit'it."

With the last ergs of his dwindling life-force, Remy triggered his powers; his hand began glowing with building kinetic energy. He placed it on the metal casing that had become his body, and it, too, began to glow.

"Hope y'all packed for a trip," Remy said, flashing a wicked smile. "I'm sure St. Pete's gonna have a *lot* t'say t'*all'a* us sinners. . . ."

# 15

THE FIRES from the chain of explosions that leveled Psi Division Headquarters were still burning when the morning rush hour began. There had been no sign of either the prisoners or their rescuers since the first report of their escape. Magneto's whereabouts were still unknown.

It was not the sort of news the Emperor wanted to hear on the day of his tenth anniversary in power. Nor was his reaction to that news something the remaining members of the war council had been eager to witness.

*"Imbeciles!"* he bellowed, slamming his fists down on the top of the war room conference table. "Incompetents! To think that that worm's sycophantic followers were within my grasp, only to have them slip through my fingers because of such gross negligence, and then to have them destroy the very facility in which they were held . . . !" He pounded the table again. "And *then* to be told that the pain and terror experienced by the agents as they died created a psychic backlash that traveled around the world, crippling or killing over ninety percent of those linked to the telepathic network at the time!" He threw his head back and roared in anger.

*"Must Doom forever be surrounded by bunglers and idiots?!"* he cried to the heavens.

It was a rhetorical question of sorts, and one that no one was willing to answer ... though Stark, Shaw, Dorma, and Wanda cast furtive glances at one another, silently daring their fellow councilors to say something in reply.

And as smart a man as he was, never let it be said that Sebastian Shaw was not up to a challenge—no matter how great the risks. It was a trait one often found in the most egomaniacal.

"Well, it's not all bad news, Your Majesty," Shaw commented. "At least that libidinous psychopath Viper paid the price for allowing them to escape."

"Yeesss ... Viper," von Doom said as he took his seat. "How unfortunate that I was denied the opportunity to personally teach her that lesson." His eyes narrowed as he focused them on Shaw. "But tell me, Sebastian—I understand that you had personally conducted one of the interviews with the prisoners. How is it, then, that *you* were not present when the facility was sabotaged?"

"I had no desire to spend the night there, Your Majesty," Shaw replied. "Not when there were far more comfortable lodgings to be had in the apartment I keep in Richmond."

"Where, I am certain, you spent the rest of the evening?" von Doom said, never breaking eye contact.

Shaw began to answer, then started. "Your Majesty, are you insinuating that *I* had anything to do with the prisoners' escape?"

Von Doom sat back in his chair and steepled his fingers. "I have not risen to this level of power by being trustful of those who serve me, Sebastian—you are no exception."

"B-but," Shaw sputtered, "what possible reason could I have for betraying you, my lord?"

"A few reasons come to mind," von Doom replied. "The prisoners were mutants. *You* are a mutant. You are also responsible for keeping your kind in control. Perhaps, with all this talk of Magneto striking me down at the celebration, you felt it was time to switch allegiances and throw in with that dog, Lensherr. Promise him that the very mutant population you oversee would be more than willing to offer up their lives in a vain attempt to place him on the seat of power."

"Your Majesty, I assure you—"

"It is also no secret that you disliked Viper—with her death, there is one less voice of dissension to be raised against you at these sessions . . . although I am certain Lady Dorma would be happy to stand in for her fallen comrade on that count."

Shaw looked across the table at Dorma. She glared at him from above her breathing mask; her eyes shone with open hatred.

"And, not to be forgotten, you have always been a man in pursuit of power. I'm certain Magneto's ceaseless banter about creating a world in which mutants are the ruling class must appeal to you on quite a number of levels." Von Doom raised a quizzical eyebrow. "Including the position you would receive as a reward for your efforts in a coup, perhaps?"

"Your Majesty, *please*—"

"But, even more importantly, Sebastian—you have not answered my question."

"Yes! Of course I was in my apartment!" Shaw bellowed. "Your Majesty, I swear I am loyal to y—"

"*Silence!*" von Doom barked. He glared at his councilor. "You think me a fool, Shaw? Or that I would not have you under surveillance twenty-four hours a day—as I do all members of this council?" Shaw noticed he wasn't the only councilor to have a surprised response to that question.

"I know all about your pathetic little affairs," the Emperor continued. "*Especially* those concerning your trysts with the so-called 'Black Queen' of the Hellfire Club!" He leapt to his feet, thrusting an accusatory finger in Shaw's face. "And yet, despite the fact that you were derelict in your duties to the Empire, thereby aiding in the death of a member of my war council, you have the unmitigated *gall* to sit there and *lie* to your Emperor!" He leaned forward, eyes practically burning with rage. "I'll ask you once more, before I tear out your miserable throat with my bare hands: Did you spend the rest of the evening in your apartment?"

Shaw shifted in his chair, trying to break eye contact with von Doom, yet unable to do so; it was as if he had been hypnotized by a cobra about to strike.

"No, Your Majesty," he said quietly.

A low growl issued from von Doom's throat. "Were you not a close friend of the Empress—" he held up his hands, to display the Mandarin's deadly rings "—it would give me the greatest pleasure to show you what each of these baubles is capable of doing to a man."

"Th-thank you, Your Majesty," Shaw replied. "You are most generous."

"Do not be so quick to offer me your thanks, mutant," the Emperor said. "Until you have given me irrefutable proof that you have not, as they say, 'gone over to the other side,' you have no place in this war council. Leave now, before I resolve the matter . . . with a public execution."

Shaw rose from his seat, glancing to the side just in time to see Dorma grinning broadly. There was nothing friendly in her shark-toothed smile. He was certain, though, that she was sorely disappointed in the Emperor for not ordering his immediate death.

The sound of approaching boot heels momentarily diverted attention away from the disgraced councilor.

Agent Harada—Ororo's new personal bodyguard—stopped a few feet from the table and stood at attention. "Excuse me, Sire."

"What is it, lackey?" von Doom rumbled.

Harada looked as though he wanted to turn and run—a thin layer of sweat was already forming on his brow—but he stood his ground, back ramrod straight, eyes respectfully averted from the royal presence. "Sire, the Empress requests your presence. The guests are beginning to arrive for the celebration."

The change in the Emperor's mood was instantaneous. "The celebration . . ." A small smile played at the corners of his mouth, and his eyes shone with merriment. "Very well—I shall join her shortly."

Harada bowed, turned smartly on his heel, and quickly headed for the exit.

Von Doom turned back to his councilors—and found Shaw standing in front of him. His joyous mood of a moment before was immediately forgotten.

"Why are you still here, Shaw?" he growled.

"I was just leaving, Your Majesty," the mutant councilor replied quickly. With a small bow, Shaw left the table, heading for the elevator at the far end of the war room.

"Oh—Sebastian?" the Emperor called after him.

Shaw halted and turned around. "Yes, Your Majesty?"

"Did you *learn* anything from the prisoner you interviewed?"

Shaw opened his mouth to speak, then closed it and stood silently for a moment. "No, Your Majesty," he said at last.

A satisfied smile played at von Doom's lips. "I thought as much." He waved a dismissive hand at Shaw. "Now, leave—your continued presence sickens me."

Ignoring the smug looks of the others, Shaw turned on his heel and, head held high, proudly strode toward the elevator.

"Well, *that* could have gone better."

Sitting on the edge of a coffee table in a Bethesda, Maryland hotel suite, Mystique looked to Magneto for a response. Grouped around him, like spandex-clad members of a cult, stood his followers, eager to hear his every word.

"I suppose so," he replied slowly. "But at least it was a successful mission."

Magneto looked around the room. Across from him, the costumed ones called Cyclops and Phoenix were seated on a couch, his legs comfortably stretched across her lap as he lay back on the cushions. From the ways in which they touched and gazed so intently at one another, it was clear they were more than friends—lovers, perhaps, or even husband and wife. On the far side of the suite were Wolverine and Nightcrawler. The gruff Canadian was the only member of his group not in costume, having scrapped the tattered remains of his yellow-and-blue outfit in favor of jeans, boots, and a red plaid shirt. The team appeared well-rested after a few hours' sleep, their injuries having faded in the short time since their escape. All in all, the former prisoners looked a great deal better than when the acolytes had first brought them before their dread lord.

Such accelerated healing had not come easily, though—not without some degree of pain. There had been a short, yet extremely torturous, period during which Scanner had used her bioelectrical talents to short out the neural inhibitors blocking their mutant powers. Had the mutant escapees not been made of sterner stuff, the treatment might have proved as fatal to them as any punishment to which the late Psi Division could have subjected them. Nevertheless, they had endured, and then these "X-Men" had been introduced to a rather plain-looking woman named Harmony. She was, as Magneto had explained, a mutant gifted with the ability to heal the most serious injuries within the space of minutes. With a simple laying-on of hands, she had treated Jean's electrical burns and cramped muscles; Kurt's damaged hands and the crippling exhaustion he had suffered as a result of the group teleportation; and Scott's bruises, cuts, and broken arm.

Unlike his teammates, though, Wolverine had had no need of Harmony's ministrations. Once the neural inhibitor was deactivated, his mutant healing powers had kicked in, instantly healing his injuries.

As for the one called Rogue...

Looking past Scott, Jean gestured toward a closed door at the far end of the suite; it led to one of three bedrooms. "I think I should check on her. She hasn't slept since we escaped, and sitting alone, replaying their last moments together over and over in her head, is only going to continue eating away at her." She glanced at Scott. "I think we *both* know what *that's* like."

Scott nodded in agreement and swung his feet back onto the floor.

"That yer expert medical opinion, 'Doctor' Grey?" Logan asked with a small smile.

Jean smiled warmly at him, then rose from the couch and walked toward the bedroom door.

Scott turned to Magneto. "You're wrong, you know," he countered. "It *wasn't* a successful mission—we lost Gambit. Even *one* death was too high a price to pay for our escape."

Magneto nodded. "One more life for which von Doom must answer—and he will, my friend."

On the other side of the room, Nightcrawler leaned over to whisper in Wolverine's ear. "Why is it that, each time he calls one of us his 'friend,' I get a chill up my spine?" he asked.

"Pro'bly 'cause we know what a snake he really is," Logan replied. "A snake lyin' in the brush, waitin' for the right moment t'strike . . ."


"Rogue?"

Stepping further into the sizable bedroom, Jean spotted her friend sitting in a chair by a window, legs drawn up against her chest. Rogue was hurriedly wiping away tears with the heels of her hands, turning her head away from Jean so she wouldn't see her crying. Jean closed the bedroom door, but made no move forward.

"Hi, Jeannie," Rogue muttered. "You feelin' okay now?"

"Yes, thank you," Jean replied. "Magneto was right—Harmony *does* have a wonderful gift for healing. Between her touch, and the deactivation of the neural inhibitor, I almost feel like my old self." She paused. "How are *you* doing?"

Rogue laughed curtly—a short, phlegmy sound without any humor. "I been better," she replied, wiping her nose with the sleeve of her bodysuit. "Too bad that girl can't do nothin' for healin' a broken heart, right?"

Jean nodded, even though she knew Rogue couldn't see her.

"He's really gone this time," Rogue said quietly, gazing out at

the bright Maryland sunshine. "After all the times he used to disappear on us, goin' who-knew-where, and then showin' up at the
front door like no time had passed, with that big, ol' stupid-lookin'
grin on his face . . ." She looked to Jean, a haunted look in her
red-rimmed eyes. "He's not comin' back, is he, Jean?"

"I honestly don't know, Rogue," Jean replied. "I certainly pray
he will." She walked over to join her friend. "Maybe Scott is right—
maybe all of this will disappear once we've corrected whatever
Doom has done, and we'll wake up in the mansion, thinking it
had been nothing more than a bad dream." She smiled encouragingly. "And Remy will be standing at the front door, with that
stupid-looking grin on his face."

Rogue nodded her head, but it was obvious that she didn't
really believe it would happen. She turned back to stare out the
window.

"I miss him so much," she said quietly.

Jean placed a gentle hand on her shoulder. "I know."

"How's your friend holding up?" Scanner asked Wolverine, tilting
her head toward the closed bedroom door.

"How'd you *expect* her t'be holdin' up?" Logan replied gruffly.
"She just watched her boyfriend die, an' with all the powers we
got in this group, none o' us could do anything t'help 'im." He
snorted. "It ain't the kinda thing ya just shrug off, kid."

Scanner nodded in sympathy. "So, what was that whole thing
about him not being able to touch her?"

Logan grunted. "Gambit an' Rogue never had what ya'd call a
'stable relationship,' but what they *did* have was somethin' special—somethin' the rest o' us can only dream about havin'." He
glanced at the door with a melancholy expression. "That girl's
gonna be a long time hurtin'. I just hope she's got the strength
t'get through it."

The door suddenly opened, and Jean stepped from the bedroom; she closed the door behind her. Both acolytes and X-Men
turned to face her.

"She's sleeping," Jean explained. She looked troubled. "I . . . thought it might be the best thing for her."

Logan grunted, but said nothing. He knew what Jean meant: she had used her telepathic powers to temporarily "shut down" Rogue's mind. He'd experienced the same thing done to him a time or two—usually by Professor Xavier—on those rare occasions when the bloodlust that arose in the heat of battle overwhelmed all rational thought. Logan didn't like being on the receiving end of a psi-blast—not one bit—but in Rogue's case, he had to agree that it was for the best. It was obvious Jean didn't like herself too much right now for having placed her friend in what amounted to a short-term coma. But without sleep, Rogue would more than likely become a liability in a fight, unable to focus her thoughts on her work. And they'd *need* her abilities in their strike against Doctor Doom—in this desperate bid to make things right once more.

To put an end to this madness.

Logan turned to Cyclops. "So, what do *we* do while we're waitin' fer Rogue t'wake up?"

"We make plans," Cyclops replied. He turned to Magneto. "Jean and I have been discussing your part in all this, and we're curious as to why Doom has allowed you, and your followers, to run free this long when he controls the world so completely."

" 'Allows'?" Magneto replied between gritted teeth, leaning forward in his chair. "He has made my life nothing short of a living hell for these past ten years, his lapdogs always snapping at my heels, always trying to run me to ground, torturing and killing my loyal acolytes—and you consider that 'running free'? Are you *insane*, boy?"

Scott shook his head. "Not in the least. But if Doom is as powerful as he clearly seems to be—even possessing the ability to 'rewire' the minds of every man, woman, and child on this planet, both human *and* mutant, and then create false memories—then he should have been able to capture you years ago . . . by *your* time."

"What are you talking about?" Magneto said. "And what kind of nonsense is this you're spouting—Doom being able to tinker with my thoughts?" He snorted derisively. "No one—mutant *or* human—controls the mind of Magneto!"

Jean gently placed a gauntleted hand on Scott's shoulder before he could continue the argument. "I think that's my cue," she said, and stepped toward Magneto. "I know you don't believe this, Magnus, but we've fought on the same side, in the past, many times—and fought against each other, as well." She gestured toward her teammates. "Against all of us."

"More of these 'false memories,' Phoenix?" Magneto asked skeptically.

"Not false," Jean replied. "True ones—of how the world should really be, without Doom in control. Of how we know all about you and your followers. Of the real reason it's so important that we put an end to Doom's empire. If you'd allow me to show you . . ." She reached forward to place her hands on his temples.

As one, the acolytes tensed, clearly expecting this to be a trick of some sort—a chance, perhaps, for a traitorous mutant to strike down their leader and prove her worth to the Emperor.

"I wouldn't do that, Magnus," Mystique said; a gun was in her hand, its muzzle pointed directly at Jean's head. "The girl's a mento—you *know* they can't be trusted. And after what we went through last night . . ."

On the other side of the room, Cyclops, Wolverine, and Nightcrawler were on their feet. Scott's fingers rested lightly on the visor buttons that, when pressed, would unleash his powerful force beams.

The term "Mexican standoff" skipped through Jean's mind as she looked at both teams.

"This is asinine," she said in disgust. She glared at Mystique, then nodded toward the gun that was trained on her head. "Put that thing away before I make it part of your anatomy."

Mystique smiled wickedly. "You *are* just moving away from

that whole peace-and-love nonsense, *aren't* you, Bird-Girl?" The gun didn't move from its target.

"Put down your weapon, Raven," Magneto ordered. "*This instant.*" His tone was that of an angry father scolding a rebellious daughter.

Mystique looked from Magneto to Phoenix, then back again. Finally, after what seemed like an eternity to Jean, she lowered the pistol, snapping the safety back in place.

"Fine. *Fine,*" Mystique said angrily. "I wash my hands of this whole mess." She glared at Magneto. "But don't come stumbling over to me, drooling on the carpet like an idiot, after she fries every synapse in your head. You'll get no sympathy from *me,* 'dread lord.' " Turning on her heel, she stomped away and entered one of the other bedrooms, slamming the door behind her.

Magneto snorted. "Children." He turned back to Jean. "You may proceed, Phoenix."

Gently, Jean placed her fingertips against his temples. "This is going to hurt a bit when I trigger your memories, so be prepared."

"Do what you must," the mutant overlord replied. "I am ready."

"All right," Jean said. "Then, close your eyes, and clear your mind."

Magneto did as he was told, settling back in his chair.

Jean closed her eyes. "Contact," she whispered.

And then she let loose with a psychic pulse that traveled deep into his subconscious—stirring memories long forgotten.

A startling transformation suddenly came over the Master of Magnetism. The weather-beaten skin tanned to a leathery toughness by the harsh environment of the Sahara dissipated, becoming softer. Atrophied abdominal muscles tightened. Ten years of hardship and excruciating injuries and crippling despair drained away. He almost seemed larger now, prouder, regal in bearing.

He remembered it all now: His shattered friendship with Charles Xavier; his numerous confrontations with the X-Men over the years; the times he fought von Doom and a dozen other power-mad tyrants for possession of the world; even his brief relationship with Rogue.

But most of all, he remembered Genosha—a tiny island-nation off the east coast of Africa. A place where, for decades, humans had ruled, openly oppressing the rights of the mutants who also lived there, treating them no better than the lowest of animals—it was a form of apartheid based not on the color of one's skin, but on their genetic makeup. That scurrilous policy had come to an end the day the United Nations handed rulership of the small country over to Magneto, in exchange for his guarantee that he would never again attack one of its members. As far as Magneto had been concerned, such promises were always made to be broken, but he had accepted the offer, if only to momentarily allay the U. N.'s fears and lull the humans into a false sense of security—while he planned for the future. He wasn't about to abandon his goals, not in the least: Genosha was to be just the first step toward making his ultimate dream of worldwide mutant rule a reality.

Until Doctor Doom had *recreated* the world—and him . . .

"He took it from me," Magneto said softly. His eyes snapped open, and lips pulled back in a snarl. "My memories! My triumphs! My dreams!" He leapt to his feet, brushing Jean aside, and shook mighty fists in the air. *"Damn him, he took it all away from me!"*

"I'm beginning to think this was not a good idea . . ." Nightcrawler muttered to Scott.

"You may be right, Kurt," Cyclops replied, "but we need Magnus at full strength, with all his memories intact—that way, he's completely aware of what's at stake here." Scott flashed a brief smile. "Besides, having Magneto angry and focused on Doom might give us the chance to find the source of the anomaly." He paused, noticing his friend's skeptical expression. "I *know* it's a risk, Kurt, but we're running out of options . . . and time."

Kurt sighed. "I hope you're right, *mein freund,*" he said. "For *all* our sakes."

"So am I . . ." Scott admitted.

On the other side of the room, adamantium claws extended

from the backs of callused hands. Logan was prepared for Magneto to lash out at his old enemies, now that his memories were restored; given the opportunity, the scrappy warrior wouldn't hesitate to carve out the heart of the mutant overlord before he could launch an attack.

Instead, Magneto's histrionic display came to an abrupt end, and a small smile played at his lips as he gazed at Jean.

"Thank you, Phoenix," he said gently. "You have made me whole again, and for that I am grateful."

"You're . . . welcome," Jean replied, uncertain whether she actually meant it. She stepped back to join her teammates.

Hands on hips, Magneto looked at Cyclops. "So, Summers—I understand from Miss Grey's telepathic primer that you are in need of my aid."

"Yes," Cyclops replied slowly.

"And what do you offer in exchange?" he asked.

"How 'bout the chance t'go on breathin', ya piece o' filth?" Wolverine replied, brandishing his claws. "I shoulda put you outta my misery while we were all buddy-buddy, Lensherr. Woulda spared us all a lotta trouble after we got done kickin' Doom's metal butt."

"Logan—stand down!" Cyclops ordered. He and Wolverine exchanged heated stares, but the feral mutant eventually sheathed his claws.

Cyclops turned back to Magneto. "What do you want?"

"Simply an understanding between us, X-Man." Magneto folded his arms across his chest. "Doom is *mine*. *You* may want him stopped, but *I* want his *head*."

"Magnus, you know I can't—" Cyclops began.

"You will not raise a hand in his defense," Magnus continued. "Nor will you prevent me from delivering the killing blow. If you wish to save the universe—an action I'm sure that you and the rest of Xavier's malcontents have grown used to doing—you will do *nothing* to keep me from exacting my revenge. Also, any attack made against me—or my people—by any member of your team in the so-called 'heat of battle'—" he glanced at Wolverine "—and you will be on your own. No one will come to your assistance, no one will provide you with the distractions you'll need to find the source of Doom's power. Are we agreed?"

Cyclops locked eyes with the mutant overlord, trying his best to ignore the concerned expressions on the faces of his friends. Then, his lips slowly pulled back in a sneer. "Agreed."

"Cyclops . . ." Kurt began.

"*I said we're agreed!*" Cyclops said sharply. "You have my word, Magnus," he added softly.

"A wise decision," Magneto hissed. He smiled, eyes alight with an undisguised look of triumph. "Then . . . welcome to the revolution, X-Men."

The quintet of heroes found nothing amusing in the statement.

With a hearty laugh, Magneto turned to his acolytes. "My friends, we strike—tonight! At the height of all the self-congratulatory back-patting, Doom and his fawning lackeys shall learn what it means to play Magneto for the fool! I shall tear the heart from his breast and hold it high for all the world to see! And then, my friends, then shall begin the glorious reign of *Homo superior!*"

On the far side of the room, Scott Summers glanced at his fellow X-Men. He knew that what he had set into motion was for the good of the mission; reversing Doom's work before time ran out was the greater threat—far more so than any betrayal Magneto might be planning for later on. No matter how distasteful it had been to ask Magneto for help, the mission *had* to be completed—billions upon billions of lives were at stake.

And yet . . .

And yet Scott couldn't help but wonder if, in order to save a universe, he hadn't just bargained away his soul to the devil himself.

# 16

THE TIME had come.

For weeks, every major city in the world had been festooned with banners and signs heralding the pending arrival of this day. Green-and-silver bunting—reflecting the colors of the Emperor's battle dress—hung from every government building and every household. In schools, children rehearsed plays and sang songs that detailed the Emperor's rise to power and the elimination of his enemies. Memorabilia designed to commemorate the occasion—from flags to buttons, T-shirts to posters, magazines to comic books—flew off store shelves as the citizens of the Empire snapped up little pieces of history. Like the days and months leading to the end of 1999, another countdown had been put into motion, though this one would culminate not in a new millennium, but in the party to end all parties—the tenth anniversary of the Rule of von Doom.

Now, hundreds of television cameras lined New Hampshire Avenue, broadcasting images to every household around the world. Paparazzi struggled against one another behind police barricades, trying to get the arriving guests to look their way for a photograph, and convince them to flash a quick smile and, perhaps, a bit of flesh, before entering the Von Doom Center for the Performing Arts on this, "the grandest night in the history of the world" (at least, that's how the Ministry of Information had phrased it). Thousands of cheering spectators gathered on the far side of the avenue, trying to catch a glimpse of the Imperial guests as they stepped from their limousines.

And keeping a watchful eye over all was the single-largest concentration of Guardsmen, Hunters, soldiers, and police officers ever seen since the first days of the Empire. The Emperor, after all, might be an arrogant, prideful man, but he was no fool. If there was any chance that Magneto might actually have the nerve to attack him on this of all nights, he would not find von Doom unprepared to properly greet him.

As for the people who were actually attending this extravaganza, they had come from all corners of the globe to pay their respects to the Royal Couple. There were politicians and publishers, athletes and artisans, supermodels and Broadway stars, all of them there to see and be seen, to utter embarrassingly-gushing statements about the awe and spectacle that were Victor von Doom, how honored and thrilled they were to have been invited to participate in such a momentous occasion as this, and how the Royal Couple's reign deserved to be celebrated in such a high-spirited fashion, considering how they had brought peace and prosperity to the Earth—this was mankind's true Golden Age. The crowds "oohed" and "ahhed" as celebrities such as Simon Williams—co-star of the box office smash *Doom's Patrol*—arrived arm-in-arm with Imperial Enchantress Wanda Maximoff, and millionaire playboy Anthony Stark was accompanied by model Tyra Banks. And, as each guest walked up the block-long red carpet to the main entrance of the arts center, security forces directed them to the Grand Foyer, where they were to greet the Man of the Decade when he arrived.

The setting was an impressive sight for those few chosen hundred who been invited to personally celebrate the greatness that was Victor von Doom—a setting meant to inspire both awe . . . and fear. Before the occupancy of the White House by the current administration, this six-hundred-foot-long gathering place had simply been a means by which to access the center's three main auditoriums. Now, though, it served as a tribute to the might of Latveria—the postage stamped-sized country that had given birth to the future king of the world. Lit by ten massive, crystal chandeliers, its tiled floor gleamed with the sort of brightness that only human hands could have accomplished—no machine could match the almost religious fervor with which the janitorial staff had applied themselves to their work in ensuring that their master would always be pleased by what he saw when he entered this nexus of entertainment. Wood-paneled walls—not part of the building's original design—proudly displayed the works of some of Latveria's finest artisans. A plush, blood-red runner stretched from the main doorway to the far side of the foyer, above which hung a large replica of the Latverian coat-of-arms. Replacing the spectacular bronze bust of John F. Kennedy that had stood to one side was a massive, marble sculpture of von Doom clad in his battle armor, helmet tucked under his left arm, right hand holding a large globe representing the Earth. Its powerful statement of complete dominance over all was not lost on anyone in the foyer.

But then, subtlety had never been a strongsuit of the monarchy.

Along with dozens of celebrities from every level of the entertainment industry and the fine arts, the members of the Senate and the House of Representatives—officials whom von Doom regarded as being no more than toadying vassals who tended the lands he owned in exchange for the honor of serving him—had assembled here at the Emperor's command, joining their spouses and the White House staff to show their allegiance to their master. Though none of their ilk had existed in his native Latveria—for Doom shared his power with no one—the Emperor had to admit that these lick-spittle politicians, with their slick appearances and nauseating talent for speaking in television broadcast-ready sound bytes, *did* have their uses, if only to continue spreading the word about how marvelous, how incredibly awe-inspiring was the man who had transformed the planet into a veritable paradise.

Nevertheless, if the opportunity ever presented itself when he no longer had need of their services, von Doom would waste no time in ordering speedy executions for each and every one of them. Politics, he felt, was a time-consuming game for fools and old men, and von Doom was neither. Nor had he the patience for such trivialities as peaceful negotiations when a swift, decisive action would resolve any conflict and immediately reestablish the indisputable fact that the Emperor was now, and always would be, in control; he had been trying to make *that* point clear to that bothersome flea Magneto for the past year. As a leader—first of Latveria, then of the world—von Doom had always ruled under the same belief as that expressed by the 19th-century German statesman Otto von Bismarck: "The great questions of the time are not decided by speeches and majority decisions, but by iron and blood."

And if blood is what it took to keep the Empire running, then let it be shed by others in the service of Doom.

A hush fell over the assembly as a tall, thin man dressed in a tuxedo stepped just inside the main doorway.

"Ladies and gentlemen, King T'Challa of Wakanda," he announced.

The gathered throng began applauding, welcoming the ruler of the small African nation. Dressed in the flowing, colorful, traditional robes of his people, T'Challa—once known to the citizens of the world by the more colorful name "The Black Panther"—strode into the room, accompanied by his five-member personal guard. Standing over six feet tall, dark eyes constantly sweeping the room, he moved with the grace of the animal from which his alter ego had taken its name, muscles rippling with each step that he took. Unlike von Doom—a gypsy who had clawed his way to power and appointed himself the ruler of Latveria—T'Challa was a true monarch, the son of T'Chaka, Wakanda's greatest king.

"Prince Namor of Atlantis," came the next announcement.

Again, applause, though this time its tone was somewhat muted. Namor—the hybrid son of an Atlantean princess and a human sea captain, known far and wide as "The Savage Sub-Mariner" ever since his first recorded appearance during the darkest days of World War II—had never entirely gained the trust of the human race, nor did he really care to. And considering the fact that he had tried on numerous occasions to rule the world on his own before von Doom took power, it often amazed the powerbrokers of Washington that this hawk-faced, belligerent egoist should be one of the Emperor's most trusted allies.

He was clad in a formfitting, black outfit of some rubber-like material that covered him from shoulders to feet; his arms, though, were bare, but for a large, golden bracelet around each wrist. An open panel in the front of the outfit exposed his chiseled torso from collar bone to abdomen; his ankles were also left uncovered, to allow a quartet of small, delicate wings to jut out to provide him with the power of flight. Around his waist hung a black belt held fast by a golden, trident-shaped buckle. A pair of small, golden rings adorned the lobe of each of his pointed ears, the cartilaged tips just brushing the edges of his black hair, which was forever shaped into a crewcut that rose shallowly from a widow's peak just above his brow. Namor gave no indication that he was even aware of the formal welcome; he merely stomped his way up the runner.

"Lord and Lady Plunder of the Savage Land."

Of all the royalty assembled in the great hall, the couple who now entered—to a smattering of applause—were the least formal ... and the least respected by all but the Emperor. In his late twenties, Kevin Plunder looked more like a movie star than a sovereign, with his squarish jaw, piercing blue eyes, deep tan, and shoulder-length blond hair, strands of which constantly bobbed in front of his face. He was dressed in a tuxedo that, even though it was tailor-made, still seemed too small for his athletic build; from his expression as he pulled at the collar of his starched white shirt, it was evident that he would have felt more at ease in the customary animal-skin loincloth and boots that he normally wore back in his Antarctic realm.

His wife looked equally uncomfortable. Dressed in a stunning, dark-green gown that complemented her mane of red hair, the former veterinarian-cum-jungle goddess known as Shanna O'Hara-Plunder had a look about her that resembled an animal sniffing around unfamiliar surroundings—head slowly turning from side to side, ears alert for any hint of approaching danger.

The royal guests were directed to their spots at the end of the line, closest to the Concert Hall doors, joining such dignitaries as the ever-silent Black Bolt, king of the Inhumans, and his fiery-tressed wife, Medusa; the Minister of Entertainment, Arcade, and his assistant, Miss Locke; and the gnomish Mole Man, who had all arrived before them.

War Council member Sebastian Shaw, however, was noticeable by his unexplained absence.

The announcer delicately cleared his throat for attention.

"Ladies and gentlemen," he said loudly, "Emperor and Empress von Doom."

As one, the guests began applauding, the sound of flesh striking flesh rising appreciably as the most powerful couple in the world entered the foyer arm-in-arm. The Empress looked dazzling in a black, full-length ball gown, snow-white tresses styled fashionably. The Emperor, on the other hand, wore his traditional battle armor—*sans* mask—and flowing green velvet cloak; the metal gleamed brightly in the well-lit hall. Ororo smiled warmly, nodding slightly in acknowledgment to each of the people she knew; von Doom, meanwhile, strode arrogantly down the carpeted pathway, ignoring everyone around him . . . except the wizened old man standing off to one side, his weight supported by a gnarled, wooden cane.

For the first time that day—perhaps for the first time in quite a while—a genuine smile came to the face of Victor von Doom. Stepping away from Ororo, he opened his arms wide and heartily embraced the visitor.

"Boris!" he said. "It is good to see you!"

"The feeling is mutual, Master," the old man said.

In his late seventies, hair and flowing beard a dazzling white set against the deep blue of his suit and the red of his silk tie, Boris was the closest von Doom had had to a true friend before his courtship of Ororo. Like the Emperor, the old man was a gypsy, one of a band of wandering free spirits who had settled in the small European country of Latveria. He was the best friend of Victor's parents, and had been appointed ambassador for the country after Victor took control of the planet.

Still clasping Boris's shoulders, Von Doom stepped back to gaze closely at him. "You are looking well, my friend."

Boris smiled warmly. "I have my good days, Master; some bad, but mostly good. Seeing all you have accomplished over the years keeps me going—I'm always afraid I'll miss out on some new wonderment of yours if I were to go and die without your permission."

To the amazement of everyone in the foyer—except, perhaps, Ororo—the Emperor actually joined the old man in a laugh.

Von Doom clapped Boris on the shoulder. "Excellent! Well said, faithful Boris! And how are my parents?"

"Strong like bulls, as ever," Boris replied. "Latveria could not have been left in more capable hands, Master. The regent sends his regards, both to you—" he nodded to Ororo, who had joined them "—and your lovely wife." The old man bent forward, leaning close to von Doom's ear so that only he could hear his next words. "But your mother worries about your health. She thinks you looked far too thin on your last worldwide broadcast. 'A homecooked meal, Boris,' she said to me. 'That is what my son needs, before he wastes away to nothing.'"

Von Doom compressed his lips and nodded thoughtfully. "I see. Then I shall have to schedule a visit to my homeland before it is too late," he said, with just a trace of humor. He glanced at Boris, and smiled. "It *is* good to see you, my old friend," he said softly.

"It is, Master," Boris agreed. He smiled. "But now, I think it is time for an old man to leave his sovereign so that he may get on with celebrating such an important night as this. We shall talk again later, at your convenience."

"Indeed, we shall," von Doom said. He turned to one of his aides, a young, round-faced man in his early twenties. "Escort the Latverian ambassador to his seat, and see to his every need."

"At once, Your Majesty!" the aide said. He looked to Boris. "If you'll follow me, sir . . ."

With a bow to the couple, Boris was led away, the tip of his cane tapping loudly against the tiled floor. Von Doom and Ororo watched him until he had stepped from sight, then proceeded toward the Concert Hall.

As they passed their friends from Antarctica, Ororo noticed the dark look that Shanna cast at the Emperor; Victor was completely oblivious to it. Though the rulers of the Savage Land had long ago reached an alliance with von Doom, still it was clear that Lady Plunder did not care for the man in the least.

Such opinions, Ororo knew, mattered little to her husband, though he was well aware of them; after all—he was *Doom*. How could he *not* know of them? But Shanna—like all his subjects around the globe—was allowed to have free will (within limits), to have her differences from the Emperor . . . as long as such convictions did not interfere with any of his carefully-tailored plans. "I have no use for slaves. What I require are loyal and devoted subjects," Victor had once said, according to Lancer. What *did* matter to von Doom, though, was that Shanna—like her boyish husband, and Namor, and T'Challa, and everyone else on the planet, *including* the Empress—should know her place.

It made for some . . . interesting discussions around the dinner table.

Reaching the entrance to the Concert Hall, the Emperor stopped to turn around and gesture to the crowd.

"Come, my friends!" von Doom said. "It is time for the celebrations to begin!"

"I think I'm going to be sick."

Backstage, in one of the dozens of dressing rooms that lined the lower halls of the arts center, Betsy Braddock sat on a loveseat, tightly hugging one of the throw pillows. Clad in bra and panties, she stared numbly at the elegant black gown Warren was holding.

"Come on, Betts—you'll be fine," Warren said, ignoring the fact that her skin had gone as white as a sheet of paper. "Look—you got this far, right?"

Betsy grimaced as her stomach made a troubling gurgle.

"Right!" Warren said, answering himself. "So, if you've made it all the way to the Big Night, it shouldn't be any problem to get through one song." He waved the gown at her. "Now, come on—get dressed."

"But, what if I forget the words?" Betsy asked, eyes suddenly wild with panic. "What if I trip on my way to the microphone? What if—"

"What if you don't get ready for the show?" Warren interjected. "I think that's the far more *pressing* issue, don't you?" He flashed a sly smile. "Or do you plan on going out there *décolleté?* You'd certainly make your mark in history *then*—although I'm not sure how the *Empress* might respond to you serenading her husband in your underwear . . ."

A wisp of a smile came to her lips. "You're terrible," she said.

"That I am," Warren agreed. "Which, may I remind you, is one of the reasons you're so head-over-heels in love with me."

Betsy tossed aside the pillow, rose to her feet, and wrapped her arms around his neck, pulling him close.

"Quite true," she said. "But I think I'll keep my clothes on, anyway."

Warren shrugged. "Von Doom's loss . . . but I can live with that."

They stood like that, gazing deeply into one another's eyes, until a knock on the door brought their attention back to more earthly matters.

"I'd better get that," Betsy said.

"All right," Warren replied.

"But you have to let go of me first," she pointed out.

"Oh, very well," Warren sighed. He removed his arms from around her waist.

Betsy quickly shrugged into a full-length terrycloth bathrobe and opened the door.

Standing in the hallway was Tommy Grunfeld, one of the art center's assistant stage managers. In his early twenties, medium of height and build—at five-foot-eleven, Betsy towered about two inches above him in her bare feet—he sported sandy hair tied back in a ponytail, and a tiny spot of facial hair—often referred to as a "soul patch"—just below the center of his bottom lip. He wore a powder-blue tuxedo that looked as though it had been rented twenty-five years ago by his father—when wide lapels were all the rage—and never returned, only passed along to the next generation of Grunfelds. A small earpiece and attached microphone were held fast to his head by a wide plastic strap, and he carried a clipboard containing what appeared to be the run-down of the show.

Tommy let out a high-pitched wolf whistle. "Wow, babe! You look like a million bucks!"

"What . . . ?" Betsy gazed down at her frumpy garment, which had opened just enough to provide a hint of cleavage. "It's a *bathrobe*, Tommy."

"Oh." Grunfeld shrugged. "Hey, what do *I* know from fashion? All I *do* know is it's got more material than anything Tina Turner is wearin'." He made an appreciative face. "Looks nice on ya, though." Looking up, he caught sight of Warren standing just beside her. "Uh . . . no offense, sir."

Warren raised a quizzical eyebrow and stuck out his bottom teeth in a vague, caveman-like expression. "You . . . *like* Worthington woo-mahn?" he grunted.

"Don't mind him, Tommy—he's had a little too much caffeine today," Betsy commented. She elbowed Warren in the stomach without turning to look at him. Grunting once more, he shambled over to the loveseat and flopped down on its cushions.

"What did you want to see me about, Tommy?" she asked.

"Just checkin' in with everybody, lettin' 'em know what the final order for the acts is gonna be." Grunfeld glanced at his clipboard. "You go on around ten, just before the Intermission."

Betsy smiled. "That's not bad at all. Who am I following?"

Another glance at the schedule. "Umm ... The Senior Class of The Massachusetts Academy in *The Fall of Attuma: An Epic Tale Told in Song and Dance*." Grunfeld sucked in his breath through clenched teeth. "Whoa—talk about your spots that really *bite.*" He glanced up. "Sorry, babe."

"Don't be," Betsy said, a twinkle in her eye. "Going on before Intermission means I'll be the first act everyone remembers when they get together in the Foyer."

Grunfeld raised an eyebrow. "Just so long as they're talkin' about you in a *good* way, babe. Keep that in mind before you go out there, okay?"

Betsy chuckled. "Oh, I will, inde—"

A phalanx of Guardsmen suddenly stomped by in the hall, catching her attention.

"What's with all the security?" she asked. "There weren't that many guards rushing about when we got here this afternoon."

"S.O.P., babe, when the Big Man's in the house, although it's usually not *this* many goons." Tommy glanced around to make sure no one but Betsy could hear him. "Must be all that talk about Magneto wantin' to blow the place up," he said quietly.

*"What?"* Betsy cried.

Tommy gestured wildly with his hands, motioning for Betsy to lower her voice. "Hey, keep it down! You wanna get me in trouble?" He nodded. "Yeah—word is he had somethin' to do with that big explosion in Virginia last night." He tilted his head to one side "What, you didn't hear the blast? It was so loud, they say you could hear it in Pittsburgh."

"We were ... busy," Betsy replied, glancing at Warren. "But I heard about it on the news this morning. I just didn't think it had anything to do with—are you *sure* he's going to try and blow up the arts center?"

"Hey, it's no big deal, babe," the assistant stage manager assured her. "With the kinda firepower we got around us, that bucketheaded maniac would *really* be outta his nut to try an' take on the Big Man on his home court—y'know what I mean?"

"I . . . guess," Betsy replied.

"Primo!" Tommy said. He patted her on the shoulder encouragingly, then glanced at his watch. "Oh, jeez. Look, I got a few more people to see. Don't worry about a thing—just concentrate on knockin' 'em dead out there, okay?"

"Okay," Betsy said.

"Break a leg, babe!" Tommy said, then hurried down the hall.

Betsy crossed her fingers and glanced up at the ceiling. "God willing, that's *all* that will be broken tonight . . ."

"All is in readiness, dread lord," Cortez reported. "We await your command to strike."

"Excellent," Magneto said.

Behind them, the X-Men and acolytes were gathered around the suite's television, watching the live broadcast from the arts center. Rogue, having awakened from her "nap," had joined them, but she sat in a corner, ignoring all attempts to draw her into a friendly conversation. Slumped in her chair, she stared at a spot on the carpet—never blinking, never moving a muscle. And though each of her teammates had tried their best to talk to her, it seemed that nothing would bring her out of her crushing depression.

Wolverine was right—she *would* be a long time hurting . . .

"Lotta security," Forge noted, pointing to the TV screen as the cameras outside the building showed glimpses of the grim-faced forces that stood guard. "Looks like von Doom's getting ready for a war."

"It appears we are expected, Father," Pietro said with a wry smile.

"Then, who am I to disappoint our host," Magneto replied with a false smile, "after he has gone to such lengths to make me feel so welcome?"

A sinister chuckle rippled through the acolytes and their leader—a sentiment not shared by the X-Men.

"Just remember to hold up your end of the bargain, Magnus," Cyclops said.

"You have my word that no innocents shall be harmed in this endeavor, Summers," Magneto said. "It's Doom I want, not his slaves." His eyes narrowed. "But should any of them become foolish enough to delay my vengeance by even a fraction of a second—"

"That's when I cut yer heart out," Wolverine interjected with a sneer. "An' have it bronzed."

"Focus on the *mission*, Logan, not your anger," Cyclops ordered. "Let Magnus run off at the mouth as much as he wants—stopping Doom is what's important here." He glanced at Magneto, and shrugged. "Besides, he can't *help* posturing—it's his nature."

"You're beginning to sound like your mentor," the mutant overlord sniped, "although I wonder how the saintly Charles Xavier would feel about his favorite student agreeing to allow their greatest enemy the chance to murder a common foe, even for the good of the universe." A vicious, arrogant smile twisted his lips. "Doesn't such behavior go against the tenets of his precious Dream—that petty, saccharine-sweet vision in which all life—even that of an armored tyrant—is sacred, and man and mutant live in ever-lasting harmony? How do *you* think he would react, Summers?"

Cyclops fell silent, trying to ignore the disappointed expressions of his teammates.

"Yakyakyak," Unuscione said angrily. "We just gonna stand around talking, or do we get around to ripping off Doom's head and stuffing it with garlic?"

"The latter, dear child," said Magneto. "Most definitely the latter." He looked around the room at his fellow conspirators. "Now, my friends, the moment is at last upon us to strike! Once Doom has fallen, this world—and everyone in it—will be changed for-ever!"

"I hope he means that in a *good* way," Nightcrawler whispered to Phoenix.

"I hope we survive long enough to find out . . ." she replied.

The voices were back—with a vengeance.

With Warren having gone off to take his seat in the audito-rium—after making certain she wouldn't appear on-stage in her unmentionables by helping her into her gown and matching opera gloves—Betsy had been sitting alone in her dressing room for the past hour, with only her thoughts to keep her company. She was waiting for Tommy to eventually come by and rap on her door to let her know it was time. Unfortunately, as the minutes passed, her pre-show jitters became so intense that she allowed her con-centration to slip.

The sound and fury that suddenly exploded in her mind was akin to waking up in the center of the New York Stock Exchange on a frantic day of trading—there were screams, shouts, even bells ringing. The intensity of the "noise" had driven her to her knees, and momentarily blinded her.

There were too many people around her, she realized as she staggered over to the loveseat; too many "voices" demanding to be heard. The thoughts pounded her mind in unrelenting waves, each breaker more powerful than the one before it, until she was sitting, doubled-over, the heels of her hands pressing against her temples.

*Get outGetOUTGETOUT!* her own thoughts screamed at the un-wanted voices.

And, to her amazement, the voices obeyed; all was suddenly calm and quiet in the mind of Elisabeth Braddock—the very same woman who, a few short days ago, had feared for her sanity.

Betsy opened her eyes, uncertain of what had just happened. True, she had been working hard to block outside thoughts for the past few days; her success at the party last night was proof that she had been getting better at it. But now, it was as though she had angrily confronted a group of guests who had overstayed their welcome and forced them out of the cluttered apartment that was her mind, then locked the door behind them.

Could her control be *that* good, in so short a period of time?

"Well, don't *question* it, you git," she scolded herself. "Just be *thankful* for it."

Nodding in complete agreement with herself, Betsy slowly eased back in the loveseat, expecting the "guests" to return at any moment, prepared for the worst. When it didn't happen, an easy smile came to her lips, and she began to enjoy the feeling of serenity that flowed through her mind. Maybe Warren was right; maybe she *would* get through this evening without any problems . . .

A fog bank was rolling in from off the Potomac River.

It was a complete surprise to the security detail of D.C. police officers on the river side of the arts center—the weather forecast had called for clear, moonlit skies and a cool breeze from the east (all due, of course, to Ororo's influence). And the fact that it had appeared without them noticing it before this second made them incredibly suspicious.

Unfortunately for the officers, the fog was upon them before anyone was able to notify the command center—and then all it took was a strong telepathic "push" from Phoenix to "shut down" their minds and render them unconscious, as she had done with Rogue.

After scanning the fallen officers to make sure none had suffered brain damage, Phoenix took to the air, heading for the roof.

Across the river, on Theodore Roosevelt Island, the X-Men and Magneto's acolytes had gathered to launch their attack. Now, they watched as the fog bank continued to move from the river to envelop the arts center; the building was quickly lost from sight.

"That is a most impressive ability of Ms. Voght's," Nightcrawler said. "I didn't think she was capable of covering such a large area in her mist-form."

"It ain't gonna work fer long, though," Wolverine commented. "All these bully-boys in one area, watchin' out fer trouble—*somebody's* gonna get wise an' let Doom know what's goin' on."

"True," Forge said. "But that tyrant's such an incredible egomaniac, he'll probably want to meet us head-on."

"I certainly hope so . . ." Magneto said, a wicked gleam in his eyes.

"It's Phoenix," Cyclops suddenly said; he was receiving information from his wife through their telepathic link. "The first obstacle's been removed—she's moving on to Target #2."

Magneto turned to his fellow conspirators. "We move—quickly."

Gathering everyone in a magnetic field, the mutant overlord flew them across the river, to land in front of the arts center. Phoenix drifted down from the roof to join them.

"Mission accomplished," she said. "All the guards on this side of the building, as well as the roof, are sleeping like babies. But we've got to move quickly—I heard some chatter over their walkie-talkies: they know we're here. It won't be long before they start heading this way."

"All right, Summers, this is where we split up," Magneto said to Cyclops. "You and your people are the first line of defense. Try and hold off Doom's lapdogs for as long as you can."

"Giving you time enough to get to Doom," Cyclops replied.

Magneto smiled without humor. "And all this time I used to think you were quite the dullard." He turned to his acolytes. "Come, my friends—we mustn't be late for the final act . . . especially when *we* are the ones who are going to write it." An evil smile twisted his features. "I wonder how the story will end . . . ?"

Moving quickly but silently, the band of rebellious mutants disappeared into the mist.

"I'm gonna enjoy carvin' my initials in that puke's face when the time comes . . ." Wolverine muttered.

"Don't bother with your initials, Logan," Cyclops said through clenched teeth as he gazed into the living fog that undulated around them. "Write your full name."

Nightcrawler turned to the young woman standing beside him. "Feeling up to this, Rogue?" He waited for her to reply, but the beautiful powerhouse only stared at the arts center, fidgeting as though eager to be somewhere else. *"Rogue?"*

The red-and-black-clad X-Man started, as though awakened from a trance. Slowly, she turned toward Kurt. "What?" she asked heatedly.

"I was asking how you felt," Nightcrawler replied.

"I'm *fine*, Kurt—just *fine,*" she said curtly. "Couldn't be better— for a woman who just lost the man she loved, that is." She glared at her teammate. "That answer your question?"

"Indeed," Kurt replied softly. Rogue grunted and went back to staring at the wall in front of her, as though she were capable of seeing through it.

But looking for what? Kurt wondered, as he gazed at Rogue's heated expression. It was obvious the girl was running on auto pilot; it would be a miracle if they could actually count on her in this fight, but excluding her from the mission had not been an option—they needed her powers.

But there was something more to her silent rage—something that went beyond mere depression. All that anger, all that grief she was so clearly bottling up inside ever since she had stepped from the hotel bedroom—Kurt knew they had to be released at some point, or they'd eventually destroy her. It was *how* she would release those emotions when the time came that was beginning to worry him.

Could she be waiting, perhaps, to get her hands on the one person she held responsible for Gambit's death? The one man who had changed an entire world to suit his twisted needs, thus forcing the X-Men to set out on this nightmarish mission that had cost them so dearly already?

And, if so, would one of her friends be forced into stopping

Rogue, before she did something she'd regret for the rest of her life?

Silently, Kurt prayed that he and his fellow X-Men would not have to be placed in such a position. In his heart, though, he knew it was just a matter of time . . .

Inside the Concert Hall, the woman known as Lancer sat bolt upright in her seat in the Royal Box—there was a loud buzzing in her ear. It took her a moment to recognize it as the alert for an incoming call on the combination receiver/transmitter she wore clipped to her right ear.

She touched a small contact on the earpiece. "Go."

"Sorry to disturb you, Sam, but there might be a situation brewing." The voice that crackled through the receiver belonged to Peter Garibaldi, the White House Chief of Security. He was also one of the few people Lancer allowed to address her by her real name.

"Hang on a second," she whispered. Moving quietly so as not to disturb the Royal Couple, Lancer rose from her seat and moved to the rear of the box.

"All right, talk to me," she whispered into the tiny microphone.

"Security detail on the roof spotted a fog rolling in from the river—big one, too."

"One not scheduled by the Empress to remind her of her last trip to London, I imagine," Lancer said.

"You got it. Then we lost contact with them." Garibaldi paused. "The detail on the roof, too."

Lancer sadly shook her head. "You'd think that walking magnet would've had the decency to wait until the show's over."

"Some people, huh?" quipped Garibaldi.

"Yeah." Lancer sighed. "All right, go to full alert—nobody in, nobody out. I want this place locked up so tight Reed Richards couldn't squeeze in here through a crack in the plaster. And if somebody *does* spot Magneto, I want to know from which direction he's coming, which wall he's probably going to blow up to get inside, and how long it'll take him to get to the Concert Hall."

"Hell, I'll even give you his aisle and row numbers if I can find my copy of the seating arrangements," Garibaldi replied.

Lancer chuckled softly. "You do that. And Peter?"

"Yeah?"

"The first person who falls asleep at the switch will answer to *me*—and they *better* hope their medical insurance payments are up-to-date when they do. Make sure you pass *that* bit of encouragement along to the troops, would you?"

"It'll be an inspiration to us all, Ms. Dunbar," replied the security chief.

Cutting the connection, Lancer turned around to find von Doom and Ororo watching her.

"Damn . . ." Lancer muttered. Crouching low, and pulling up the hem of her dark-blue ball gown so she wouldn't trip, she moved to speak with them, motioning to Harada to join in the conversation.

Von Doom turned back toward the stage to watch Bernadette Peters as she soulfully performed "Someone to Watch Over Me." The Emperor nodded politely as she looked toward the Royal Box. "Is there a problem, Lancer?" he asked softly.

"Could be," she admitted, and glanced at Ororo. "An unexpected fog bank that just rolled in from the Potomac—Security's having some trouble seeing."

"He comes," the Emperor murmured. "At last, he comes." The tone of malicious joy in his voice was unmistakable.

"That would be *my* guess, Your Majesty," Lancer said. "But this really isn't the time or place for a knock-down/drag-out—not with all these people here probably getting caught in the middle."

"What would you suggest, Lancer?" Ororo asked.

"It might be best if we were to leave, Your Majesty," Lancer replied.

Miss Peters finished her last song to an energetic round of applause. Von Doom and Ororo joined in, the sound of his metal-encased hands coming together ringing loudly throughout the auditorium. When the applause at last died down with Miss Peters' exit from the stage, the Emperor turned to his bodyguard, a sneer on his lips.

"You think I should *run* from him, Lancer? Should I cower in fear, and allow others to snatch from my hands the victory over that wretch that should be *mine,* and mine alone?"

"Now, you *know* I didn't mean it like that, Your Majesty," Lancer replied. "But you pay me to watch your back, and that's *exactly* what I'm trying to do—if you'll *let* me."

"There will be no talk of running, Lancer," the Emperor stated flatly. "*Let* that mutant dog come. Doom stands ready for him."

Lancer sighed. "Somehow, I just *knew* you were going to say that . . ."

"Ladies and gentlemen—Miss Elisabeth Braddock."

A polite smattering of applause greeted Betsy as she stepped out onto the stage of the Concert Hall and nodded in acknowledgment to the orchestra conductor; he smiled and did likewise. The "voices" greeted her, too—mostly blasé comments about her being "Worthington's songbird" from those who recognized her, or questions about who she was, and how in the world she had wound up on the evening's card from those who didn't—but she forced them down and out of her mind. *Nothing* was going to spoil this moment for her. Somewhere, out there in the seemingly endless rows of seats, she knew, Warren was watching her, probably holding his breath and crossing his fingers, trying to look calm while his heart nervously pounded in his chest.

She felt the same way.

Yet, knowing that the most important person in her world was out there, confident in every way that she would have no trouble in getting through what could be the most important *moment* of her *life,* she wondered how she could even have *thought* about disappointing him . . . or herself, for that matter.

She reached the microphone without tripping over the stand, or bumping into its foam-covered diaphragm and causing a screech of eardrum-rattling feedback to echo throughout the hall. So far, so good. Now she just had to make it to the end of her set . . .

"Good evening," she said to the crowd. "Although I'm certain others before me have expressed these same sentiments, I'd just like to say what an honor it is to be here tonight, on such a special occasion." She glanced toward the Royal Box. "And for such a special honoree."

The audience applauded enthusiastically, less for her sentiment and more for the man in the iron suit, who smiled politely and nodded in approval.

Betsy smiled demurely. *Never let it be said I don't know how to suck up big-time to royalty . . .*

When the applause died down, she turned to the conductor. He nodded and signaled for the orchestra to begin playing the introduction to her first number.

For the next twenty minutes, Betsy opened her heart to the people around her—and the billions watching across the world—singing of hopes dashed and dreams realized, of bitter disappointments and wondrous expectations, of tragic losses and soaring victories.

But most of all, she sang of love. Of its magic and its miraculous healing powers. Of its inspirations and wonderments. Of how she had found its true meaning in the touch of the one man in all the world who meant everything to her—the man who was her life, her heart, her soul.

And when she had finished, when the last sweet note had faded into the shadows around her, an unusual silence enveloped the Concert Hall.

Nervously, eyes tightly shut, Betsy bit down on her lower lip for a moment, wondering what could have gone so wrong that the audience wouldn't even respond. And if the audience hated her singing, then what must the Royal Family have thought of her? Slowly, she opened her eyes and glanced toward the Royal Box—

—and was stunned to see the Emperor and Empress rise to their feet and applaud.

Following that cue—apparently having been waiting for the Royal Family's reaction—everyone in the auditorium did likewise. They cheered loudly, the sound growing in volume until the arts center seemed to vibrate.

And as the house lights came up, Betsy looked out into the audience, to find Warren standing front row, center, beaming proudly. He pointed to her and silently mouthed the words, "You *did* it, Betts. Nobody but *you.*"

She stood there, tears of joy running down her cheeks, soaking up the cheers and applause that made the years of frustration, the snide questions about her talent, even the voices in her head seem worth all the struggle; reveling in this moment that she wished might never end—

And then the first explosion rocked the building.

# 17

**R**OGUE! CLEAR a path!" Cyclops yelled. "Get those people out of there before they get caught in the crossfire!"

Nodding in acknowledgment but saying nothing, Rogue flew toward the south side of the arts center and began hammering away at the marble wall.

Cyclops turned to the other male members of his team. "Wolverine! Nightcrawler! Keep an eye out for more of those Hunters Magneto warned us about—we don't need a repeat of a few days ago."

Nightcrawler watched Rogue as she tore away great chunks of the arts center's façade, her lovely features now contorted with rage. To Kurt, it looked less like she was creating an emergency exit for the guests trapped inside, and more like she was tunneling into the building to find the true target of her anger. If she made it inside alone . . .

"Cyclops," Nightcrawler said, "I think, perhaps, I should help Rogue instead . . ."

Cyclops shook his head. "She's a big girl, Kurt—she can take care of herself." He turned to Phoenix. "Jean, you're with me. We have to find Doom before Magneto does."

"What *about* Lensherr, Summers?" Wolverine asked. "If I see 'im, ya want me t'escort 'im t'Doom's private box?"

Cyclops glared at him for a moment, then thrust a warning index finger in Wolverine's face. "Don't push me, Logan—not now."

Wolverine snarled. "Point that finger somewhere else, one-eye—before I go upsettin' yer wife."

"Stop it!" Phoenix snapped. "We don't have time for this!" She stared heatedly at Wolverine. "You want to take your aggressions out on someone, Logan?" She pointed over his shoulder. "Take it out on them!"

Wolverine turned. The artifical fog that was Amanda Voght was lifting, presumably because she was joining Magneto's forces on the other side of the building. Their position exposed by the light of the full moon, the X-Men had known it wouldn't take very long for trouble to find them—and now it was here.

Stomping their way was a group of Hunters—a quartet of men and women who, even in a normal world, the X-Men would have considered enemies.

In her mid-twenties, The White Rabbit was an attractive woman who looked more like a disgruntled Playboy Bunny than a super-villain, dressed in white go-go boots and one-piece bathing suit, over which were worn the sort of plaid vest, gold pocketwatch, and blue velvet waistcoat that might have attired her anthropo-morphic namesake in the classic story *Alice in Wonderland*; a ri-diculous pair of artificial bunny ears protruded from her shoulder-length blond hair, and a fluffy tail was sewn onto the back of her swimsuit, just above her posterior.

Diablo was a green-and-purple-clad sorceror of indeterminate age. Thin as the proverbial rail, with a pencil-thin mustache and a sharp, hawk-like beak for a nose, he was a master of the black arts, conjuring demons and bewitching his victims with but a wave of his hand and a few simple words. Unfortunately, having to rely on oral spells was a terrible drawback for the sorceror, since he possessed what is commonly referred to in boxing as "a glass jaw."

A swift shot to the molars, and Diablo would wind up kissing the ground as though it were a long-lost lover.

The assassin known as Deadly Nightshade was an African-American woman in her early twenties, wearing thigh-high, black leather boots and the briefest of black leather bikinis, a pair of gunbelts wrapped around her shapely waist; her head was framed by an immense Afro, the size of which made one immediately think of the R&B group The Commodores at the height of their musical careers. However, despite the fact that she looked like someone who had spent far too much time watching female "blaxploitation" films of the 1970s during her formative years, Nightshade was as talented a markswoman as Cyclops was with his power beams.

A bunny. A pantywaist. A Pam Grier wannabe. Not exactly the kind of group normally expected to provide serious trouble for any *single* member of the X-Men, let alone the entire team.

The man *leading* the pack of Hunters, however, was an entirely different story.

He was a bear-sized man with a wild mane of golden hair, deadly fangs, and an even deadlier set of claws. A raving sociopath who lived for the thrill of the hunt, for the pleasure of the kill. A mutant, who, *on his own,* had come close to wiping out the entire complement of the X-Men's roster on quite a few occasions.

His name was Sabretooth; in this, or any other reality, he was Logan's oldest—and most lethal—enemy.

And Wolverine always looked forward to the next opportunity when he could literally wipe that malicious grin off his inhuman sparring partner's face—usually by dragging it along the side of a building.

With a malicious smile, Logan triggered his claws.

"You folks head in," he growled to Cyclops and Phoenix. "I might be here a while." And then, with a lion-like roar, he charged at his adversaries.

Cyclops turned to Nightcrawler. "Kurt—"

Torn between aiding his colleague and teleporting into the

building to track down Rogue, Nightcrawler froze, his thoughts racing over what to do next. Against Sabretooth and his three accomplices, his rational mind argued, it was a certainty that Logan could handle the situation; Rogue, on the other hand, was in the midst of severe depression. For all Kurt knew—and the good Lord knew he wasn't a psychologist—she might not be looking to punish Doom for Gambit's death; rather, she could be planning to force him to end her suffering—so she could spend the rest of eternity by Remy's side.

And yet, the image of Logan, standing atop a pile of corpses in the center of the Salem Center death camp, flashed through his mind. He couldn't allow such carnage to happen again.

The piercing scream of the White Rabbit as she leapt away from Wolverine's slashing claws helped Kurt come to a quick decision.

"All right, Scott," Nightcrawler replied. "I shall try to keep him out of trouble . . . though it would be far easier to ask me to stop the Hulk from tearing down the towers of the World Trade Center."

"Next time," Cyclops said with a wry smile.

Nightcrawler nodded. "Good luck with your help, *mein freuden.*" Turning on his heel, he raced over to help Wolverine, though it was obvious that it was the Hunters—with the exception of Sabretooth—who were the ones in most need of aid, if only to provide them with any chance of surviving this encounter with the feral X-Man.

Cyclops looked to Phoenix. "Let's go."

A flash of bright-green eyes, and Phoenix hoisted them both into the air. They flew quickly above the stampeding crowds that poured through Rogue's hastily-made side exit, moving deeper into the arts center.

Of Rogue herself, there was no sign.


*"Where is he?"* Magneto bellowed to the panicked patrons as they raced for the exits. "Where is your 'beloved ruler'—that tin-plated madman who dared to toy with the mind of Magneto?"

As to be expected, no one stopped to answer him; within seconds, he was alone.

Standing in the lobby of the arts center, hips on hips, Magneto hurled destructive bolts of magnetic energy at the walls, the ceiling, the fine *objets d'art* that had represented all that was best in Latveria. Everything shattered beneath the devastating volley. The building shook violently, as it had when he had fired the first volley that blew in the north wall, throwing aside subterfuge for a line of attack more suited to his personality: direct confrontation.

It had certainly gotten everyone's attention.

*"DOOM!"* he shouted. "Your executioner has arrived! Come forth, so we may put a swift end to this nonsense you've created!"

"Y'all can't have him, Erik," said a familiar, Southern-tinged voice from above.

Magneto looked up. There, on the second floor landing, was Rogue. As he watched, she took to the air, floating down to land directly in his path.

"What's this?" Magneto asked. "Summers and I had an agreement, Rogue: *none* of you are allowed to interfere."

"Cyclops can go *hang* for all I care," Rogue said. "This here business is just between Doom an' me."

"And what sort of 'business' would *that* be, child?" Magneto asked, clearly annoyed by this interruption.

Rogue snarled. "Me *killin'* him."

"Is that so?" Magneto said, raising a quizzical eyebrow. He seemed more amused than threatened by this young woman, as he gazed at her smoldering, hate-filled eyes. Slowly, though, he came to an understanding. "Ah. I see. He killed your—" he sneered "—boyfriend, Gambit, and so he must pay the ultimate price. 'An eye for an eye,' yes?"

"Somethin' like that," Rogue said. Her voice was flat, emotionless.

Magneto chuckled. "If only your idealistic teacher could see you all now. *You* want to kill von Doom. *Cyclops* is willing to step aside and allow me first blood. How Charles's heart would break."

He shook his head. "But I'm sorry, child. While I empathize with your situation—truly, I do—and would dearly enjoy seeing you take that first step toward darkness, I cannot allow it. Doom is *mine* to punish." He moved to one side, to go around her and continue on his way.

*"No,"* Rogue said flatly. She stepped into his path again, hands curled into mighty fists.

"Don't force me to kill *you* as well, X-Man," Magneto warned.

"Take yer best shot," Rogue growled.

Razor-sharp claws suddenly raked across her back, and Rogue cried out in pain. Blinking back tears, she turned to face her cowardly attacker, only to be bludgeoned with a hundred blows across her face and body, delivered within the space of a heartbeat by the super-swift Quicksilver. She staggered back, dazed, into the arms of the reptilian Mellencamp, who wasted no time in sinking his powerful teeth into her left shoulder and clamping down tightly, like some saurian pit bull. Rogue screamed and thrashed wildly, but could do nothing to pull herself free.

Quicksilver came to a halt beside Magneto. "Having some trouble, Father?"

"A momentary diversion, my son," he replied. "Though I had no need of assistance, I am still grateful for your timely intervention." He looked around. "Where are the others?"

"Unuscione and Cortez are dealing with the Hunters. Mellencamp and I have already confronted the Guardsmen; they have momentarily withdrawn—" Pietro smiled "—probably to repair all their damaged armor. Vindaloo and Scanner are handling the armed forces without."

As if on cue, a wall of fire erupted in front of the building—Vindaloo's napalm-like flames at work. The screams of those caught in the blast were cut short by the window-shattering explosions of limousines and police vehicles as their gas tanks ignited.

"Forge and Voght are providing cover for us," Pietro continued. "And Mystique has already been here for quite some time."

Magneto nodded, clearly pleased with the report. "And the X-Men?"

"Like *this* one—" Pietro gestured toward Rogue, who was trying to pry open Mellencamp's jaws "—they're starting to make their way inside."

"To be the ones who reach Doom first," Magneto rumbled, a sneer on his lips. "To keep me from my vengeance."

"Then, *go*, Father," Pietro said. He lashed out with a booted foot, ending Rogue's struggles with a swift kick to the head. "Mellencamp and I shall deal with this . . . minor annoyance."

"As ever, my son, you do your father proud," the mutant overlord said. Without looking back, he moved deeper into the building, determined to find the man who had dared to toy with his mind.


"Your Majesty, we should leave," Lancer said.

Around the Royal Box, the guests were in a panic, stampeding for the exits as the building swayed from an almost continuous series of explosions created by the powerful, destructive energies being unleashed both inside the arts center and outside the grounds. Bits of plaster began to rain down from the Concert Hall ceiling, and the lights started flickering.

Von Doom glared at his bodyguard. "You think I fear a handful of traitors and their cretinous leader? Doom fears *no one!*"

"I didn't say you did, Sire," Lancer replied. "But my job is to keep you and the Empress safe from harm, and I can't very well do that in a place the size of an aircraft carrier. Too many spots in here for someone to hide and wait for that split-second when Security might become distracted by an attack made just to draw our attention away from you. I wouldn't put something like that past Magneto."

"Lancer is right, my love," Ororo said calmly. "This space is too confined for a confrontation with your enemies, and too many innocents would be caught in the crossfire. But if we were to lure him away, perhaps to The Mall, where there is far more room in which to maneuver . . ."

The Emperor paused to consider the logic of his wife's explanation. After a few moments, he slowly nodded in agreement, and smiled warmly. "Once more, my love, you demonstrate why Doom chose you as his mate—not only for your ravishing beauty, but your intelligence."

Von Doom rose to his feet and held out his hand. Ororo gently took it, laying her fingers across his gauntleted palm.

"Come, my dear," the Emperor said. "We must prepare to—" a wicked smile came to his lips "—properly greet our guests."

"Warren! Warren!" Betsy cried. "Where are you?"

Stumbling through the uppermost floor of the arts center, Betsy had spent the better part of a fifteen minutes searching for her missing beau; they'd become separated after the initial explosion, during the audience's mad dash for the exits. Betsy had been swept away on the tide of humanity that had surged across the stage, barely saving herself from being trampled to death by ducking into a women's bathroom before the hem of her gown had the opportunity to trip her up as she ran.

"Aero-taxi service, Ma'am?" a male voice asked, from just behind her.

Betsy turned and looked up. Warren was hovering in the air just past her left shoulder. He had tossed aside his jacket and undone the harness he usually wore that kept his wings hidden under his clothes; now, they were spread wide, flapping gently, their feathers a magnificent white against the shadows of the darkened hallway and the moonlit sky outside.

Betsy ran to him and threw her arms around him as he settled to the ground. He gently stroked her hair and hugged her back.

"I was starting to think I'd never find you," Warren said softly. He kissed the top of her head.

"You can't lose me *that* easily, Mr. Worthington," Betsy said, her cheek pressed against his chest.

"Well, I never *want* to lose you that easily, Ms. Braddock," he replied.

The chatter of gunfire from outside drew their attention to a giant picture window at the front of the building. Down on the street, and around the arts center, man and mutant clashed, and man was clearly losing. The air was rent by the screams and moans of the injured and dying. Half a dozen cars were aflame, the thick, black smoke that wafted up from their smoldering husks lifting high above the district, blocking the light of the moon.

"It feels like the world is coming apart at the seams," Betsy said quietly, looking out at the chaos unfurling below them. Warren gently placed an arm around her waist.

"Don't worry, hon," he said reassuringly. "Doom will have all this back under control by morning." He winced as he saw a limousine explode. "I just wish we were able to tell what's the safest way out of here so we could *make* it to the morning."

"There ... might be a way for me to find out," Betsy said hesitantly, turning to face him.

Warren raised a quizzical eyebrow. "And how, pray tell, Ms. Braddock, would that be possible?"

Betsy paused, chewing on her bottom lip for a moment, trying to find the right way to explain her ... peculiar situation. Or at least a way that wouldn't make it sound as though she'd lost her mind.

*Well ... the direct approach is usually the best way,* she thought. *Just go ahead and tell him.*

"You remember that night after my performance for Arcade?" she asked.

A wolfish grin lit Warren's handsome features. "How could I forget?"

She playfully slapped him on the arm. "I meant *before* that, you big, blue idiot—when we were in Central Park, and you asked me if I could read your mind?"

Warren paused, obviously searching his memory for that particular conversation; then, his eyes widened in surprise. "What? You mean you really *are* a mind reader?"

Betsy flashed a small smile. "Something like that. But only recently."

"Oh, great," he replied sarcastically. "It's bad enough I have to watch what I say out loud around you—now I've got to be careful about what *thoughts* might be running through my head." He smiled and tapped the end of her nose with his index finger. "That's not fair, you know."

"Darling, you're a *man,*" Betsy said playfully, reaching up to stroke his cheek. "I could read your mind *long* before this happened." She smiled. "You know, you're taking this much better than I expected."

"Hey, hon, you're talking to a guy with *blue skin* and *wings,*" Warren replied. "When you wake up every morning and get reminded of that little fact by your reflection in the bathroom mirror, everything else seems kinda run-of-the-mill after that. Besides, there are certainly *worse* things you could have told me than that you're turning into a budding mento—like you're really some trained assassin who used to work for the Japanese mobs." He smiled. "Now, *that* would surprise me." He paused. "Well, at least it explains those headaches you were having. Still having them?"

Betsy nodded. "Yes, but they're not as bad as before. I seem to have some influence over them—at least for now."

Another explosion—close to their position—rocked the building, and they held tightly to one another.

"I believe you said something about finding us a way out of here . . . ?" Warren urged.

"I'll do my best." Betsy stepped back from him and closed her eyes. "Now, be a quiet little bear and let Mother find us a way out of here."

"I'll try to keep the gunfire down to a minimum," Warren said sarcastically.

Taking a deep breath, then slowly releasing it, she reached out with her mind, scanning the floors above by allowing the thoughts around her to filter in, giving her some indication of where the forces of Magneto and von Doom were currently clashing. She eventually made contact with the unconscious minds of the security detail stationed on the roof—exactly *how* she was able to do *that* she didn't know—and discovered they were all in some sort of deep sleep. That was good, in a way—it meant she and Warren wouldn't be shot while trying to make their escape.

"The roof seems to be the safest bet," she told Warren as she opened her eyes. She pointed toward a nearby EXIT sign that hung above a door leading to the fire stairs. "This wa—"

—and then her thoughts were suddenly touched by another mind.

It this wasn't like her other, horrid experiences, though, with voices raging in her head and tearing at her sanity; these were the thoughts of a woman like her—someone with similar abilities, though Betsy could immediately tell that this other person was in complete control of the psychic madness they shared.

And there was also a familiarity to this voice that had inadvertently entered her mind—a gentle tone that gave her comfort, calmed her fears, made her feel as though everything would be all right. A name suddenly formed in her thoughts:

"Jean . . . ?" she whispered uncertainly.

"Scott—it's Betsy!" Phoenix cried. "She's here—" her eyes widened in surprise "—and so is Warren!"

Standing beside his wife in the Grand Foyer, Cyclops opened his visor to release a devastating stream of energy that scattered the riot gear-clad police officers charging their way.

"Where?" Cyclops asked. "We could certainly use their help!"

Phoenix concentrated for a moment as her husband continued to hold at bay what seemed to be most of the cops in the district. "They're—No! They're leaving—flying away!"

Cyclops grunted. "Just as well—they probably wouldn't have recognized us, anyway. Where's *Doom?*"

Another psychic probe went forth, searching the building for their adversary. "He's also on his way out—two floors down, heading north." Phoenix started. "Scott . . . Ororo's with him."

"I guess that's to be expected, hon," Cyclops replied. "They *are* the Royal Couple, after all."

The two heroes' discussion was interrupted by the arrival of a coterie of National Guard troopers, armed to the teeth and ready to take on all comers.

"Take 'em out!" ordered a man wearing sergeant's stripes. More than a dozen M-16 rifles swung around to target the young couple.

"Well, *this* is bad . . ." Phoenix muttered.

Cyclops grabbed her arm and pulled her into the abandoned Concert Hall just as the shooting began.

"Let's find an exit, all right?" he said as they dashed down the center aisle. "Hopefully, it'll be the same one Doom winds up at . . ."

Lancer never expected—in a world where men and women flew under their own power and unleashed incredible, destructive energies stored within their own bodies—that something so commonplace as a bullet would end her life.

Leading the Royal Couple from the Concert Hall, through the back stage area, and toward an underground garage in which the Emperor's limousine was parked, every step of the escape had been a major hassle. It seemed that, each time the arts center was rocked by another explosion, von Doom would move to run off and go in search of the very mutants who were trying to find *him*. It was only the logical arguments of the Empress—ones guaranteed to play directly to her husband's mountain-sized ego—that had stayed his ill-considered actions, and kept the line moving.

But, as Lancer, Harada, and another male bodyguard—recruited during their exit from the Royal Box—escorted the Emperor and Empress to the exit leading to the garage, she was surprised to find Arcade waiting for them, a big grin etched on his face.

"What are you doing here, Minister?" she asked suspiciously.

"Well, I was running for my life from all those crazy mutants attacking the place, sweets, when I heard you folks tromping this way," he explained, and turned to von Doom. "Are you all right, Your Majesty?"

"I am unharmed, Arcade," the Emperor replied, clearly annoyed by the man's presence, "but I am most eager to show these loutish mutants the error of their ways. Now, remove yourself from my path."

Arcade ignored the command and nodded toward the EXIT sign above his head. "Taking them out the back way, Lancer?"

"Exactly why are you so curious, Minister?" Lancer asked. "And if the way out of this war zone is so clearly marked, then why haven't you made use of it?" She raised a quizzical eyebrow. "Unless, maybe, you're not looking to escape, but merely delay *us* from doing so . . . ?" Her hands crackled with energy. "Step aside, before I—"

And then one of the bodyguards standing beside her pulled a gun from inside his tuxedo jacket, and calmly shot her in the head.

Lancer was dead before she hit the floor.

Harada joined her a moment later, cut down by Miss Locke as she stepped from the shadows behind him.

As the Royal Couple watched, the remaining bodyguard changed shape, instantly becoming a blue-skinned, red-haired woman in an abbreviated white gown.

"Mystique," von Doom said with a sneer. His gauntleted hands clenched into fists. The gems of the Mandarin's rings flared brightly.

"Now, just hold off with flashing the costume jewelry, Vic," Arcade warned. "I know you've got enough deaths for everybody on those fingers of yours, but keep this in mind: the odds're good that, before you get a chance to take all three of us out of the picture, one'a us will *still* manage to help the Empress gain some unwanted weight—say, a few ounces of lead in her brain pan?"

"Do not hesitate on my behalf, Victor," Ororo said, head held high.

"But I must, beloved," the Emperor replied. "What sort of ruler—

what sort of *man*—would I be if I were willing to sacrifice my very heart . . . even for the good of the Empire?" Von Doom shook his head. "No. The time to strike will present itself . . . and soon. Fools such as these *always* err when they are most certain they possess the upper hand."

Mystique kept her eyes on the Emperor, her gun aimed squarely at the center of his forehead. "I take it, Arcade, this means *you're* Pietro's Washington contact," she said to the Minister of Entertainment.

Arcade nodded. "Since Day One, sweets. How else could Petey have managed to smuggle his old man around the Empire without gettin' caught, or find the best route t'get him back to the States?" He chuckled. "Y'know, if it hadn't been for Viper—God rest her *gentle* soul—and her overactive libido, I never would've found out *half* the things I did about all those war council meetings." He sighed. "Too bad she had t'go an' bite the Big One, huh? Cost me my best source of info."

"You are a *worm*, Arcade," Ororo said, a look of disgust contorting her features. "An ugly, little worm, without a shred of decency."

*"Ouch."* Arcade laughed sharply, and acted as though he were wiping a tear from the corner of his right eye. "Sticks and stones, babe. I've been called *worse* in my time." He turned to von Doom. "Looks like you and the Missus have a problem here, Vic—what with a revolution going on, and the two of you about to die, I mean. I'm not surprised, though—you keep stepping on the little people on your way to the top, and eventually they're gonna start wanting to step on *you.*" He smiled. "And I got some pretty big boots in the car, just itchin' for the opportunity to stomp a mudhole in your—"

"I will *enjoy* destroying you, maggot," von Doom said evenly; it wasn't a threat—merely a statement of fact.

Arcade shook his head in mock sadness. "See? It's *that* kind of attitude that makes a man rethink his alliances and go with a winning team. And to be quite honest with you, Vic, odds are

Mags is gonna do a *much* better job of takin' care of your ol' pal, Arcade, then *you* ever did. And *that's* the kind of employer/employee relationship I like." He snorted derisively at Ororo. "And as for you, Miss High-an'-Mighty, Miss Partridge-Family-makes-for-great-music—hope you don't mind me playin' 'Tiny Bubbles' for your funeral procession." He grinned. "You know *I'll* be lovin' it."

"Oh, just shut the hell up, Arcade," Mystique said curtly. She turned to glare at him. "Enough talk. Let's just kill them and—"

Her order, however, was cut short as a blast of frigid energy—fired by the power ring on the Emperor's right index finger—enveloped her, coating her in a substance akin to liquid nitrogen.

Ororo reacted as well, summoning a powerful blast of wind that slammed Miss Locke against a wall. The comely woman's face suddenly unhinged and dropped off, to reveal the circuitry and memory chips that had given her artificial life.

"I seem to have broken your toy, Arcade," Ororo said, her eyes flashing angrily.

The Minister of Entertainment was no longer smiling.

The blast of fire that shot forth from the ring on the Emperor's left thumb put a swift end to any useless pleas for mercy he might have been about to voice. The hallway quickly filled with the stench of melting polyester and burning flesh.

Then, a sadistic grin lighting his features, von Doom lashed out with a gauntleted fist and shattered the frozen remains of the shapeshifter that stood before him. Separated from her body, Mystique's head bounced twice off the tiled floor, then snapped in half.

"Cretins," von Doom rumbled. He turned to leave.

"My husband, what of Lancer?" Ororo asked, pointing to the lifeless body at their feet. The young woman's hair was soaked with blood, the blond locks now a ghastly crimson hue. "And Agent Harada?"

Von Doom watched dispassionately as the life fluid of his security people pooled around his metal-booted feet.

"True heroes of the Empire," the Emperor said curtly. "They gave their lives in the service of Doom—that is reward enough for anyone." He took Ororo by the arm. "Come, my dear—our people have need of us this night."

So saying, he led her toward the garage entrance, leaving behind a trail of bloody footprints.


"Come on, punk!" Wolverine bellowed. "Whattaya waitin' for?"

Teetering on unsteady legs, clothing torn, body bruised and bloodied, Logan flashed his claws, waiting for Sabretooth's final charge. Around them lay the unconscious bodies of the other Hunters in the bear-like mutant's team. Nightcrawler had taken care of them all on his own—they really *had* been no serious threat for a solitary X-Man—while Wolverine had had his time occupied with just keeping his old enemy at bay.

"Get inside, elf!" Wolverine had ordered when he saw that Nightcrawler had completed his work. "Go help Cyke and Jeannie find Doom 'fore Roma decides it's time t'turn off the lights!"

Nightcrawler hadn't been happy about leaving his friend behind, but Wolverine was right about time running out for the universe, and, knowing the countless decades of animosity toward one another that Logan and Sabretooth shared, it was perhaps best to stay out of their way and concentrate on completing the mission. He had hurried off to assist Cyclops and Phoenix, confident that Wolverine wouldn't be too long in resolving this matter.

Unfortunately, with all the madness the X-Men had experienced in this topsy-turvy world, Logan had made the mistake of forgetting that the feral villain *also* possessed an adamantium-laced skeleton—and claws.

Logan slipped on a patch of his own blood as Sabretooth rushed to meet his challenge. Sparks flew as metal-coated bioweapons clashed.

"That the best you got?" Wolverine hissed, ignoring the pain that ripped through his body when the animalistic sociopath had raked his claws across his abdomen.

"*Wait* for it, runt," Sabretooth growled. "It gets *better.*"

And then, with an ear-to-ear grin splitting his haggard face, he unexpectedly broke off the attack and jumped back.

Before Wolverine could go on the offensive—or even question his foe's motives for a sudden withdrawal—a fusillade of armor-piercing bullets tore into his back, his neck, his legs. Sabretooth's military support, it appeared, had finally arrived.

The rounds rattled around inside him, glancing off the super-strong metal that protected his bones—but not his organs. Logan staggered about in blinding pain, unable to see, unable to stand.

Then something slammed into his chest—hard. Flesh tore. Blood spurted from his wounds, coating his eyes, filling his mouth.

Blinking his eyes rapidly, wiping the heels of his hands across his face to wipe away the arterial spray, Logan finally succeeded in clearing his vision—just in time for him to see Sabretooth plunge his adamantium-tipped claws into the Canadian's chest.

Logan howled.

The Imperial limousine tore out of the arts center parking garage like the proverbial bat out of hell.

As it rounded the north corner of the building, heading for New Hampshire Avenue, the car plowed through a group of superpowered combatants clashing on the driveway to the main entrance where, a few hours before, guests had begun arriving for what had promised to be a magical evening—instead of a mind-numbing Caught off-guard by the charging automobile, Scanner and Vindaloo were the first to fall beneath its wheels.

The front of the arts center suddenly exploded outward, showering man, mutant, and Hunter alike with chunks of masonry that crushed bones, and shards of glass that tore at flesh and sliced through arteries. The force of the blast carried across the avenue, tossing aside cars, emergency vehicles, and anyone who had been foolish enough to remain behind to view the spectacular battle.

And from the rubble of the shattered building stepped Magneto.

Lips twisted in a hate-filled snarl, he gazed at the destruction spread before him and roared.

*"DOOM!"* he shouted. "Where are you, you steel-shrouded maggot?"

His eyes narrowed as he caught sight of a limousine fleeing the scene, its roof emblazoned with the seal of the Empire.

"Run all you like, human!" Magneto cried. "You only race all the faster to make your appointment with Death!"

He took to the air, flying high above the carnage he had wrought, and pursued the Imperial limousine as it rocketed through the streets, turning onto Constitution Avenue. To the right, along the edge of The Mall, crowds that had gathered to cheer the Royal Couple as they returned to the White House after the gala now ran in blind panic to escape the conflict heading their way.

With a burst of speed, the limousine tore up the avenue, heading for the mansion; another minute at the most, and the von Dooms would be safe.

But then the car was torn asunder by powerful magnetic forces.

The Royal Couple and their driver were thrown from the remnants of the vehicle, to land in a heap on the asphalt. The driver died instantly, his neck snapping as he struck the pavement. The Empress cried out in pain, the weight of her body falling fully onto her right arm as the limb swung beneath her; the snap of her ulna as it broke could plainly be heard.

Clad in his battle armor, the Emperor, of course, was unharmed.

"It is *over*, von Doom!" Magneto bellowed at the Emperor. "This fantasy world you have somehow created comes to an end *tonight*, with your death!"

"Try your best, mutant!" the Emperor shouted. "Doom stands ready!"

Magnetic forces and ring-generated powers tore the air between them, filling the night-drenched city with the light and heat of a small sun. Buildings suddenly caught fire. Automobiles exploded. Those people unfortunate enough to have been standing close to the energy burst internally combusted. Heedless of the damage they were causing, neither mutant overlord nor tyrannical genius wavered in their resolve to destroy the other.

The phrase "Hell on Earth" flashed through the mind of more than one person that night.

And then a momentary lull in the battle came when the energies unleashed by the Mandarin's power rings proved to be too much for the Emperor's armor to handle. Roaring with frustration, he tore the smoldering gauntlets from his burned hands and threw them to the ground.

Taking advantage of his enemy's weakness, Magneto lashed out with a powerful magnetic bolt, ensnaring von Doom and pulling him high into the night sky. As the Emperor fought to free himself, Magneto closed his hand—and von Doom's armor collapsed inward, crushing flesh and bone.

The Emperor screamed; Magneto, on the other hand, found it all quite amusing.

A bolt of lightning suddenly tore through the sky, to strike Magneto full in the chest. He cried out in pain, releasing his hold on the Emperor, who tumbled toward the ground. Before von Doom impacted, though, a powerful wind gusted beneath him, carrying him a hundred yards from the mutant overlord, then gently setting him upon the grass.

Summoning another gale-force wind, Ororo used it to lift herself into the air. Eyes literally flashing in anger, cradling her broken arm against her chest, she flew directly toward Magneto, who was dazedly floating above The Mall, wheezing for breath. The center of his crimson outfit was charred through to his chest; the exposed skin was likewise blackened.

"*You dare?*" Ororo shouted. "You *dare* to lay hands upon the greatest man the world has ever had the privilege to know? Even more, you dare to attack the husband of one who controls the very *elements?*"

Above the battlefield, an angry storm was beginning to take shape, its strong winds and ominous rumbling mirroring its mistress's dark mood. The air filled with the strong odor of burning ozone.

"Ah, my dear Storm," Magneto said, shaking his head sadly. "If you but knew the truth about your 'beloved' mate, and the ways in which he has deceived you. I am certain you would be quite angered—and, perhaps, greatly embarrassed." He sneered. "However, I have neither the time nor the patience to educate you. But I will say this: because we have, in the past, had occasion to fight as allies, I shall give you the opportunity to remove yourself from my path—" he gestured toward her broken arm "—without further injury."

"And allow you to murder my husband?" Ororo snarled. "Never!" The air around them shook mightily as a massive thunderhead boomed just above them. It sounded as though a bomb had been dropped in the center of the capitol.

"I thought as much," Magneto said; he almost sounded melancholy.

With but a glance, he caused the iron in Ororo's blood to form a clot at the base of her brain. Ororo screamed in agony for a moment, left hand clasping the back of her head, eyes squeezed shut tightly; then she moaned pitifully and blacked out. Magneto caught her before she could fall, cradling her gently in his arms as he descended to ground level. He touched the back of her head with the tip of a finger, dispersing the clot, then placed her on the grass.

Glancing up, he saw Cyclops, Phoenix, and Nightcrawler racing toward him. The mutant overlord rose into the air once more.

"Magnus, wait!" Cyclops shouted. "If you kill Doom, we'll never find out how to repair the damage he's done!"

"See to your comrade, X-Men," Magneto called down, ignoring Cyclops's plea. "You may question what remains of that maggot after I am done with him." He flew off to finish his work.

Cyclops knelt beside his wife as she delicately gripped Ororo's left wrist between thumb and middle finger. *Jean?*

Phoenix breathed a sigh of relief. *She's all right, Scott. There's a broken arm that needs a splint, but I've got a strong pulse. He wasn't trying to kill her, thank God.* She gazed at him, eyes filled with concern. *But what* are *we going to do about Magneto?*

*I know* exactly *what to do* . . . Cyclops thought.

"Kurt!" he barked. "To hell with my agreement with Magnus! If we don't stop him from killing Doom, we'll never find out what he used to change the world—or how we can change it back!" He pointed toward the Emperor. "Grab him and bring him back—Jean and I will hold off Magneto!"

"Wait!" Nightcrawler shouted, pointing to the western sky. "What's that?"

*"DOOM!"*

Rogue appeared to come out of nowhere, streaking like a missile toward the Emperor. Her outfit was shredded, her face speckled with blood, but nothing had removed the look of utter hatred that seemed permanently etched into her features.

Before anyone could react, she punched von Doom in the chest with enough force to send him careening across The Mall, to land at the steps of what had once been the Lincoln Memorial. Circuits in his armor sparked and smoldered; the odor of burnt plastic wafted into the air.

*"You're* the reason Remy's dead!" Rogue shouted hysterically, hovering above the grassy field. "If it hadn't been for *you*, the world wouldn't have changed, an' we wouldn't have tried to fix it, an' Remy wouldn't have been infected with that stinkin' virus, an'—"

"Wh-what are you prattling on about, stripling?" von Doom gasped—clearly, the blow had injured him. "How is Doom responsible for the actions of some costumed imbecile he has never met?" Slowly, he staggered to his feet. "Were it not for the constant interference of cretins such as yourself and your churlish band of misfits, Doom would not have to—"

*"SHUT UP! SHUT UP!"* Rogue screamed, tears streaming down her cheeks. "I don't wanna *hear* anymore of your stinkin' lies!"

She flew toward him again, picking up speed as she drew closer. "All I want is t'see you *dead!*"

She drew back her fist, prepared to deliver the fatal blow—

—only to be smashed aside by a surge of magnetic energy that sent her flying past the monument, toward Independence Avenue, to slam, hard, into the side of a fuel tanker-truck as it moved along the thoroughfare. The powerful shockwave generated by the resulting explosion violently shook the ground for miles around, and sent the gathered combatants tumbling in all directions.

Lying in the center of the blast crater, unconscious but otherwise unharmed, Rogue would be out of the fight for quite a while.

"Doom is mine!" Magneto shouted, to no one in particular. "*Mine* must be the hand that slays him!"

The mutant overlord turned back to his target as the Emperor rose to his feet, preparing to meet the attack.

"And now, your reign of terror comes to an end, human!" Magneto shouted. "Tomorrow's sun shall rise over the new empire of *Homo superior!*" Powerful magnetic forces crackled around his hands, and he prepared to loose them on von Doom—

—only to be blindsided by another airborne mutant. The impact sent him tumbling through the night sky.

"Watch those hands, friend!" Warren said. "The Emperor doesn't know where they've been!"

Before the mutant overlord could react, Warren had grabbed him underneath the arms and hauled him into the storm-lashed sky, pulling him as far from the Emperor as possible.

"Damn all you infernal do-gooders!" Magneto raged. "Even with your minds rewired by that tyrant, *still* do you constantly find ways in which to interfere with my plans! Well, no more, I say! Von Doom *dies* this night, and no man—no *mutant*—shall keep Magneto from taking his revenge!"

His hands began to glow brightly. Bolts of magnetic energy crackled between his fingertips, becoming more powerful by the second. Wrenching himself out of Warren's grip, Magneto turned in mid-air—and placed both hands flat against the winged mutant's chest.

Warren screamed—a high-pitched keening that could be heard even above the rumble of the storm. His shirt started to burn, then the azure flesh beneath it. His body convulsed spasmodically; his wings stopped beating.

And then, like Icarus cast down from the heavens, Warren plummeted toward the ground so very far below.

*"WARREN!"* Betsy cried. "Oh, my God, my God . . ."

They could have escaped all this insanity; could have kept flying and put themselves far and away from any danger.

But when Warren had looked back in time to see Magneto tear apart the Imperial limousine, he had insisted on going back. It was madness, she had said—sheer and utter madness for him to think he had any chance against such a man as Magneto; a man who could match the Emperor strength for strength, and decimate the ranks of the finest soldiers in the Empire.

But he wouldn't listen. Dropping Betsy off on the far side of Constitution Avenue, in front of the National Academy of Science, he had soared away to protect his leader, ignoring her pleas to come back.

And now . . .

Paying no attention to the war being fought around her—or the level of danger in which she was placing herself—Betsy raced across the battlefield, watching his descent with growing panic. He was falling faster and faster, wings fluttering uselessly; above him, Magneto sneered, then floated away toward his original target.

Betsy screamed when Warren struck the ground near the Reflecting Pool; the sound of bones breaking was unmistakable.

Hands pressed over her mouth, she slowly walked toward him, not wanting to see his condition, but unable to stop herself. Warren lay on his back, arms and legs splayed at unnatural angles, wings spread wide on the grass. His clothes were smoldering, and the stench of ozone and burnt flesh that flooded her nostrils almost made Betsy retch. A small scream escaped her lips, the sound muffled by her gloved hands, and tears streamed down her cheeks.

And then Warren moaned; his wings gently fluttered.

He was still alive.

Betsy gasped. "Warren . . . ?" She ran to his side as he struggled—and failed—to sit up.

"Hey . . . Betts . . ." he said weakly. He inhaled shallowly, and something rattled within his chest. "Guess this is . . . what I get for . . . trying to impress . . . my girl, huh?"

Despite her tears, Betsy forced herself to smile encouragingly as she knelt beside him and cradled his head in her lap.

"You stupid, stupid man," she said, gently stroking his face. "A nice bouquet of flowers would have been just as impressive."

"I'll . . . remember that . . . next time . . ." Warren replied. Each word, each breath was a labor for his damaged lungs. His face suddenly contorted horribly, and he gasped, unable to breathe.

*"Help us! Someone please help us!"* Betsy cried. She frantically looked around for a paramedic, or a police officer—somebody. *Anybody.* But her pleas were lost amid the clash of mutant energies that crackled across the night sky, and the dull thud of flesh striking flesh. From off in the distance, the high-pitched wail of sirens could be heard as emergency teams raced to the scene.

"Guess everybody's a . . . little busy . . ." Warren muttered. The pain appeared to have subsided, but the azure color of his skin had noticeably paled, and his handsome features looked strained.

"Shhh," Betsy whispered, placing a finger to his lips. "Don't speak." She leaned forward to gaze into his glassy eyes, and her lavender hair descended like a curtain over both their faces. She angrily swept it back, draping it over her right shoulder. Warren laughed softly, brushing aside a loose strand that lay across the bridge of his nose.

"You sang like . . . an angel," he said, grinning lopsidedly. "You know that? So beautiful . . ." He grimaced as his body was wracked by another painful spasm; it subsided after a few agonizing moments. "Kinda funny, don't you think . . . since *I'm* the one . . . with the wings . . ."

"Please, baby—*don't talk,*" Betsy insisted. "You've got to save your strength."

"You British women . . ." Warren gasped. "Insatiable . . ." He chuckled—a weak, phlegm-drenched sound that rattled up from his lungs.

"Oh, God . . ." Betsy moaned. She was in a panic, her thoughts jumbled as each screamed to be heard over the others, until her mind was filled with white noise. After what seemed like an eternity of confusion, one thought was able to force its way to the front of her mind: *GET HELP.*

"Warren, I'm going to find a doctor, or a paramedic," she said. "I'll be right back, okay? Just please, *please* hang on."

She started to rise, but Warren grasped her hand and pulled her back down. "No . . . don't go . . ." he said, slowly shaking his head. His voice was growing fainter.

Betsy opened her mouth to say something—some words of encouragement, or even anger, telling him he had no right to give up, not when they still had a whole lifetime ahead of them to explore—but in her heart, she knew it was too late.

Too late for anything more than good-byes.

So did Warren. Tenderly, he reached up to stroke her cheek. "You really *are* . . . the most beautiful woman . . . in the world . . . you know . . ."

Betsy took his hand and brushed her lips against his fingers. "Warren, I . . ." she began, then fell silent, unable to speak. A tear dropped from the corner of her left eye, to splash on Warren's cheek.

"Don't leave me . . ." she sobbed.

Warren smiled. "Love you, Betts . . ." he whispered.

And then he was gone.

*"Die, you worm! In the name of all that is holy, why don't you die?"*

Floating a dozen feet above The Mall, Magneto unleashed another blast of energy that caught von Doom squarely in the chest. The Emperor skidded across the grassy field, then lay still for a moment.

*"What is the meaning of this?"* Magneto bellowed, pointing at von Doom as he struggled to a sitting position on the grass.

As one, both mutants and humans stared in shock at the sight before them.

Armor smoldering, velvet cloak burned away, the Doombot looked down to see the tangle of wires and circuit boards that protruded from its chest.

"Damn . . ." it muttered in an electronic gurgle.

# 18

S HE WAS going into shock.

Kneeling on the grass, Warren's lifeless body cradled in her arms, Betsy stared blankly at the tableau laid out before her.

The battle had come to an abrupt halt with the startling revelation that the man who had ruled an entire planet for a decade— or, far more truthfully, for only one short month, in the "real" world—was in actuality an automaton.

And then the rain began to fall.

Betsy didn't feel the drops striking her exposed skin, or soaking her expensive gown, or drenching her hair, washing some of the lavender color from her locks. Her makeup began to run as well, exposing a bright red tattoo that extended from just above her left eyebrow to just below her left eye; it looked like a stylized "J." In all the years she'd possessed it, Betsy could never remember how or why she had chosen to have such a noticeable mark etched onto her face, but Warren had always liked it.

"Warren . . ." Betsy whispered, and looked down at him. Now that he was no longer troubled by pain, he looked so peaceful, as if he were resting. She bent down to kiss his lips one last time, and was shocked to discover how cold they felt.

"Oh, my God . . ." said a small voice beside her.

Slowly, Betsy lifted her head and looked up. A red-headed woman and a dark-haired man, both clad in colorful spandex costumes, were standing next to her.

"Oh, Betsy," the woman said, eyes brimming with tears. "I am so very, very sorry."

Betsy stared at the woman; her glassy eyes began to clear.

"You," she said softly. "Yours was the voice I heard inside my head."

The woman nodded and knelt beside her. "That's right, Betsy. I'm Jean. Do you remember me?"

"I . . ." Betsy began; her eyes started to glaze over once more. "Did you know Warren?"

"We *both* did, Betsy," the costumed man replied. "He was our friend—as you are, too."

"I—I don't remember . . ." Betsy said hesitantly. Her gaze drifted back toward Warren; staring blankly at his stilled features, she gently stroked his hair.

"Betsy, I . . . I know it might sound a bit . . . *cold,* given the circumstances, but I could *help* you remember," Jean said. "Would you like me to do that?"

Betsy's eyes cleared, the fog that shrouded her thoughts suddenly lifting; her body began to tremble with uncontrolled anger. She turned to glare heatedly at this costumed woman kneeling beside her. What in God's name was *wrong* with these people? Couldn't they see she was consumed by grief? Were they blind to the fact that she was cradling the dead body of a man who had meant the world to her—and who had been needlessly taken from her by the same superpowered madman who was leading them? Hadn't they a *shred* of decency, or was it some sort of requirement among Magneto's followers to be able to so callously ignore the suffering they caused?

"Haven't you people done enough already?" she said, her features contorted with hate.

Jean started. "What . . . ?"

"*You're* the ones who started all this fighting, aren't you?" Betsy snapped. "Magneto's superpowered toadies? Didn't any of you have the *slightest* idea about what might happen if you attacked the Emperor at a public event? About what the cost in human life might be once all the shooting started?" Her lips pulled back in a snarl. "Or was your precious revolution all too damned important for such considerations? So *what* if lives are lost, so long as your master's blasted dream of mutant superiority comes *true*, right?" Her eyes blazed with anger. "Perhaps if you'd taken the time to put a little more *thought* into your plans, figured out a way that wouldn't have involved laying waste to half of Washington, then Warren wouldn't have had to ... wouldn't have ..." She closed her eyes to blink back tears, then turned her head away.

Jean placed a consoling hand on her shoulder; Betsy shrugged it off, her attention focused once more on Warren. She angled her head above his face, using her darkening hair as an awning of sorts to protect it from the rain.

"You're wrong, Betsy," Jean said gently. "I know how it looks, I know how you feel right now, but you're *wrong* about us. *We're* the ones trying to put an *end* to all this madness."

Betsy laughed—a sharp, bitter note—and wiped away the raindrops that had collected on Warren's stilled features. "I'd say you're a little too late for that, then—wouldn't *you?*"

"I ..." Jean began, then stopped. "Yes," she said softly.

Betsy glanced up as the man's bright yellow boots came into view. He crouched down in front of her.

"Warren was my friend, Betsy," he said, his voice strained with grief. "I valued his friendship, as I have yours. Please believe me: I didn't want this to happen. I just did what I thought was right, for the good of the mission." He shook his head. "I don't know— maybe if I'd reacted faster when Magneto was helping Ororo, gone back on my word earlier ..." His head lowered. "I didn't mean for any of this to happen," he whispered.

Betsy opened her mouth, ready to discharge a stream of choice invectives and tell him what he could do with his sympathy, but the pain that was so clearly etched on his features made her stop and reconsider.

"No," she finally said. "I imagine you didn't."

The man slowly looked up. "Betsy, it's *important* that you remember who we are, and what you mean to us," he said. "What Jean and I, and the other X-Men, are up against is too big to tackle on our own—we need our friends by our side. We need *you*. Will you help us?"

Betsy shrugged; she didn't care one way or the other.

The man turned to Jean and nodded. Gently, she placed her fingertips against Betsy's temples. "This may sting a bit..."

*"How?"* Magneto roared. "How can this be? To have come so close to having my revenge, only to have it stolen away by a . . . a *robot?*"

He landed beside the faux von Doom as it sat on the grass. Sparks tumbled from its shattered casement, to be quickly extinguished by the heavy downpour, and the rosy complexion of its face and hands had faded; its skin now looked like white candle wax. The automaton looked up at him, and flashed that same infuriating, condescending smile that had haunted the dreams of Erik Lensherr every night of his long exile in the Sahara—which, as it turned out, had been a dream of sorts itself.

"You have *lost*, mutant," the robot burbled. "Though you have caused your fair share of trouble this night, and revealed to the world that its beloved ruler has been living vicariously through this metal shell, *still* is Doom triumphant." It waved a gauntleted hand at the fiery ruins around them—at the lifeless bodies, and the thick smoke, and the decimated field. "By morning, Washington shall be restored to its full glory, and all this shall be but a distant memory—the fading remnants of a dream lost upon awakening. You, as well; now that you have played your final hand, I find myself quickly growing tired of this game. You have led me a merry chase, Magneto, but the time has come for Doom to put away his toys and move onto far more important matters." The android chuckled. "Despite your best—though ultimately pathetic—efforts, mutant, it is *my* dream, *my* empire, that shall endu—"

Magneto savagely ripped it apart with a bolt of magnetic force, then threw back his head and roared.

*"Come out and face me, you mind-twisting worm!"* he screamed to the heavens.

But the rumble of the storm was the only reply he received.

Jean had been right—having her memories jump-started hurt like hell. But the pain was worth undergoing the process in order to have her true life fully restored to her.

Betsy remembered everything now: her brother Brian's costumed identity as the super heroic Captain Britain, and the knowledge that both siblings had gained extraordinary powers from their father, a former citizen of Otherworld; her kidnapping at the hands of the "real" Arcade and Miss Locke, and Brian's efforts to free her from Murderworld; then her days as a fashion model in London, and her months as a S.H.I.E.L.D. Psi Division agent; from her time as the X-Man called Psylocke to the moment when her life had changed forever—the Siege Perilous, an event of cosmic proportions that, somehow, had transferred the mind and soul of Elisabeth Braddock into the body of a Yakuza-trained assassin named Kwannon.

And Warren; she remembered everything about Warren, as well. Their first awkward dates, when he would try to impress her by playing the suave millionaire playboy, and she would act the part of the *femme fatale*, all slinky body movements and sensuous gazes—that sort of behavior hadn't lasted long, mainly because he wasn't all that suave, and she had run out of double-entendres to spice up her conversation; they'd settled for just being their true selves, and seeing where that would take them. The time he'd encouraged her to sing in public for the first time, draped across the grand piano in the center of the Starlight Room like Michelle Pfeiffer in *The Fabulous Baker Boys*. Their moonlit flights above Manhattan, his arms secure around her waist, giggling hysterically as she felt the cool rush of air against her face.

There was more: Their adventures with the X-Men. Their attempts to live a normal life together in a world of spandex-clad madmen and alien invasions and universe-threatening disasters. Her brush with death, after Sabretooth had gravely wounded her, and Warren's subsequent, perilous journey to the mystical realm called The Crimson Dawn to retrieve the Ebon Vein, an elixir that saved her life and granted her the power to teleport through shadows. His battle with Kuragari, the self-proclaimed "Shogun of the Shadows," who later captured Betsy and tried to use her as his pawn in his quest to take control of the Crimson Dawn.

And his offering of a portion of his own life-force to the Dawn in order to free her from that living hell. He had been living on borrowed time since then, never knowing whether he might "wake up dead"—as Betsy had put it—in a year, a month, a day. "But, if it means that for another year, month, or day I'm with *you,*" he had said, "then it was *worth* it."

Her heart ached from the memories. So many experiences together; so much love they had shared; so many sacrifices made—for their friends, for each other. And to have it all restored now, when it was too late...

Sobbing gently, Betsy turned away from Jean—only to spot Warren's murderer standing beside the shattered remains of the Doombot.

"Magneto..." A low growl issued from her throat.

She leapt to her feet, face flushed with uncontrollable rage. Before Phoenix or Cyclops could move to stop her, she was racing across the field.

"Betsy—don't!" she heard Jean say.

But hate had added wings to Betsy's feet; they'd never catch up to her in time to prevent her from avenging Warren. As she closed on her target, anger growing with each step, she focused her mental powers, creating the special weapon that had become her trademark as an X-Man. Rose-colored energy crackled around her right hand, forming a stylized knife that jutted six inches from her fist.

It was called a psychic blade, and it could terrible things to an unprotected mind.

*"MAGNETO!"* Betsy screamed.

The mutant overlord turned to meet the challenge, and looked surprised to find another of Xavier's students bearing down on him. Before he could react, she leapt forward, pouncing on him, screaming unintelligibly as she pushed him backward with her left hand.

Betsy raised the dagger high above her head—and then plunged it deep into his skull.

Magneto screamed as the blade sliced through every synapse in his brain. His body shook, hands clenching and unclenching; flecks of bloody spittle flew from his open lips, staining his crimson and purple outfit.

Betsy thought it was all quite amusing.

She held the dagger in place for a few seconds, watching as Magneto twisted in agony, unable to free himself from the mental assault to which he was being subjected. Then, opening her fist, Betsy made the blade vanish, as though it had never been there.

Eyes widened in shock yet unseeing, Magneto moaned loudly and collapsed, landing on his back. He began twitching spasmodically.

"I hope you burn in *hell* for what you've done," Betsy said with a satisfied sneer.

And then she vanished from sight.

Cyclops and Phoenix reached the spot where Betsy had been standing a moment after her sudden disappearance.

"Psylocke?" Cyclops called out. "Where are you?"

"Could she have used her shadow-powers?" Phoenix asked. "Teleported somewhere else?"

Cyclops nodded. "Possibly. But why?" He glanced down at their unconscious enemy; the terrified look on Lensherr's face sent a chill up his spine. "She had Magneto right where she wanted him, and you know Betsy—she's never been the type to leave something half-done. She's got to be around here."

Phoenix glanced around the area, her face lined with concern. "Yes, but where could she have gone . . . ?"

She was standing in a vast, dark space.

Confused by her new surroundings, Betsy looked around, but could see nothing. She could tell the room was large, though, from the way the echo carried when she moved her foot across the floor.

"Greetings, X-Man," said a raspy voice from the darkness. "I welcome you to the Royal Mansion."

Betsy started; it sounded as though it had come from just over her shoulder, but she hadn't heard anyone moving about.

"The White House?" she asked. "But, how did I get here?"

A few feet away, a spotlight clicked on, illuminating a throne-like chair, its back turned toward her. It took her a moment to realize that someone was sitting in it.

"You are here because I *wished* you to be here, Psylocke," the voice ordered. "Now, approach. We have much to discuss, you and I, and a short amount of time in which to do it."

Hesitantly, Betsy moved forward, stepping around the chair to face its occupant. Her attention, however, was caught by a brightly glowing object that floated a few inches above the open hands of her host. It was shaped like a small box, measuring approximately six inches on each side, and shone with the brightness of daylight.

"Dear God . . ." she gasped. Though she had never seen such a device first-hand, Betsy immediately recognized it from descriptions in the Xavier Institute's computer files.

It was a Cosmic Cube.

Small in size though it might be, the original Cube had been designed years ago by the scientists of the infamous organization A.I.M.—under the watchful eye of their living computer, MODOK— as the source of ultimate power: capable of rewriting the laws of

physics and turning fantasy into reality with just a thought. Shortly thereafter, it had been stolen by the Red Skull—an insane villain trained during the blackest days of World War II by none other than Adolf Hitler himself to become the ultimate Nazi. The Skull's plans for creating a "Fourth Reich," as well as his goal of achieving world domination, had ultimately been ruined by the timely intervention of Captain America. The Cube had been thought destroyed during their battle, but that was never the case: Though *one* Cube might be destroyed, *another* always seemed to pop up somewhere in the world, allowing whoever possessed it to make their dreams come true.

Like the dreams of an armored madman who had wished to become the emperor of the world.

Betsy took a step backward, wanting to put as much distance between her and the device as possible.

"Cease your trembling, mutant!" the Cube's owner snapped. "I have no patience for your paltry fears."

Forcing herself to look away from the Cube, Betsy turned to face the device's owner. He was a wizened old man with sharp, sunken features; the light of great intelligence still burned from beneath shadows cast by bushy eyebrows. His thinning, unkempt hair was a brilliant white, his face lined and creased with incredible age. Betsy figured he had to be at least a hundred years old, give or take a year, but the familiar silver armor and green velvet cape in which he was clad were brand-new—though a month's worth of dust had accumulated on the battle dress, dulling their original shine.

"Who—who are you?" Betsy asked haltingly.

"I?" the old man said softly. "Do you not *recognize* me, mutant?"

Betsy slowly shook her head.

The old man shifted in his chair, sitting up straighter; he almost looked regal in stature now.

"I," he said proudly, "am Doom."

* * *

*"Zum teufel!* Where did Psylocke go?" Nightcrawler asked.

He stood beside Cyclops and Phoenix on The Mall; all three of them were soaked to the skin by the unrelenting weather. Lying on the ground in front of them were Magneto and Rogue, Kurt having rescued the insensate Southern Belle from the blast crater in the center of Independence Avenue.

"I haven't the slightest idea, Kurt," Cyclops responded. "One minute, Jean and I were running over to stop Betsy before she might have killed Magneto, and the next . . ."

"A greater disappearing act than any *I* could come up with," Nightcrawler said.

Cyclops nodded and turned to his wife. "Jean, is there any chance you could scan the area, see if you can pick up her thoughts, like you did back in New York?"

"I'll let you know in a minute," Phoenix replied. Closing her eyes, she placed her fingertips to her temples; her brow furrowed with intense concentration.

While they waited, Cyclops pulled Nightcrawler aside. "Any sign of Wolverine?"

Kurt shook his head. *"Nein.* I have not seen any sign of our feral friend—or Sabretooth—since we split up at the arts center." He frowned. "I tried to search the area around the building, but the escalation of the fighting between the guards and Magneto's acolytes forced me to withdraw." He looked around. "Where is Ororo?"

"We had to turn her over to Doom's security forces," Cyclops explained. "She'd been injured and, rather than get into a shooting match with a bunch of soldiers over who had the right to take care of the 'Empress,' Jean and I elected to let them get her to a hospital."

A distant explosion caught their attention; fires were still raging near the arts center, despite the downpour. Nightcrawler sucked in his breath between gritted teeth.

"It should not be taking Logan this long to rejoin us," he noted, a look of concern plainly etched on his face, "even if it *was* Sabretooth he was facing . . ."

Their conversation was interrupted by the soft sound of moaning from below. Looking down, they saw Rogue start to awaken. Nightcrawler crouched down and helped her to a sitting position.

"How do you feel, *mein freund?*" he asked.

"I—" Rogue began, then lowered her head. "Like a damn fool, Kurt. I shouldn't've lost my head like that, an' let Magneto sneak up on me." She pounded the ground with her fist. "An' now I done lost my chance t'get at Doom . . ."

"You mean *him?*" Nightcrawler asked. He sifted through the shattered remains of the android and picked up its head. The infuriating smile of Victor von Doom shone brightly in the flashes of lightning.

"He's a *Doombot?*" Rogue asked.

"A stand-in for the real one," Cyclops said. "But we'll find him."

"And there will be no more talk of 'getting' him, yes?" Nightcrawler asked. "Remember, Rogue: You are an X-Man, not a killer. Remy would not want to see you throw away your life in some blind quest for vengeance. Such behavior would despoil his memory, and the love he had for you."

Rogue grunted in reply and looked to the side, to find Magneto lying beside her. His eyes had closed, the mask of horror he had earlier worn now faded away with his consciousness. "W˙ ˍat happened to Magnus?" she asked.

"Betsy," Cyclops replied. "There was an . . . accident . . ." He stepped to one side, to allow her an unobstructed view of Warren. Scott had folded his wings around him, to provide some protection from the rain.

"Oh, Lord . . ." Rogue whispered in shock, a hand to her mouth. "Where is she?"

"We do not know," Kurt said. "She just . . . vanished—" he gestured toward Magneto "—after venting her frustrations on our friend here. Jean is trying to scan for her."

Phoenix's eyes popped open. "I've found her!" she announced. She glanced at her teammates. "She's with Doom—the *real* one."

*"Unglaublisch,"* Nightcrawler muttered under his breath.

"Where is she?" Cyclops asked.

Phoenix pointed to the east, along Constitution Avenue—and the world famous home that stood just off from it.

"The White House—of course," Cyclops said. "Let's move, people!"

Sprinting across the storm-soaked Mall, the quartet of heroes raced toward the great mansion, unaware of the vaporous cloud that slowly drifted around Magneto.

*"You're* Doctor Doom?" Betsy asked, nonplused. Her head was spinning from the revelation. "But—" she gestured at his aged appearance "—but how . . . ?"

The Emperor grunted in disgust. "Why is it that all you so-called 'heroes' must stammer and needlessly prattle on whenever you are confronted by events so clearly beyond your ability to comprehend? Can you not merely accept what is before your eyes?"

"But you're so *old,"* Betsy replied. "And you're holding the *Cosmic Cube,* for heaven's sakes! How would you *expect* me to respond?"

The old man smiled wolfishly. "Ah. You *recognize* the Cube for what it is—the ultimate power in the universe. Therefore, you must realize that only Doom is capable of controlling such forces; that only Doom could have used them to create the perfect world you had come to accept as fact—until the meddlesome antics of your misanthropic teammates proved to you otherwise."

"Yes, I know all about you, 'Emperor,' and what I *realize* is that Doom is responsible for turning my whole world upside down, solely to placate his precious ego," Betsy replied with a sneer, "and, therefore, is directly responsible for the death of the only man I have truly ever loved."

"Ah, yes." Von Doom shook his head in mock sadness. "Poor

Worthington—cut down in the prime of his youth, all because he sought to defend a man with a 'precious ego' from assassination. A wasted effort, of course, but clearly a heartfelt one." He pointed a warning finger at Betsy. "Do not seek to shift blame where it does not belong, girl. *I* did not cause him to attack Magneto; what he did, was done of his own volition. Such has always been the downfall of you costumed fools." The old man smiled. "I assure you, however, that he will be remembered as a hero of the Empire."

"Why?" Betsy asked. "Why do that, when you could just *wish* him back with the Cube?" A rose-colored light suddenly filled the darkened chamber as she formed her psychic dagger. *"Do it,"* she ordered, grabbing him by the throat. "Bring him back."

"Have a care, mutant—you address *Doom,* not some petty street thug," the Emperor replied with a snarl.

"From what I hear, you cheeky little monkey," Betsy replied with a similar snarl, "there are times when people who are dealing with you can't tell the difference between one and the other, either."

"Such insolence!" Von Doom chuckled. "You have *spirit,* girl, to dare pit your meager telepathic abilities against the might of Doom—when he holds the very powers of Creation *itself* in his hands." He laughed—a short, barking noise laced with phlegm. "If I so desired, stripling, I could flay the skin from your bones, plunge you into the Earth's molten core—all with merely a thought. And you threaten Doom with a mental *toy?"*

"I'm *willing* to pit my blade against your little gift box," Betsy replied sharply. "Think you can wish *fast* enough to beat me, Doctor?" She drew back her arm, preparing to drive the blade deep into his mind.

"I do," von Doom said. In his hands, the Cube flared brightly.

Without warning, Betsy was stunned to find herself floating in space, hundreds of miles above the Earth; the planet stretched out far below her. She gasped involuntarily, and the void rushed to fill her lungs. The icy coldness quickly seized upon the areas of her flesh not protected by her gown and opera gloves, draining her strength, her consciousness. Slowly, her struggles ceased; her eyes rolled up in her head—

And then she was back in the chamber.

Gasping for air, she dropped to the floor, coughing and wheezing until she was certain her windpipe would tear from the abuse, rubbing her bare skin to shake off the chill that gripped her. Eventually, forehead pressed against the cool tiles, she was able to regain her breath; the burning sensation created by the void's frigid embrace left her body.

"I *trust* you have learned your lesson, child," the old man said menacingly. "Enfeebled though he may be, Doom is ever your superior."

"I'll ... keep that ... in mind ..." Betsy rasped, wiping away tears. A thin line of drool ran from her gaping mouth to the chamber floor; her throat felt as though it was on fire. Yet, unwilling to remain prostrated before this man whom she hated so much, she wiped the spittle off her chin with the back of her hand, and slowly rose to her feet.

"Do not delude yourself into thinking Doom is a benevolent man, mutant," the Emperor warned. "Were you of no use to my plans, I would banish you to limbo, wipe you from the minds of every man, woman, and child on this planet, as easily as I shall soon do to that upstart, Lensherr. It would be as though you had never existed."

"But that's something I don't understand," Betsy said, ignoring the pain that shot through her larynx with the utterance of each syllable. "Why in heaven's name, if you had complete mastery over the world, would you *allow* someone like Magneto to run free? With the power of the Cube, you could have simply wished *him* out of existence before all this madness was set in motion."

Von Doom shrugged. "Merely for entertainment purposes. With the accursed Fantastic Four finally eliminated, I found there were often moments when I grew bored with this perfect world; my enemies were either dead, or had been fashioned into willing, unquestioning followers—there were no challenges left to face."

His eyes lit up with malicious joy. "And then I came upon a most *wonderful* idea: I would take my greatest rival and set him loose in my new world, to see what he would do—much like a laboratory rat placed in a maze. True, I could have located him at any time merely by using the Cube, but, through his remarkable ingenuity in finding ways by which he, time and again, could elude the Hunters that were dispatched after him, he kept my interest piqued. After that, I allowed him to form his underground network of spies and saboteurs—such additional levels to the game kept the chase from becoming dull." A trace of a smile came to his lips. "I must admit, the destruction of Paris was truly inspired— I never would have thought Lensherr capable of such widespread slaughter." He chuckled softly.

"I'm so glad you find senseless death something to laugh about," Betsy said sarcastically. "It adds a whole new layer of slime to your already-sparkling personality."

Von Doom ignored her. "But then, something . . . unplanned occurred," the old man said with noticeable hesitation.

Betsy's eyebrows rose. From what she had heard about the villain, the great Victor von Doom was not the type to ever come right out and admit he had made a mistake. To hear such an admission now . . .

"What happened?" she asked. Despite her situation, von Doom's comment had made her curious.

The old man frowned. "A slight . . . miscalculation by one of my technicians created an imperfection in the Cube—one I have been unable to correct."

"Is that why you've aged as much as you have?"

Von Doom nodded. "Unlike the previous versions of the Cube designed by A.I.M., this particular device operates by absorbing the life-energies of its possessor—the more detailed the reality, the more tampering done to the timestream, the greater the drain on the individual. As you can probably surmise, I have been *quite* detailed in the construction of my world."

Betsy started. "You mean you're *dying?*"

"That is so," von Doom replied. "At my current rate of deterioration, I estimate that I have no more than thirty days left in which to live."

"And what will happen when your time is up?"

"Before I draw my last breath, before Death comes to lead me into her realm of never-ending darkness, I will order the Cube to destroy this world, and everyone on it," von Doom replied.

"That's insane!" Betsy said. "Isn't there some way for you to turn it off *now*, before it ever comes to that?"

"And why would I *want* to do that, girl?" the wizened Emperor replied; his tone was that of an adult addressing a child. "If *Doom* cannot rule the Earth for all eternity, then *no one* shall."

Betsy shook her head emphatically. "No—there *has* to be another way."

"There *is* an alternative ..." von Doom said slowly.

Betsy eyed him warily. "What are you talking about?"

"It is the very reason I summoned you, girl: to offer you a rare opportunity," von Doom said, a sinister gleam in his eyes. "Take possession of the Cube, and your lover will not have to die. Take the Cube, and this night and all its madness need never have occurred."

"Why me?" she asked. "Why not Ororo, or one of your super-powered lapdogs? I'm sure they'd be more than willing to help you."

"Indeed. But you have lost so much more that they ever have—so much, in fact, that I believe you would be willing to give up almost *anything* for the opportunity to restore your precious Mr. Worthington to life." The old man smiled wolfishly. "Is that not so, Ms. Braddock?"

A chill ran up Betsy's spine as she realized what von Doom was saying. "And what do you want from me in return?"

Von Doom shrugged. "Merely a small service: That you take my place and maintain this reality, in exactly the same form in which I recreated it, under my guidance. You will do as I tell you, and, in exchange, you are free to resurrect Worthington, even start your lives over with new identities, if that is what you wish. The

Cube can make it *all* a reality." He paused. "Of course, you will never leave this chamber again, but you can still exist outside these walls, by placing part of your consciousness within the shell of an android created in your image—as I had been doing, until tonight. In this way, you will be able to move about the world, sharing your days with your handsome mutant as the mighty empire of von Doom continues to flourish."

"But then, *I'll* be the one who dies in a month's time," Betsy said.

"Of course," von Doom replied. "And then I shall find another troubled soul to take *your* place; then another, and another, ad infinitum." He leaned forward in his chair. "But it will be a month that you would otherwise be unable to spend with Worthington, would it not? A month that could seem like an entire lifetime of happiness, with your lover by your side—alive, unharmed, ready to take you in his arms once more." He raised a quizzical eyebrow. "Are you *willing* to make such a sacrifice, Ms. Braddock? Are you willing to risk your life, your world . . . for love?"

Betsy suddenly trembled and turned away, placing a hand to her mouth so Doom wouldn't hear her choking back a sob. He was the devil incarnate, she realized—a sadistic old man reveling in the torment he was putting her through, offering her her heart's desires in exchange for her soul.

As for the Cosmic Cube . . .

It was a Monkey's Paw; she knew that. Like the fictional talisman in the short horror story, it was a device created to give its bearer whatever their heart desired—money, power, the return of a loved one, long dead. But there was always a terrible price to be paid for its use—the Paw always perverted the wish, turned it against the one who uttered it, made a dream into a nightmare.

But, she was *already* living the nightmare, wasn't she? Her world had been turned upside down, restructured by one of mankind's greatest enemies with just a tiny box and a dream. And she had lost the only man she had ever truly loved, seen him taken from her by another egomaniacal dreamer who, if he ever learned of the Cube's existence, would only use it to rewrite history to suit his own needs and place himself in power.

In one evening, everything she had come to accept as fact had been revealed as a lie—her life, her career, her history. A façade created by her subconscious, and an unusual combination of mystical and mutant super-powers—an eye of harmony in the raging storm that was the mind of Victor von Doom.

A dream that, even now, was fading into memory.

But no, she suddenly realized—not everything had been a lie. Even before the world was turned inside-out, she had had Warren's love, and he, hers. Despite Doom's machinations—perhaps even because of them—their love had endured, grown even stronger. Though they had forgotten their friends, their dedication to the visions of Charles Xavier, their lives as "super heroes," not even the villainy of an all-powerful tyrant could keep them apart.

Was it *wrong* to want things to go back to the way they had been, Betsy asked herself—even if it meant putting the world back under the control of a tyrant?

At least with Doom in control, there would be a world of order, where there were no more half-mad mutant overlords tearing across the countryside, destroying the lives of innocent people—she'd see to that herself, without Doom's tutelage. A world of peace and prosperity, where a blue-skinned, winged romantic and a British noblewoman trapped in the body of a Japanese karaoke singer could live Happily Ever After.

Would it really be so bad, Betsy wondered, to—just this once—be selfish enough to have *her* dream—to hold Warren in her arms again, run her fingers through his golden hair, giggle uncontrollably when he flashed his boyish grin, feel the warmth of his body beside her late at night?

To learn the answer, she would only have to pay a small price: her immortal soul.

A worthy exchange, she told herself, for love.

"Damn you, von Doom," she said at last, her voice barely above a whisper. "You know I can't live without him..."

"That is so," von Doom replied. "And that is *why*, in the end, Doom is always the victor. Now—step forward ... and take hold of the Cube."

Taking a deep breath, she steadied herself, then reached for the small, glowing box. She felt its hypnotic pull, calling to her, whispering to her enticingly like a lover. Urging her to open Pandora's Box and release the demons that savagely plucked at her heartstrings.

All it would take was a gentle touch, and a simple wish ...

*Warren, please forgive me. . . .*

# 19

**B**ETSY—*NO!*" cried Jean Grey from behind her.

She turned. Gathered on the far side of the chamber were Cyclops, Phoenix, Rogue, and Nightcrawler. Her fellow X-Men. Her friends.

Her saviors from eternal damnation.

"Bah," the wizened Emperor growled, and spat on the floor.

"It's *over*, Doom," Cyclops said. "Shut down the Cube, or we'll shut it down *for* you."

"Imbecile!" von Doom sniped. "You think restoring the world is as simple as flicking a light switch—I order the Cube to deactivate itself, and you awaken in your beds as though from a dream, wondering if any of this ever happened?" He snorted derisively. "At this point, the Cube is so unstable that it would require the full life-force of its possessor to calm its increasingly uncontrollable energies, if only to provide them with enough time to change back all that I have done—to 'lock in' the matrix, so to speak, so that all will become as it had been, before my great plans were set into motion."

"And when were you going to mention *that* bit of information?" Betsy snapped.

Phoenix looked to her husband, her features etched with concern. "Scott, unless someone else takes control of the Cube and puts everything back to normal, Roma will have no other choice but to take action herself."

"And wipe out the entire universe to stop it," Cyclops said. "I know."

Betsy's eyebrows rose dramatically. "I beg your pardon?"

"We are, as the saying goes, 'racing the clock,' " Nightcrawler explained. "By recreating the world in Doom's image, the Cube has created an instability in the omniverse that we must correct before—"

"Before the universe is wiped out by Roma in order to stop it," Betsy concluded. "Yes, I heard that part."

"How very interesting . . ." von Doom muttered, clearly intrigued by this information. "I had *no* idea the Cube could be that powerful."

"Still set on destroying the world before you die, Doctor?" Betsy asked. "Or are you going to hand over the Cube now?"

"Regained your spirit, have you, now that your friends are here?" von Doom replied. He shrugged. "Perhaps I shall set events into motion myself, rather than wait for this Roma to rob me of such a grand opportunity." He reached for the Cube—

—only to be yanked back by Nightcrawler as the blue-skinned teleporter suddenly appeared beside his chair, pinning the old man's arms against the throne.

"I believe you have had *enough* fun with your toy, *Herr Doktor,*" Kurt said sternly. "Now, it is time for the adults to put your things away and tidy up what you have so callously broken while we were away."

"I will see you *dead*, mutant," the Emperor spat, struggling to free himself. "Crushed beneath my boot heel."

"Would that be before or after you have chased me down the hallway with your walker, Grandfather?" Kurt asked sarcastically. "Now be still, before I forget you are a doddering old fool and turn you over to Rogue. She is most eager to speak with you in

private—if you understand my meaning." There was a sinister tone to his voice that surprised even Betsy.

Von Doom gazed evenly at Betsy. "It appears that we are back where we began, Ms. Braddock. Since I am unable to use the Cube, the world—and, quite possibly, the safety of the universe itself—is now yours for the making . . . *if* you have the strength of will to control it."

"*I'll* do it," Cyclops said without hesitation. He took a step toward the throne.

"*No,*" Betsy said.

Cyclops halted; he looked confused by her reaction.

"Oh, stop playing the noble martyr, Scott, and think of your *wife* for a change," Betsy said, with more than a touch of anger. "You and Jean have struggled enough, *suffered* enough, to help the Professor try and realize his dream for a better world. You're always putting the team ahead of yourselves, constantly giving of yourselves—" she glanced at Phoenix "—but I know that, in the backs of your minds, you're always wondering when the day will come when one of you doesn't come back from a mission. And whether you'll have had the chance to say how much you love each other before that happens." She shook her head. "That has to *stop.*"

She smiled at them both. "Don't you see? You should be *happy* for once in your lives; enjoy the times you have together." A trace of sadness crept into her dark eyes. "They're so precious, and they pass so quickly. What the two of you have is something *special*— as special a love as the one Warren and I have—" she winced "—*had* . . ." Her voice trailed off for a moment, then she cleared her throat. "You shouldn't be so willing to just casually toss it aside everytime there's a crisis."

"Betsy, I know how badly you want to be able to bring Warren back with the Cube," Cyclops said, "but there's more at stake here than that."

"I know that now," Betsy said. "And I *still* want to go through with this."

"But, you *don't* have to," Cyclops argued. "Would Warren *really* want you to sacrifice yourself just because you feel lost without him?"

"It's *my* choice, Scott," Betsy replied. *"My* decision. *Someone* has to be willing to give up their life for the safety of the universe—why does it always have to be you or Jean?" She smiled. "You shouldn't have a monopoly on saving the world, you know. It gives the rest of us terrible inferiority complexes." Not wishing to discuss the matter any further, she turned to face the Cube. "All right—let's get this over with."

"Betsy—" Jean began.

"Be *happy,* my friends," she said softly, and stepped forward. Her hands began to close around the Cube—

And the far wall of the chamber suddenly exploded inward, sending chunks of concrete and adamantium hurtling through the darkened room with missile-like speed. The X-Men dove for what little cover was available; von Doom was protected by the Cube's power.

Then, Magneto strode into the room.

He struck quickly, wordlessly, immobilizing Phoenix with the same blood-controlling defense he had used on Ororo, rendering Jean unconscious before she was able to defend herself. As Phoenix collapsed, Cyclops moved to open his visor and unleash his power beams—only to be attacked by Pietro, who ran past his father to rain a furious series of blows upon Scott's head; the insensate leader of the X-Men soon joined his wife on the floor.

Rogue raced forward to aid her fallen comrades, but the Southern Belle was intercepted by a powerful forcefield—courtesy of the arriving Unuscione—that slammed into her, then crushed her against a wall of the chamber and held her there. As Rogue struggled to free herself, a thick fog flowed into her nostrils and mouth, cutting off her breath. The red-and-black-clad powerhouse gasped for air for a few moments, then went slack.

Unuscione deactivated the forcefield, and Rogue pitched forward, unconscious, onto the floor. A moment later, the same fog that had stopped her breathing flowed out of her body, to solidify into the form of Amanda Voght.

Nightcrawler was the only one who succeeded in reaching the mutant overlord, by teleporting across the chamber. But his attack was ended before the first punch had been thrown, cut down by the powerful electrical charge of an amplified taser fired by Forge as he and Cortez joined his master.

And then Magneto turned to face Betsy.

*"You,"* Betsy growled. "How could you have—" She shook her head. "It doesn't *matter* how you survived. It just means I'll have to be sure I *finish* the job this time." She stepped forward, a newly-formed psychic blade glowing around her right hand.

"It seems, my dear Psylocke," Magneto explained, "that the circuitry lining my helmet which had long enabled me to avoid detection by the dreaded 'Psi Division' is also capable of protecting my mind from serious mental injury . . . though the *pain* I experienced at your hands was quite overwhelming." He sneered. "Allow me to return the favor."

He waved a hand in her direction, and a bolt of magnetic energy caught Betsy full in the chest, tossing her backward and slamming her against a wall. She collapsed in a heap onto the chamber floor, mind and body wracked with blinding pain; the psychic blade vanished.

Apparently satisfied that the X-Men would not present him with any further trouble, the mutant overlord continued his approach toward the man he had come to destroy.

"You *dare* to step unbidden into the palace of Doom?" the armored tyrant said in a reedy voice to his longtime enemy. The Cube began to glow brighter. "With but a thought, mutant, I shall—"

"Be *quiet,* you impotent old worm!" Magneto shouted, and struck von Doom across the face with the back of his gauntleted hand. The former Emperor tumbled from his throne, to lie in a heap on the floor, his breaths coming in short, labored gasps.

Separated from its master, the Cosmic Cube merely floated in midair, as though certain that a new owner would soon come along to take possession of its wondrous gifts.

Magneto, of course, was more than willing to fill that position. Kicking von Doom aside, he sank into the soft-cushioned throne and placed both hands around the source of ultimate power.

"Somebody havin' a party an' ferget t'invite me?" shouted a gruff voice.

Everyone but Magneto and von Doom turned to look as Wolverine staggered into the chamber through the hole created by the mutant overlord. He was covered from head to toe in blood, and his street clothes hung in tatters on his hirsute frame. His arms, legs, and face were a mass of scar tissue, and there was a particularly nasty gash across his chest; if it weren't for his unique healing factor, he obviously would have been dead quite some time ago.

"Logan," Betsy whispered gratefully as the magnetically-generated pain she was suffering began to abate. Gazing upon her blood-soaked teammate, an old punchline came to mind: "If you think *I* look bad, you should see the *other* guy." She could only imagine the sort of condition in which Logan had left his unknown sparring partner; it sent a chill up her spine.

Using the wall for support, she pulled herself back onto her feet. "Wolverine!" she shouted. "Doom's been using a Cosmic Cube to create all this insanity—you've got to stop Magnus from trying to take possession of it!"

Logan looked across the chamber to see Magneto cradling the Cube in his hands, staring into its milky depths as though hypnotized. The device pulsed with a blindingly-sharp, white luminescence.

"Glad t'be o' service," Wolverine said with a sinister smile. He triggered his claws—the tips were tinted a disturbingly bright crimson—and ran straight for Magneto.

"No!" Pietro yelled. "My father shall not be stopped now—not when he is about to make his life's work—his long-cherished dream—a reality!"

"Then I'm *just* the guy t'be givin' 'im a wake-up call!" Wolverine barked, and charged at the mutant overlord, claws raised to strike a killing blow.

But Quicksilver was too fast. In the blink of an eye, the white-haired speedster was upon him, unleashing a flurry of blows that rocked the scrappy Canadian. Frustrated and angry, Logan snarled and blindly lashed out with his claws, but Pietro managed to stay just outside their range, ducking and weaving with blinding speed as he continued his assault.

It was only a matter of time before one of them fell.

The Dream was alive.

Seemingly unaware of the battle being fought mere steps away from him, Magneto continued to stare at the Cube, an odd smile bowing his lips.

*This* was the moment for which he had lived—and fought—so long to see happen. The moment when he possessed absolute power over the universe itself—the kind of power that would at last make *Homo superior* the dominant species on this planet. The moment when humanity faced its possible extinction—and trembled at the realization.

And now that he had such inimitable control over the universe—even more, over the very forces of Creation—no one would ever take it away from him.

A quote sprung unbidden into his mind—something Pietro had told him had been attributed to the mutant overlord by Hollywood screenwriters apparently hoping to curry favor with the Emperor:

" 'And Darkness and Decay and the Red Death held illimitable dominion over all,' " he whispered.

No truer words had ever been spoken.

The Dream was dying.

Lying on the floor of the chamber, von Doom gazed longingly at the Cube as it floated ever so tantalizingly close to his outstretched hand. But it belonged to Magneto now; he could see the hungry look in the mutant's eyes—the same look *he* had possessed when he had come to realize just how much power was at his command. Knowing that, with but a thought, he could become a veritable god, re-fashioning the world as he saw fit.

A heady experience, to be sure.

And von Doom had been the first to do it—something no one else had ever accomplished with lasting success: become absolute master of the world. He had eliminated his greatest enemies. Punished the accursed Reed Richards and his three fellow meddlers for their many years of insolence. Recreated the world in his image in less than a day, and ruled it for one brief month—but had made that month last for an decade. The rapid aging, the isolation, the realization that death was imminent—they had all been worth the struggle, the suffering, just to attain his life's ambitions.

But now, he was going to lose it all—including, quite possibly, his very existence . . .

The Dream was dead.

Even from a few feet away, Betsy could hear the siren call of the Cube in her mind; for a moment, as an image of Warren appeared to form in front of her, she considered answering it, taking a tentative step toward the device. She wanted Warren back so badly; even now, as Magneto surrendered to the hypnotic song, she still had the opportunity to seize control of it, use its awesome powers to—

No, she told herself.

The longing was there, the need to have Warren by her side in this most dire of situations, as the world came apart around them, but Scott had been right—there *was* far more at stake here than an overwhelming desire to be reunited with a loved one, no matter how painful it was to face that truth. She had to be strong—for her friends; for herself. It's what Warren would have expected her to be.

It's what an *X-Man* would be.

No, she told herself; *she* wouldn't use the Cube. But she could still try to take it away from Magneto before *he* did.

Activating her psi-blade, she rushed forward, praying she could end this living nightmare before it became even worse. She back-handed Forge as he moved to intercept her—breaking his nose as she pushed him aside—then drove a fist into Cortez's sternum before he could defend himself, leapt over one of Unuscione's deadly forcefields, never breaking stride, and drew back her dagger to strike at the mutant overlord newly perched on the throne—

But she was too late.

"Now, at last," Magneto said softly, "the Age of *Homo superior* begins!" He closed his hands around the Cube—and screamed.

Tendrils of energy suddenly erupted from the tiny box, wrapping around him, bonding to his flesh, to his mind. Magneto twisted violently, eyes bulging from their sockets, mouth moving soundlessly, his body clearly wracked with terrible pain.

Halting her attack, Betsy dropped to the floor, narrowly avoiding a stray bolt of cosmic power as it lanced across the room. The hairs on the back of her neck stood on end; the air was alive with the unleashed energies of Creation.

And then, with a high-pitched keening like the wail of a thousand lost souls, the Cube flared even brighter, its cosmic lightning flowing outward, spreading across the chamber in an ever-expanding wave of chaos force—a wave that, Betsy realized with mounting horror, would ultimately overwhelm the entire planet.

"Warren . . ." she whispered.

It took Cyclops and Phoenix first, flowing over them—consuming them. They vanished in a burst of multicolored light. Rogue, Nightcrawler, Unuscione, Wolverine, and Quicksilver were next, followed by Forge, Cortez, and Voght; one moment they were there, then . . .

Momentarily frozen with fear, Betsy could only stare helplessly as each of her friends were taken, absorbed by the power of the Cosmic Cube to be reshaped, recreated, by whatever dark urges lurked within the mind of Erik Lensherr, driving him ever onward to attain his perverted dream of world domination.

And now it was her turn. Every fiber of her being was screaming at her, telling her to run before it was too late—but where could she run *to*, when no place on Earth was safe from the effects of the Cube?

As the wave approached, Betsy took a step back—and gasped as a gauntleted hand closed around her ankle. She looked down to find von Doom staring back at her. His eyes burned with anger.

"Doom *never* concedes defeat, girl," the old man said. "Not while he still has one last hand to play." He pressed a hidden stud on his armor's chestplate—

And then the Chaos Wave enveloped them, too.

"Supreme Guardian!" Saturnyne cried. "Look!"

Standing beside the scrying glass, she pointed at its surface—the darkness that had long obscured their view of Earth 616 was beginning to clear. As she, Roma, and Professor Xavier watched, a crystal clear image of the planet, as seen from space, began to take shape.

"They've done it," Xavier said. He turned toward Saturnyne, trying—and failing—to keep a smug expression off his face.

But the Omniversal Majestrix wasn't looking at him—she was staring, mouth agape, eyes wide, at the glass. Confused, Xavier turned back—

—in time to see a massive wave of energy roll across the planet, its destructive forces tearing across land and sea, changing the entire surface of the world in the space of a few heartbeats.

And then the scrying glass went dark once more.

"Dear God . . ." Xavier muttered. Eyes wide with shock, he slowly turned to the Supreme Guardian; her features were stretched tight with fear. "Your Majesty—"

"They have *failed*, Charles Xavier," Roma whispered hoarsely. "They have failed, and now matters are even worse . . ."

# COMING NEXT

## X-MEN™/MAGNETO™
## THE CHAOS ENGINE: Book 2

by Steven A. Roman

Illustrated by Mark Buckingham

Cover art by Bob Larkin

ISBN: 0-7434-3490-0

After failing in their mission to destroy the Cosmic Cube, the X-Men have now fallen under the thrall of their longtime enemy Magneto, who uses the Cube to bring about his dream for all mutantkind: the day when *Homo sapiens superior* freely walk the Earth, not as equals to the human race, but as their *masters*.

The only hope the world has to survive the mutant overlord's reign is in the hands of Professor Charles Xavier and the one X-Man *not* affected by the reality-changing powers of the Cube: Betsy Braddock—the ninja-trained telekinetic known as Psylocke. But unknown to any of the players in this cosmic chess match is that there is one *final* participant waiting in the wings, and he is about to make his first move. . . .

## ALSO AVAILABLE

### X-MEN™
### SHADOWS OF THE PAST

by Michael Jan Friedman

Illustrations by Ladronn

Cover art and design by Steranko

ISBN: 0-7434-2378-X

Years ago, an alien invasion of Earth was stopped through the efforts of a young Charles Xavier, though the victory cost him the use of his legs. Now, Xavier claims to have evidence of the invaders' pending return, and he sends the X-Men on a series of missions to seize key pieces of technology from the installations abandoned by the aliens after their previous failed attempt. The purpose is to create a defensive weapon capable of repelling the approaching strike force. But is the invasion real—or does Professor X have a different, *hidden* agenda . . . ?

# SPIDER-MAN™
# REVENGE OF THE SINISTER SIX™

by Adam-Troy Castro

Illustrations by Mike Zeck

Cover art by Mike Zeck and Phil Zimelman

ISBN: 0-7434-3466-8

Peter Parker, the amazing Spider-Man, has made an astonishing discovery: he might have a sister! Unfortunately, a manipulative super-villain known as the Gentleman—who had a hand in the deaths of Peter's parents—has somehow brainwashed her into becoming the deadly super-villainess known as Pity! Together with Doctor Octopus, Electro, the Vulture, and Mysterio, they've formed the newest incarnation of the Sinister Six, a group dedicated to destroying Spider-Man!

But there is something more than just the death of Spider-Man on the Sinister Six's agenda; something that has caused Col. Sean Morgan and his hi-tech anti-espionage agents of S.A.F.E. to become involved. But even with help from his allies, Spider-Man discovers that nothing he can do will stop the Sinister Six from achieving their goal of revenge!

Your comments on *X-Men: The Chaos Engine*
are welcomed. Contact author Steven A. Roman
at starwarpco@aol.com.